OL

POCKET GUIDE

BRUCE SMITH WITH MARK WEBB

CollinsWillow
An Imprint of HarperCollins*Publishers*

First published in 2000
by Collins Willow
an imprint of HarperCollins*Publishers*
London

© Bruce Smith 2000

1 3 5 7 9 8 6 4 2

All rights reserved. No part of this publication may be reproduced, stored in a retrieval system, or transmitted, in any form or by any means, electronic, mechanical, photocopying, recording or otherwise, without the prior written permission of the publishers

The Author asserts his moral rights to be identified as the author of this work

A CIP catalogue record for this book is available from the British Library

ISBN 0 00218921 6

The HarperCollins website address is:
www.**fire**and**water**.com

Printed in Great Britain by
Clays Ltd, St Ives plc

CONTENTS

Introduction	5
Sydney 2000	6
Torch Relay	6
A Potted History	7
Day-By-Day Event Schedule	10
Did You Know?	17
Past Olympic Games	19
Medal Tables	20
The Venues	31
Great Britain – All Time Medals	43

Events A to Z

Archery	73
Athletics	76
Badminton	84
Baseball	88
Basketball	93
Beach Volleyball	97
Boxing	100
Canoe/Kayak Slalom	105
Canoe/Kayak Sprint	108
Cycling: Mountain Bike	112
Cycling: Road Race	115
Cycling: Track	118
Diving	122
Equestrian: Dressage	126
Equestrian: Jumping	129
Equestrian: Three-day Event	132
Fencing	135
Football	139
Gymnastics: Artistic	144
Gymnastics : Rhythmic	149
Gymnastics: Trampoline	151
Handball	153
Hockey	156
Judo	160
Modern Pentathlon	164

Rowing	167
Sailing	171
Shooting	176
Softball	180
Swimming	185
Synchronised Swimming	190
Table Tennis	193
Taekwondo	197
Tennis	200
Triathlon	205
Volleyball	208
Water Polo	212
Weightlifting	215
Wrestling	219
Sydney 2000 Dates	224

Bibliography:

The Complete Book of the Summer Olympics, by David Wallechinsky, published by Little Brown and Company, 1996.

Chronicle of the Olympics, DK Publishing Inc., 1996

Daily Telegraph newspaper

Atlanta Herald newspaper

Disclaimer: In a book of this type it is inevitable that some errors will creep in. While every effort has been made to ensure that the details given in this annual are correct at the time of going to press, neither the authors, editor nor the publishers can accept any responsibility for errors within.

Introduction

The *Greatest Show on Earth* is just one of the many phrases that has been used to describe the Olympic Games. If the lead-up to Sydney 2000 is anything to go by, then that claim will not fall short. One thing is for sure – Sydney will be the place to be during September and October of Y2K. More than 15,300 athletes and officials will descend on the country's largest city to take part in traditional and some brand new events for the best part of three weeks and let's not forget the 7,000 or so that will follow on in their footsteps for the Paralympics straight after. Sydney is a wonderful city at the best of times but will be brimming with excitement and entertainment as six years of planning finally come to fruition.

Events at Sydney 2000 are classified in over 40 different headings – many of those, such as "Athletics: Field" contain a variety of different events. Understanding and following even a handful of the events is the best most people can hope to do. The aim of this Pocket Guide is to help you get inside, understand and follow not just the Olympic Games but also each of the events that bolt together to form the total event!

Whether you are watching in the stands or watching on TV, you will find a wide variety of useful and plain anorak-style information packed into these 224 pages. Central to it all is the Events A-Z section, with pages devoted to each of the events. This includes an introduction to the sport or sports, a review of the event in the last Olympic Games in Atlanta, plus an outline guide to the rules. This is topped with some useful facts and definitions of some of the terms that will be used by the commentators. Note that the rules are only outlines and are in no way meant to be definitive nor official, although they will certainly provide you with more than the basics.

Elsewhere you will also find details of all the venues that will be used plus a useful wad of statistics about past Games and medal winners.

In your pocket or on the arm of your favourite chair, the *Olympics 2000 Pocket Guide* is a vital companion for any serious sports fan.

Author's Notes

Comments about this book can be sent to Bruce Smith at:
PO Box 382, St. Albans, Herts, AL2 3JD
alternatively he can be contacted via email at:
SmithBruce@Hotmail.com

Sydney 2000

The host city, Sydney, was awarded the Games of the XXVIIth Olympiad – known as the Millennium Games – on 23 September 1993 in Monte Carlo. It was a case of third time lucky for Australia because this was the third of three consecutive bids to be made by an Australian city to stage the Olympic Games. Sydney, Australia's largest city, has a population of approximately 3.7 million people and Australia is one of the few countries to have been in attendance at every summer Olympic Games since they began in 1896. The original home of the Olympic Games was Greece, and in 2004 the Games will return to Athens.

Torch Relay

A Torch Relay will have brought the Olympic Flame from Olympia, Greece to Sydney in accordance with Rule 68 of the Olympic Charter. The torch will have travelled through all the Oceania countries who are represented by a National Olympic Committee. The Sydney Olympic Torch Relay will have been the longest in the history of the event.

The Flame was kindled in the Temple of Hera at Olympia on 10 May 2000 and was then carried by a relay of runners into the Panathenean Stadium in Athens, where the Flame was handed to a representative of the Sydney Organising Committee. From there around 12,000 people carried it on a 38,000 mile journey lasting 100 days culminating with its arrival in Stadium Australia for the Opening Ceremony on 15 September 2000. On its journey it will have travelled by every conceivable means of transport, from foot to plane, from boat to camel!

Nova Paris-Kneebone, the first Aboriginal athlete to win an Olympic Gold medal – in hockey – was the first runner to carry the torch in Australia. The honour of carrying the torch on the final mile into the stadium was given to a Sydney resident.

A Potted History

In the beautiful Valley of Olympia, hundreds of years before the birth of Christ, Greeks gathered together to pay respect to their gods and compete in individual contests to establish the best athletes of the day. The first recorded date of these Olympic Games is 776 BC and the Games were held every four years until 394 AD, thus lasting 1,170 years. The ancient world was turned on its head many times during this turbulent period but the Games continued in some form or another until emperor Theodosius decreed their end. It is interesting to speculate whether the current edition of the Games will last for that long and whether the 'city states' of the modern world will get tired of courting the Games. Perhaps the Games will return to a permanent site one day, perhaps they will become just another commercial enterprise, a slave to the media companies that generate the required funds. Or maybe the Games will continue to welcome athletes in the right spirit of friendly competition and rivalry with the support of a sport-loving public.

The first 13 Olympic Games featured only a foot race run the length of the stadium – approximately 200 metres. Over time the Olympic Games became a five-day festival with additional religious festivities and events such as the chariot race, a bareback horse race, the pentathlon, various foot races, boxing, upright wrestling and the pankration (meaning 'all kinds of fighting'), which was apparently a vicious contest that combined wrestling, boxing, and judo. The final event involved runners suited up in coats of armour running the 400 metres.

Women and girls were excluded from the Olympic Games but an alternative event, known as the Herannic Games, was set up in honour of Hera, the wife of Zeus. These were held regularly, two years after each Olympic Games.

You can travel by road or train to the site of ancient Olympia today and view the remains of the buildings but before 1875 there was little to see of the site which had been covered over during hundreds of years of neglect. The Olympic Games were remembered only by the verse of the Greek poets of the time, who were hired to celebrate the victories of the leading athletes of the time and the towns which produced them.

In 1875, amidst a renewed interest in the ancient world and what it had to offer, German archaeologists started a six-year project that unearthed the entire city of Olympia. A French nobleman, Baron Pierre de Coubertin, visited the site and was inspired by the ideals of the ancient Games. He believed that an international sports competition could promote world peace, and his efforts led to the formation of the International Olympic Committee. Today there are almost 200 nations that have Olympic committees.

The first modern Games were held in 1896 in Athens, Greece. Since then, with only three exceptions – 1916, 1940, and 1944 – they have been held every four years. Unlike the ancient games, which attracted competitors to one site from around the ancient world, the modern Olympics thrives on moving to one of the world's great cities every four years. The competition for the honour of holding the Games is much sought-after.

The early Games included recognition of competitors in areas other than sports, and prizes were awarded in fine arts from 1912 up to 1948. Sydney continues this tradition by running an arts festival in parallel. The first official Olympic Winter Games was 1924 and two Winter Games were held two years apart in 1992 and 1994 so that they would be offset from the Summer Games.

In 1900, women began to compete in lawn tennis and other events followed until the situation today is that almost all events are held for both sexes. The idea of the Olympic village was established for the first time in the 1932 Games in Los Angeles.

The Games try to be nothing more than to be the pinnacle of the various sports that are featured but nevertheless they are sometimes mixed up with world events. They collided with Nazi politics in 1936 Berlin but the Games went ahead as planned. Back in Germany in 1972 Arab terrorists took hostage and then killed 11 Israeli athletes but the Games continued. In 1980 the United States government led several nations in staying away from the Moscow Games in protest against the Soviet Union's invasion of Afghanistan. In 1984, the Soviets led a tit-for-tat boycott of the Los Angeles Games.

The ceremonial aspect of the ancient Games has remained, reflecting de Courbertin's belief that the Games could act as a sporting bridge between nations otherwise in conflict. In 1896 70,000 spectators witnessed 258 athletes from 13 different countries in the opening ceremony in which the King of Greece declared the Games of the first modern Olympiad officially open. These days athletes from each participating country parade into the stadium, following their national flag. The athlete chosen by his or her teammates to lead the delegation carries each flag. Athletes from Greece are always given the honour of entering the stadium first. Athletes of the other countries follow them in alphabetical order. The host country's team enters last.

A national leader of the host country welcomes the athletes and declares the Games officially open. An athlete and one official then recite the Olympic oath. A flock of doves are usually released, and the Olympic flame is lit.

In the closing ceremony, the flag from the country hosting the next Olympic Games is raised, and that country's invite the world to their country in four years for the next Games. Finally, the Games are declared officially closed, the Olympic flame is extinguished, and the Olympic flag is lowered. A great big party, involving the athletes themselves, then ensues.

DAY-BY-DAY EVENT SCHEDULE

The following pages contain a day-by-day guide to events at the Olympics. These are listed in alphabetical order for each day and not in chronological order of occurrence as many occur throughout the day at different times. The key to the various venues is also listed below.

Abb.	Venue
BC	Baseball Centre
BCG	Brisbane Cricket Ground
Binnie	Binnie Pavilion (No. 3)
Bruce	Bruce Stadium, Canberra
BS	Baseball Stadium
Buring	Buring Pavilion (No. 4)
BVC	Beach Volleyball Centre
DGV	Dunc Gray Velodrome
EC	Equestrian Centre
Hindmarsh	Hindmarsh Stadium, Adelaide
MBC	Mountain Bike Course
MCG	Melbourne Cricket Ground
PWS	Penrith Whitewater Stadium
RALC	Ryde Aquatic Leisure Centre
Ross	Ross Pavilion (No. 2)
SA	Olympic Stadium
SC	Softball Centre
SCC	Sydney Convention Centre
SD	Sydney SuperDome
SEC	Sydney Entertainment Centre

Abb.	Venue
SECH	Sydney Exhibition Centre Hall
SFS	Sydney Football Stadium
SH	Sydney Harbour
SHC	State Hockey Centre
SIAC	Sydney International Aquatic Centre
SIAP	Sydney International Archery Park
SIRC	Sydney International Regatta Centre
SISC	Sydney International Shooting Centre
SSC	State Sports Centre
TEN	Tennis Centre
TC	Triathlon Course

Wednesday, 13 September

Event	Venue
Football	MCG
Football	Bruce
Football	BCG
Football	Hindmarsh

Thursday, 14 September

Event	Venue
Football	MCG
Football	Bruce
Football	Hindmarsh
Football	BCG

Friday, 15 September

Event	Venue
Opening Ceremony	SA

Saturday, 16 September

Event	Venue
Badminton	Ross
Basketball	The Dome
Beach Volleyball	BVC
Boxing	SECH3
Cycling Track	DGV
Equestrian 3-Day	EC
Fencing	SECH5
Football	Hindmarsh
Football	SFS
Football	Bruce
Football	BCG
Gymnastics Artistic	SD
Handball	Binnie
Hockey	SHC
Judo	SECH 1&2
Shooting	SISC
Swimming	SIAC
Table Tennis	SSC
Triathlon	TC
Volleyball Indoor	Buring
Volleyball Indoor	SEC
Water Polo	RALC
Weightlifting	SCC

Sunday, 17 September

Event	Venue
Archery	SIAP
Badminton	Ross
Baseball	BS
Baseball	BC
Basketball	The Dome
Beach Volleyball	BVC
Boxing	SECH3
Boxing	SECH3
Canoe/Kayak Slalom	PWS
Cycling Track	DGV
Equestrian 3-Day	EC
Fencing	SECH4&5
Football	MCG
Football	Bruce
Football	Hindmarsh
Football	BCG
Gymnastics Artistic	SD
Handball	Binnie
Hockey	SHC
Judo	SECH 1&2
Rowing	SIRC
Sailing	SH
Shooting	SISC
Softball	SC
Swimming	SIAC
Table Tennis	SSC
Triathlon	TC
Volleyball Indoor	Buring
Volleyball Indoor	SEC
Water Polo	RALC
Weightlifting	SCC

Monday, 18 September

Event	Venue
Archery	SIAP
Badminton	Ross
Baseball	BC
Baseball	BS
Basketball	The Dome
Beach Volleyball	BVC
Boxing	SECH3
Canoe/Kayak Slalom	PWS
Cycling Track	DGV
Equestrian 3-Day	EC
Fencing	SECH5
Fencing	SECH4
Gymnastics Artistic	SD
Handball	Binnie
Hockey	SHC
Judo	SECH 1&2
Rowing	SIRC
Sailing	SH
Shooting	SISC
Softball	SC
Swimming	SIAC
Table Tennis	SSC
Volleyball Indoor	Buring
Volleyball Indoor	SEC
Water Polo	RALC
Weightlifting	SCC

Tuesday, 19 September

Event	Venue
Archery	SIAP
Badminton	Ross
Baseball	BC
Baseball	BS
Basketball	The Dome
Beach Volleyball	BVC
Boxing	SECH3
Canoe/Kayak Slalom	PWS
Cycling Track	DGV
Equestrian 3-Day	EC
Fencing	SECH5
Football	SFS
Football	MCG
Football	Hindmarsh
Football	BCG
Gymnastics Artistic	SD
Handball	Binnie
Hockey	SHC
Judo	SECH 1&2
Rowing	SIRC
Sailing	SH
Shooting	SISC
Softball	SC
Swimming	SIAC
Table Tennis	SSC
Tennis	TCEN
Volleyball Indoor	Buring
Volleyball Indoor	SEC
Water Polo	RALC
Weightlifting	SCC

Wednesday, 20 September

Event	Venue
Archery	SIAP
Badminton	Ross
Baseball	BC
Baseball	BS
Basketball	The Dome
Boxing	SECH3
Canoe/Kayak Slalom	PWS
Cycling Track	DGV
Equestrian 3-Day	EC
Fencing	SECH5
Football	MCG
Football	Bruce
Football	Hindmarsh
Football	BCG
Gymnastics Artistic	SD

Event	Venue
Handball	Binnie
Hockey	SHC
Judo	SECH 1&2
Rowing	SIRC
Sailing	SH
Shooting	SISC
Softball	SC
Swimming	SIAC
Table Tennis	SSC
Tennis	TEN
Volleyball Indoor	Buring
Volleyball Indoor	SEC
Water Polo	RALC
Weightlifting	SCC

Thursday, 21 September

Event	Venue
Archery	SIAP
Badminton	Ross
Basketball	The Dome
Beach Volleyball	BVC
Boxing	SECH3
Cycling Track	DGV
Equestrian 3-Day	EC
Fencing	SECH5
Gymnastics Artistic	SD
Handball	Binnie
Hockey	SHC
Judo	SECH 1&2
Rowing	SIRC
Sailing	SH
Shooting	SISC
Softball	SC
Swimming	SIAC
Table Tennis	SSC
Tennis	TEN
Volleyball Indoor	Buring
Volleyball Indoor	SEC

Friday, 22 September

Event	Venue
Archery	SIAP
Athletics	SA
Badminton	Ross
Baseball	BC
Baseball	BS
Basketball	The Dome
Beach Volleyball	BVC
Boxing	SECH3
Diving	SIAC
Equestrian 3-Day	EC
Fencing	SECH5
Gymnastics Trampoline	SD
Handball	Binnie
Hockey	SHC
Judo	SECH 1&2
Rowing	SIRC
Sailing	SH
Shooting	SISC
Softball	SC
Swimming	SIAC
Table Tennis	SSC
Tennis	TWEN
Volleyball Indoor	Buring
Volleyball Indoor	SEC
Water Polo	RALC
Weightlifting	SCC

Saturday, 23 September

Event	Venue
Athletics	SA
Badminton	Ross
Baseball	BC
Baseball	BS
Basketball	The Dome
Beach Volleyball	BVC
Boxing	SECH3
Cycling Mountain	MBC

Diving	SIAC
Fencing	SECH5
Football	Hindmarsh
Football	BCG
Football	SFS
Football	MCG
Gymnastics Trampoline	SD
Handball	Binnie
Hockey	SHC
Rowing	SIRC
Sailing	SH
Shooting	SISC
Softball	SC
Swimming	SIAC
Table Tennis	SSC
Tennis	TEN
Volleyball Indoor	Buring
Volleyball Indoor	SEC
Water Polo	RALC
Water Polo	SIAC
Weightlifting	SCC

Sunday, 24 September

Event	Venue
Athletics	SA
Baseball	BC
Baseball	BS
Basketball	The Dome
Beach Volleyball	BVC
Boxing	SECH3
Cycling Mountain	MBC
Diving	SIAC
Fencing	SECH4
Football	SFS
Football	Bruce
Gymnastics Artistic	SD
Handball	Binnie
Hockey	SHC
Rowing	SIRC
Sailing	SH
Sync. Swimming	SIAC
Table Tennis	SSC
Tennis	TEN
Volleyball Indoor	Buring
Volleyball Indoor	SEC
Water Polo	RALC
Weightlifting	SCC
Wrestling GR	SECH 1&2

Monday, 25 September

Event	Venue
Athletics	SA
Basketball	The Dome
Beach Volleyball	BVC
Diving	SIAC
Equestrian Jumping	EC
Gymnastics Artistic	SD
Handball	Binnie
Hockey	SHC
Sailing	SH
Softball	SC
Sync. Swimming	SIAC
Table Tennis	SSC
Tennis	TEN
Volleyball Indoor	Buring
Volleyball Indoor	SEC
Water Polo	RALC
Weightlifting	SCC
Wrestling GR	SECH 1&2

Tuesday, 26 September

Event	Venue
Baseball	BS
Basketball	The Dome
Beach Volleyball	BVC
Boxing	SECH 3&4
Canoe/Kayak Sprint	SIRC
Cycling Road	Road
Diving	SIAC

Equestrian Dressage	EC
Football	SFS
Football	MCG
Gymnastics Artistic	SD
Handball	Binnie
Hockey	SHC
Sailing	SH
Softball	SC
Sync. Swimming	SIAC
Tennis	TEN
Volleyball Indoor	SEC
Water Polo	RALC
Weightlifting	SCC
Wrestling GR	SECH 1&2

Wednesday, 27 September

Event	Venue
Athletics	SA
Baseball	BS
Basketball	SD
Boxing	SECH 3&4
Canoe/Kayak Sprint	SIRC
Cycling Road	Road
Diving	SIAC
Equestrian Dressage	EC
Hockey	SHC
Sailing	SH
Taekwondo	SSC
Tennis	TEN
Volleyball Indoor	Buring
Volleyball Indoor	SEC
Water Polo	RALC
Wrestling GR	SECH 1&2

Thursday, 28 September

Event	Venue
Athletics	SA
Basketball	SD
Boxing	SECH 3&4
Canoe/Kayak Sprint	SIRC
Diving	SIAC
Equestrian Jumping	EC
Football	SFS
Gymnastics Rhythmic	Ross
Handball	The Dome
Hockey	SHC
Sailing	SH
Sync. Swimming	SIAC
Taekwondo	SSC
Tennis	TEN
Volleyball Indoor	Buring
Volleyball Indoor	SEC
Wrestling Freestyle	SECH 1&2

Friday, 29 September

Event	Venue
Athletics	SA
Basketball	SD
Boxing	SECH 3&4
Canoe/Kayak Sprint	SIRC
Diving	SIAC
Equestrian Dressage	EC
Football	SFS
Gymnastics Rhythmic	Ross
Handball	The Dome
Hockey	SHC
Sailing	SH
Sync. Swimming	SIAC
Taekwondo	SSC
Volleyball Indoor	SEC
Water Polo	RALC
Wrestling Freestyle	SECH 1&2

Saturday, 30 September

Event	Venue
Athletics	SA
Basketball	SD
Boxing	SECH 3&4
Canoe/Kayak Sprint	SIRC
Cycling Road	Road

Diving	SIAC
Equestrian Dressage	EC
Football	SA
Gymnastics Rhythmic	Ross
Handball	The Dome
Hockey	SHC
Modern Pentathlon	BS
Sailing	SH
Taekwondo	SSC
Volleyball Indoor	SEC
Water Polo	RALC
Water Polo	SIAC
Wrestling Freestyle	SECH 1&2

Sunday, 1 October

Event	*Venue*
Basketball	SD
Boxing	SECH 3&4
Canoe/Kayak Sprint	SIRC
Closing Ceremony	SA
Equestrian Jumping	EC
Gymnastics Rhythmic	Ross
Handball	The Dome
Marathon	SA
Modern Pentathlon	BS
Volleyball Indoor	SEC
Water Polo	RALC
Water Polo	SIAC
Wrestling Freestyle	SECH 1&2

DID YOU KNOW?

- The modern Olympic motto is:
  Citius, Altius, Fortius
  which is Latin for: Swifter, Higher, Stronger. It was written by Father Henri Didion, headmaster of the Aucueil School near Paris.
- A total of 180 Gold medals will be awarded at the Sydney Olympic Games.
- Australia is one of only two countries to have been in attendance at every summer Olympic Games since they began in 1896.
- The Olympic Flame will have been carried by about 12,000 people over 60,852km around the world and across Australia for 100 days before the Games. It will also have been fired into and out of space via one of the NASA Space Shuttle's.
- It is estimated that there will be an extra 1.32 million visitors to Sydney from overseas and an extra 174,000 visitors to Sydney from within Australia.
- Due to the Australian quarantine laws, the equestrian events for the 1956 Games in Melbourne were actually held in Stockholm, Sweden!
- Boycotts: The Olympic Games have been the subject of several boycotts:

  1976 – 32 nations declined to attend the games, most of them from black Africa, because the IOC would not ban New Zealand after a Kiwi rugby team had toured racially-segregated South Africa earlier that year.

  1980 – 64 nations boycotted the games in Moscow as a protest against Russia invading Afghanistan on December 27, 1979.

  1984 – The Games in Los Angeles are boycotted by 14 Eastern Bloc nations, lead by the USSR in a supposed protest over the overcommercialisation of the games by America. Most believe however that it was as a pay-back for the boycott of the Moscow Games by the USA.
- The United States' Marion Jones is aiming for an unprecedented five gold medals in the women's 100m, 200m, 4 x 100m and 4 x 400m relays, and the long jump.

- The Marathon run of legend was 25 miles. In the first modern Games it was set at 26 miles. In London in 1908 the race was extended to 26 miles, 385 yards (42.195km) so that the royal party could see the start and finish in front of them. The distance stuck.
- During the semi-final of the Cycling 1,000 metre sprint in Tokyo in 1964, Giovanni Pettenella of Italy and Pierre Trentin of France stood motionless for 21 minutes 57 seconds, each waiting for the other to lead off. The length of this standoff set an Olympic record, and standing still was later limited to a maximum of three minutes.
- Equestrian Three Day Event – in the 1932 Los Angeles Games, only two countries managed to finish. The United States won the gold medal, the Netherlands silver, and the bronze went unclaimed.
- The first women's Olympic Football final was held in Sanford Stadium in Athens, Georgia in 1996. It attracted a world-record attendance for a women's sporting event of 76,481.
- The defending Judo gold medallist in Atlanta – David Shashaleshvili – did not get to defend his Olympic title. The Georgian went to the wrong venue for his first round match and found himself out of the tournament.
- The most famous no-show occurred at the 1972 games in Munich, where American sprinters Hart, Robinson and Robert Taylor walked into the ABC television studios only to see their quarter-final heats in the 100m already under way. Only Taylor made it to his heats, barely making it but ultimately going on to win the silver medal!

PAST OLYMPIC GAMES

Sydney sees the Olympic Games return to Australia after an absence of 44 years. Melbourne in 1956 is the only other time the Olympics have been held in the Southern Hemisphere. A full list of all Olympic venues is given below.

Year	No	Location	Dates	Nations
1896	I	Athens, GRE	Apr 6-15	14
1900	II	Paris, FRA	May 20-Oct 28	26
1904	III	St. Louis, USA	July 1-Nov 23	13
1906	–	Athens, GRE	Apr 22-May 2	20
1908	IV	London, GBR	Apr 27-Oct 31	22
1912	V	Stockholm SWE	May 5-July 22	28
1916	VI	Berlin, GER	Cancelled (WWI)	–
1920	VII	Antwerp, BEL	Apr 20-Sept 12	29
1924	VIII	Paris, FRA	May 4-July 27	44
1928	IX	Amsterdam, NET	May 17-Aug 12	46
1932	X	Los Angeles, USA	July 30-Aug 14	37
1936	XI	Berlin, GER	Aug 1-16	49
1940	XII	Tokyo, JPN	Cancelled (WWII)	–
1944	XIII	London, GBR	Cancelled (WWII)	–
1948	XIV	London, GBR	July 29-Aug 14	59
1952	XV	Helsinki, FIN	July 19-Aug 3	69
1956	XVI	Melbourne, AUS	Nov 22-Dec 8	72
1960	XVII	Rome, ITA	Aug 25-Sept 11	83
1964	XVIII	Tokyo, JPN	Oct 10-24	93
1968	XIX	Mexico City, MEX	Oct 12-27	113
1972	XX	Munich, W. GER	Aug 26-Sept 10	122
1976	XXI	Montreal, CAN	July 17-Aug 1	88
1980	XXII	Moscow, USSR	July 19-Aug 3	81
1984	XXIII	Los Angeles, USA	July 28-Aug 12	140
1988	XXIV	Seoul, S KOR	Sept 17-Oct 2	160
1992	XXV	Barcelona, SPA	July 25-Aug 9	172
1996	XXVI	Atlanta, USA	July 20-Aug 4	197
2000	XXVII	Sydney, AUS	Sept 15-Oct 1	
2004	XXVIII	Athens, GRE	Aug 13-29	

MEDAL TABLES

Listed below are the medal tables which have resulted from 26 Olympiads, listed in different formats to give an idea of who the outstanding individuals and nations have been over the century and a bit of the modern Games.

Team with Most Medals by Games

Year	Location	Country	G	S	B	Tot
1896	Athens, GRE	Greece	10	19	18	47
1900	Paris, FRA	France	26	37	32	95
1904	St. Louis, USA	USA	78	84	82	244
1906	Athens, GRE	France	15	9	16	40
1908	London, GBR	Britain	54	46	38	138
1912	Stockholm SWE	Sweden	23	24	17	64
1916	Berlin, GER	–				
1920	Antwerp, BEL	USA	41	27	27	95
1924	Paris, FRA	USA	45	27	27	99
1928	Amsterdam, NET	USA	22	18	16	56
1932	Los Angeles, USA	USA	41	32	30	103
1936	Berlin, GER	Germany	33	26	30	89
1940	Tokyo, JPN	–				
1944	London, GBR	–				
1948	London, GBR	USA	38	27	19	84
1952	Helsinki, FIN	USA	40	19	17	76
1956	Melbourne, AUS	USSR	37	29	32	98
1960	Rome, ITA	USSR	43	29	31	103
1964	Tokyo, JPN	USSR	30	31	35	96
1968	Mexico City, MEX	USA	45	28	34	107
1972	Munich, W. GER	USSR	50	27	22	99
1976	Montreal, CAN	USSR	49	41	35	125
1980	Moscow, USSR	USSR	80	69	46	195
1984	Los Angeles, USA	USA	83	61	30	174
1988	Seoul, S KOR	USSR	55	31	46	132
1992	Barcelona, SPA	CIS	55	38	29	112
1996	Atlanta, USA	USA	44	32	25	101

Men: Most in a Single Games

Male athletes who have won the most medals in a single Summer Olympics up to Atlanta in 1996. Note that totals include individual, relay and team medals.

No	Men	Sport	G	S	B
8	Aleksandr Dityatin USSR (1980)	Gymnastics	3	4	1
7	Mark Spitz, USA (1976)	Swimming	7	0	0
7	Willie Lee, USA (1920)	Shooting	5	1	1
7	Matt Biondi, USA (1988)	Swimming	5	1	1
7	Boris Shakhlin, USSR (1960)	Gymnastics	4	2	1
7	Lloyd Spooner USA (1920)	Shooting	4	1	2
7	Mikhail Voronin, USSR (1968)	Gymnastics	2	4	1
7	Nikolai Andrianov, USSR (1976)	Gymnastics	2	4	1
6	Vitaly Scherbo, UT (1992)	Gymnastics	6	0	0
6	Li Ning, CNN (1984)	Gymnastics	3	2	1
6	Akinori Nakayama, JPN (1968)	Gymnastics	4	1	1
6	Takashi Ono, JPN (1960)	Gymnastics	3	1	2
6	Viktor Chukarin, USSR (1956)	Gymnastics	4	2	0
6	Konrad Frey, GER (1936)	Gymnastics	3	1	2
6	Ville Ritola, FIN (1924)	Track/Field	4	2	0
6	Hubert Van Innis, BEL (1920)	Archery	4	2	0
6	Carl Osburn, USA (1920)	Shooting	4	1	1
6	Louis Richardet, SWI (1906)	Shooting	3	3	0
6	Anion Heida, USA (1904)	Gymnastics	5	1	0
6	George Eyser, USA (1904)	Gymnastics	3	2	1
6	Burton Downing, USA (1904	Cycling	2	3	1
6	Alexei Nemov, RUS (1996)	Gymnastics	2	1	3

Women: Most in a Single Games

Female athletes who have won the most medals in a single Summer Olympics up to Atlanta in 1996. Note that totals include individual, relay and team medals.

No	Women	Sport	G	S	B
7	Maria Gorokhovskaya, USSR (1952)	Gymnastics	2	5	0
6	Kristin Otto, E GER (1988)	Swimming	6	0	0
6	Agnes Keleti, HUN (1956)	Gymnastics	4	2	0

No		Sport	G	S	B
6	Vera Caslavska CZE (1968)	Gymnastics	4	2	0
6	Larisa Latynina, USSR (1956)	Gymnastics	4	1	1
6	Larisa Latynina, USSR (1960)	Gymnastics	3	2	1
6	Daniela Silivas, ROM (1988)	Gymnastics	3	2	1
6	Larisa Latynina USSR (1964)	Gymnastics	2	2	2
6	Margit Korondi HUN. [1956]	Gymnastics	1	1	4
5	Kornelia Ender, E GER (1976)	Swimming	4	1	0
5	Ecaterina Szabo, ROM (1984)	Gymnastics	4	1	0
5	Shane Gould, AUS (1972)	Swimming	3	1	1
5	Nadia Comaneci, ROM (1976)	Gymnastics	3	1	1
5	Karin Janz, E GER (1972)	Gymnastics	2	2	1
5	Ines Diers, E GER (1980)	Swimming	2	2	1
5	Shirley Babashoff, USA (1976)	Swimming	1	4	0
5	Mary Lou Retton, USA (1984)	Gymnastics	1	2	2
5	Shannon Miller, USA (1992)	Gymnastics	0	2	3

Men: Career All-time Winners

Male athletes who have won the most Olympic medals in their career up to Atlanta in 1996. Note that totals include individual, relay and team medals.

No	Men	Sport	G	S	B
15	Nikolai Andrianov, USSR	Gymnastics	7	5	3
13	Boris Shakhlin, USSR	Gymnastics	7	4	2
13	Edoardo Mangiarotti, ITA	Fencing	6	5	2
13	Takashi Ono, JPN	Gymnastics	5	4	4
12	Paavo Nurmi, FIN	Track/Field	9	3	0
12	Sawao Kato, JPN	Gymnastics	8	3	1
11	Mark Spitz, USA	Swimming	9	1	1
11*	Matt Biondi, USA	Swimming	8	2	1
11	Viktor Chukarin USSR	Gymnastics	7	3	1
11	Carl Osburn USA	Shooting	5	4	2
10	Ray Ewry, USA	Track/Field	10	0	0
10	Carl Lewis, USA .	Track/Field	9	1	0
10	Aladar Gerevich, HUN	Fencing	7	1	2
10	Akinori Nakayama, JPN	Gymnastics	6	2	2
10	Aleksandr Diyatin USSR	Gymnastics	3	6	1
9	Vitaly Scherbo, BLR	Gymnastics	6	0	3

9	Martin Sheridan, USA	Track/Field	5	3	1
9	Zoltan Halmay, HUN	Swimming	3	5	1
9	Giulio Gaudini, ITA	Fencing	3	4	2
9	Mikhail Voronin, USSR	Gymnastics	2	6	1
9	Heikki Savolainen, FIN	Gymnastic	2	1	6
9	Yuri Titov, USSR	Gymnastics	1	5	3

* Includes gold medal as preliminary member of 1st place relay team.
NB: Medals won by Ewry (2, 0, 0), Sheridan (2, 3, 0) and Halmay (1, 1, 0) at the 1906 games are not officially recognised by the IOC.

Women: Career All-time Winners

Female athletes who have won the most Olympic medals in their career up to Atlanta in 1996. Note that totals include individual, relay and team medals.

No	Women	Sport	G	S	B
18	Larissa Latynina, USSR	Gymnastics	9	5	4
11	Vera Caslavska, CZE	Gymnastics	7	4	0
10	Agnes Keleti, HUN	Gymnastics	5	3	2
10	Poling Astaknova, USSR	Gymnastics	5	2	3
9	Nadia Comaneci, ROM	Gymnastics	5	3	1
9	Lyudmila Tourischeva, USSR	Gymnastics	4	3	2
8	Kornelia Ender, E GER	Swimming	4	4	0
8	Dawn Fraser, AUS	Swimming	4	4	0
8	Shirley Babashoff, USA	Swimming	2	6	0
8	Sofia Muratova, USSR	Gymnastics	2	2	4
7	Krisztina Egerszegi, HUN	Swimming	5	1	1
7	Irena Kirszenstein Szewinka, POL	Track/Field	3	2	2
7	Shirley Strickland, AUS	Track/Field	3	1	3
7	Maria Gorokhovskaya, USSR	Gymnastics	2	5	0
7	Ildiko Sagine Ujlaki Rejto, HUN	Fencing	2	3	2
7	Shannon Miller, USA	Gymnastic	2	2	3
7	Merlene Ottey, JAM	Track/Field	0	2	5

Men: Most Gold Medals

No	Man	Sport	G	S	B
10	Ray Ewry, USA	Track/Field	10	0	0
9	Paavo Nurmi, FIN	Track/Field	9	3	0
9	Mark Spitz, USA	Swimming	9	1	1
9	Carl Lewis, USA	Track/Field	9	1	0
8	Sawao Kato, JPN	Gymnastics	8	3	1
8 *	Matt Biondi, USA	Swimming	8	2	1
7	Nikolai Andrianov, USSR	Gymnastics	7	5	3
7	Boris Shakhlin, USSR	Gymnastics	7	4	2
7	Viktor Chukarin, USSR	Gymnastics	7	3	1
7	Aladar Gerevich HUN	Fencing	7	1	2

*Includes gold medal as preliminary member of 1st place relay team.

Women: Most Gold Medals

No	Women	Sport	G	S	B
9	Larissa Latynina, USSR	Gymnastics	9	5	4
7	Vera Caslavska, CZE	Gymnastics	7	4	0
6	Kristin Otto, E GER	Swimming	6	0	0
5	Agnes Keleti, HUN	Gymnastics	5	3	2
5	Nadia Comaneci, ROM	Gymnastics	5	3	1
5	Poling Astakhova, USSR	Gymnastics	5	2	3
5	Krisztina Egerszegy, HUN	Swimming	5	1	1
5	Jenny Thompson, USA	Swimming	5	1	0
4	Kornelia Ender, E GER	Swimming	4	4	0
4	Dawn Fraser, AUS	Swimming	4	4	0
4	Lyudmila Touristcheva, USSR	Gymnastics	4	3	2
4	Evelyn Ashford, USA	Track/Field	4	1	0
4	Janet Evans, USA	Swimming	4	1	0
4	Fanny Blankers Koen, NET	Track/Field	4	0	0
4	Betty Cuthbert, AUS	Track/Field	4	0	0
4	Pat McCormick, USA	Diving	4	0	0
4	Amy Van Dyken, USA	Swimming	4	0	0
4	Barbel Eckert-Wöckel, E GER	Track/Field	4	0	0

Men: Most Silver Medals

No	Man	Sport	G	S	B
6	Alexandr Dityatin, USSR	Gymnastics	3	6	1
6	Mikhail Voronin, USSR	Gymnastics	2	6	1
5	Nikolai Andrianov, USSR	Gymnastics	7	5	3
5	Edoardo Mangiarotti, ITA	Fencing	6	5	2
5	Zoltan Halmay, HUN	Swimming	3	5	1
5	Gustavo Marzi, ITA	Fencing	2	5	0
5	Yuri Titov, USSR	Gymnastics	1	5	3
5	Viktor Lisitsky, USSR	Gymnastics	0	5	0

Women: Most Silver Medals

No	Women	Sport	G	S	B
6	Shirley Babashoff, USA	Swimming	2	6	0
5	Larissa Latynina, USSR	Gymnastics	9	5	4
5	Mario Gorokhovskaya, USSR	Gymnastics	2	5	0
4	Vera Caslavska, CZE	Gymnastic	7	4	0
4	Kornelia Ender, E GER	Swimming	4	4	0
4	Dawn Fraser, AUS	Swimming	4	4	0
4	Erica Zuchold, E GER	Gymnastics	0	4	1

Men: Most Bronze Medals

No	Man	Sport	G	S	B
9	Heikki Savolainen, FIN	Gymnastics	2	1	6
5	Daniel Revenu, FRA	Fencing	1	0	5
5	Philip Edwards, CAN	Track/Field	0	0	5
5	Adrianus Jong, NET	Fencing	0	0	5

Women: Most Bronze Medals

No	Women	Sport	G	S	B
5	Marlene Ottey, JAM	Track/Field	0	2	5
4	Larissa Latynina USSR	Gymnastics	9	5	4
4	Sofia Muratova, USSR	Gymnastics	2	2	4

Most Individual Medals

	No.	Athlete	Sport	G	S	B
Men:	12	Nikolai Andrianov, USSR	Gymnastics	6	3	3
Women:	14	Larissa Latynina, USSR	Gymnastics	7	4	3

Does not include team events.

All-Time Standings 1896-1996

All-time Summer Games medal standings. NB: The counts include the 1906 Intercalated Games which are not recognized by the IOC.

	Country	*G*	*S*	*B*	*Total*
1	United States	832	634	553	2019
2	USSR (1952-88)	395	319	296	1010
3	Great Britain	169	223	218	610
4	France	175	179	206	560
5	Sweden	132	151	174	457
6	Italy	166	135	144	445
=	East Germany (1956-88)	159	150	136	445
8	Hungary	142	129	155	426
9	Germany (1896-36, 92-)	124	121	134	379
10	West Germany (1952-88)	77	104	120	301
11	Finland	99	80	113	292
=	Australia	86	85	121	292
13	Japan	92	89	97	278
14	Romania	63	77	99	239
15	Poland	50	67	110	227
16	Canada	48	78	90	216
17	Netherlands	49	58	81	188
18	Bulgaria	43	76	63	182
19	Switzerland	46	69	59	174
20	China	52	63	49	164
21	Denmark	38	60	57	155
22	Czechoslovakia (1924-92)	49	49	44	142
23	Belgium	37	49	49	135
24	South Korea	38	42	46	126
25	Norway	45	41	38	124
26	Greece	28	42	43	113
27	Unified Team (1992)	45	38	29	112
28	Cuba	44	33	31	108
29	Yugoslavia (1924-88, 96-)	27	31	32	90
30	Austria	18	31	34	83
31	New Zealand	29	12	29	70
32	Russia	26	24	18	68
33	Spain	22	25	17	64
34	Turkey	30	16	13	59

	Country	G	S	B	Total
35	South Africa	19	18	21	58
36	Brazil	12	13	29	54
37	Argentina	13	21	16	50
38	Kenya	14	17	16	47
39	Mexico	9	13	19	41
40	Iran	5	13	18	36
41	Jamaica	5	16	9	30
42	North Korea	8	6	12	26
43	Estonia	7	6	10	23
44	Great Britain/Ireland	6	11	3	20
45	Ireland	8	5	6	19
46	Ethiopia	8	1	7	16
=	Egypt	6	5	5	16
48	India	8	3	4	15
=	Portugal	3	4	8	15
50	Nigeria	2	5	7	14
=	Mongolia	0	5	9	14
52	Czech Republic	4	3	4	11
=	Morocco	4	2	5	11
54	Indonesia	3	4	3	10
=	Pakistan	3	3	4	10
56	Uruguay	2	1	6	9
=	Trinidad & Tobago	1	2	6	9
=	Philippines	0	2	7	9
59	Venezuela	1	2	5	8
=	Chile	0	6	2	8
61	Algeria	3	0	4	7
=	Latvia	0	5	2	7
63	Uganda	1	3	2	6
=	Tunisia	1	2	3	6
=	Thailand	1	1	4	6
=	Colombia	0	2	4	6
=	Bohemia	0	1	5	6
=	Puerto Rico	0	1	5	6
69	Croatia	1	2	2	5
=	Chinese Taipei	0	3	2	5
71	Peru	1	3	0	4
=	Bahamas	1	1	2	4
=	Lithuania	1	0	3	4

	Country	G	S	B	Total
=	Namibia	0	4	0	4
=	Lebanon	0	2	2	4
=	Slovenia	0	2	2	4
=	Ghana	0	1	3	4
=	Luxembourg	2	1	0	3
=	Slovakia	1	1	1	3
=	Israel	0	1	2	3
=	Malaysia	0	1	2	3
82	Armenia	1	1	0	2
=	Costa Rica	1	1	0	2
=	Syria	1	1	0	2
=	Japan/Korea	1	0	1	2
=	Surinam	1	0	1	2
=	Tanzania	0	2	0	2
=	Cameroon	0	1	1	2
=	GB/USA	0	1	1	2
=	Haiti	0	1	7	2
=	Iceland	0	1	1	2
=	Moldova	0	1	1	2
=	Russia/Estonia	0	1	1	2
=	UAR	0	1	1	2
=	Uzbekistan	0	1	1	2
=	Zambia	0	1	1	2
=	The Antilles	0	0	2	3
=	Georgia	0	0	2	2
=	Panama	0	0	2	2
100	Australia/New Zealand	1	0	0	1
=	Burundi	1	0	0	1
=	Cuba/USA	1	0	0	1
=	Denmark/Sweden	1	0	0	1
=	Ecuador	1	0	0	1
=	GB/Ireland/Germany	1	0	0	1
=	GB/Britain/Ireland/USA	1	0	0	1
=	Hong Kong	1	0	0	1
=	Ireland/USA	1	0	0	1
=	Zimbabwe	1	0	0	1
=	Azerbaijan	0	1	0	1
=	Belgium/Greece	0	1	0	1
=	Ceylon	0	1	0	1

	Country	G	S	B	Total
=	France/USA	0	1	0	1
=	France/GB/Ireland	0	1	0	1
=	Ivory Coast	0	1	0	1
=	Netherlands Antilles	0	1	0	1
=	Senegal	0	1	0	1
=	Singapore	0	1	0	1
=	Smyrna	0	1	0	1
=	Tonga	0	1	0	1
=	Virgin Islands	0	1	0	1
=	Australia/Great Britain	0	0	1	1
=	Bermuda	0	0	1	1
=	Bohemia/Great Britain	0	0	1	1
=	Djibouti	0	0	1	1
=	Dominican Republic	0	0	1	1
=	France/Great Britain	0	0	1	1
=	Guyana	0	0	1	1
=	Iraq	0	0	1	1
=	Mexico/Spain	0	0	1	1
=	Mozambique	0	0	1	1
=	Niger	0	0	1	1
=	Qatar	0	0	1	1
=	Scotland	0	0	1	1
=	Thessalonika	0	0	1	1
=	Wales	0	0	1	1

Combined Totals

Countries	G	S	B	Total
USSR/CIS/Russia	466	381	343	1190
Germany/East Germany/West Germany	360	375	390	1125

THE VENUES

Over 30 different sites – stadiums, arenas and natural areas – will play host to an Olympic sport. Of the main facilities, around three-quarters have been newly constructed for the specific purpose of hosting the games, while existing venues have been refurbished and overlaid to bring them up to the required standard.

The focal point of the Games will be the Sydney Olympic Park at Homebush Bay, a twenty-minute ride by train or car from the city centre, which can also be reached by boat from Circular Quay in around 30 minutes – although this route will only be open to officials and some competitors. In addition to the various venues at Homebush Bay will be the Athlete's Village where some 15,300 athletes and officials will be housed during the games and a further 7,000 for the Paralympics, which follow straight after. At the end of the Games the village will become a new Sydney suburb for some 5,000 residents. The most striking feature of the Olympic Park though will be its homage to the environment where nothing goes to waste and where everything is recycled – even the tables in the media centre have been constructed from recycled cardboard!

For atmosphere, Darling Harbour will be one of the best places to be. Located around the 'back' of the city centre behind the more recognisable Circular Quay, it is full of life even on the most average of days. It is sure to be abuzz with people and street entertainment throughout the Games and will have spice added to it by the location of Chinatown and the Water Gardens at the inland end. Its exhibition halls and the Entertainment Centre will stage many of the indoor events, while the small malls and plethora of fast food stores and a good number of quality restaurants will keep those attending watered and fed.

The Sydney hinterland and the spectacular Harbour will be the backdrops to many other events ranging from the Western Suburbs to the stretch of ocean beyond the Sydney Harbour Heads themselves. The Games have not forgotten some of the other big Australian cities with three others hosting many of the preliminary football matches – from the Gabba in Brisbane to the MCG in Melbourne – the site of the last Olympic Games to be held in Australia in 1956.

SYDNEY OLYMPIC PARK – HOMEBUSH BAY

SUPERDOME
Capacity:	18,000	Basketball
	15,000	Gymnastics
Events:	16-21 Sept	Gymnastics: artistic
	22-23 Sept	Trampoline
	24-25 Sept	Gymnastics: artistic
	27 Sept – 1 Oct	Basketball

Built at a cost of some £80 million for the Games, the venue lives up to its name and like all the new venues at Homebush Bay it is environmentally friendly and, according to one statistic released by the organising body, will save some 25,000 tonnes of greenhouse gases over the next five years – compared to a similar non-environmentally designed arena.

The SuperDome will play host to the artistic gymnastics for eight days, sandwiching the trampolining in between, before utilising its full 18,000 capacity to host the final stages of the basketball championships. Four huge video screens will ensure everyone gets to see the best of the action as soon as it has happened.

INTERNATIONAL ARCHERY PARK
Capacity:	4,500	
Events:	16-22 Sept	Archery

Located on the fringes of the Olympic Park at Homebush Bay, Archery Park is part of an area known as the Millennium Parklands, a recreational area that will be further developed after the Games and will include a lot of natural afforestation including woods and mangroves. A temporary 4,500-seat stand will allow spectators to see the action, aided by a video screen and a state-of-the-art scoreboard.

BASEBALL STADIUM
Capacity:	20,000	
Events:	19-28 Sept	Baseball
	30 Sept-1 Oct	Modern Pentathlon

Success in Atlanta and a burgeoning national baseball league have helped provide the impetus for Sydney to acquire a first-rate baseball stadium. Not that such a facility wouldn't have been built anyway but the use it will get after the games for a growing sport is a positive factor.

The Baseball Stadium opened its doors for business in 1998 and also doubles as the Sydney Showground which moved from its old home alongside the Sydney Cricket Ground, and hosts the world famous Royal Easter Show every year.

Capacity crowds of 20,000 are expected for most of the games with the majority seated in a grandstand and with the traditional bleachers being replaced with grass banks. The stadium includes a 20-metre wide concourse, which runs right the way around the facility. Spectators will also notice the extensive use of timber in the design.

As well as hosting the baseball competition, the final stages of the modern pentathlon will be staged at the venue.

THE DOME AND PAVILIONS

Capacities:	The Dome	10,000
	The Pavilions	6,000 (each)

Events:		
	16-23 Sept	Badminton
	16-26 Sept	Basketball
	16 Sept - 1 Oct	Handball
	30 Sept - 1 Oct	Modern Pentathlon – shooting and fencing
	28 Sept - 1 Oct	Gymnastics: rhythmic
	16-28 Sept	Volleyball

The Dome is one of the most amazing features at the Olympic Park not least because so much of its construction is from natural hardwoods. On its own it can seat 10,000 but it can also be used as one large venue when the three adjacent Pavilions are opened up. The three Pavilions each hold around 6,000 people and the four facilities together total some 22,000 square metres of floor space.

For the Games the four facilities will be used individually to host a bigger variety of sports than any other venue.

TENNIS CENTRE
Capacities: Centre Court   10,000
                     Court 1   4,000
                     Court 2   2,000
                     Match Courts   200 (each)
Events: 19-28 Sept   Tennis

The 10,000-seat capacity centre court is the showpiece of the Tennis Centre and its position and lightweight roof should ensure that the vast majority of spectators will be able to watch the games in shade. Outside the main court are two show courts – Courts 1 and 2 with 4,000 and 2,000 capacities respectively. In addition there are a further seven match courts with room for around 200 spectators at each plus six practice and warm-up courts for competitors. The surface on all the courts is Rebound Ace – a cushioned acrylic surface which competitors will be familiar with from the Australian Open.

STATE HOCKEY CENTRE
Capacity: 15,000
Events: 16-30 Sept   Hockey

The hockey centre is one of the newer fixtures at Homebush Bay but forms part of one of its oldest – the State Sports Centre. A new state-of-the art water-based carpet has joined the old original synthetic surfaces and its floodlight towers are one of the first features you notice when you arrive at the Olympic Park. The old pitches have also been re-surfaced to provide top quality warm-up and practice pitches.

The new grandstand holds 15,000 and, like the floodlights, its roof is a distinctive feature with the whole centre nestling alongside and behind the imposing Aquatic Centre.

STATE SPORTS CENTRE
Capacity: 5,000
Events: 16-25 Sept   Table Tennis
              27-30 Sept   Taekwondo

The State Sports Centre is the oldest of the venues being used for the Games at the Homebush Bay site. It opened in 1984 and can cater for some 25 different sports although during the Games it will play main host for only the table tennis and taekwondo events. Anybody who has the chance to walk through the inner sanctum will be able to view "The Hall of Champions" – a tribute area to Australian sporting icons which includes some memorabilia that dates back to the late 1800s.

SYDNEY INTERNATIONAL AQUATIC CENTRE

Capacity:	12,000	
Events:	16-23 Sept	Swimming
	22-30 Sept	Diving
	24-29 Sept	Synchronised Swimming
	23 Sept	Water Polo
	30 Sept-1 Oct	Water Polo
	30 Sept-1 Oct	Modern Pentathlon – swimming

Having done a few lengths myself in the pool, it came as no surprise for me to hear it described by IOC President, Juan Antonio Samaranch, as "the best swimming pool I have seen in my life." Because it is. Bright and cheerful, the water areas that greet you within the centre in the family leisure area, even before you get to the main Olympic pool, are spectacular.

The addition of extra seating hung onto the top of the building to expand the capacity was completed with several months to spare as part of the final overlay work at the Olympic Park. The 50-metre 10-lane competition pool has a movable bulkhead, which allows it to be partitioned into two 25-metre pools, and it can even be capped off for other events (including ice galas). The diving pool is also located here.

STADIUM AUSTRALIA

Capacity:	110,000	
Events:	15 Sept	Opening Ceremony
	22 Sept-1 Oct	Athletics
	30 Sept	Football
	1 Oct	Closing Ceremony

The large arches that mark the rise of the two main stands make Stadium Australia a landmark that can be seen from just about any vantage point around Sydney. The 110,000-seat stadium would just about fit under the Sydney Harbour Bridge and, at a cost of £275 million, is the most expensive facility ever built in Australia.

In the two years leading up to the games it was used to stage a plethora of events and continued to set record crowds for whatever sport it hosted. In March 1999 it drew a crowd of 104,583 for a RFL double-header while the 107,042 it drew for the Wallabies and the All Blacks, remains a world record for a rugby union match.

The Olympic centrepiece will host the opening and closing ceremonies as well as the majority of the athletics events and football final. After the Games the capacity will be reduced to 80,000 and the infrastructure is in place to allow the two main stands to be placed onto wheels that will allow the venue to be reconfigured to host both cricket and Aussie Rules football.

SYDNEY DARLING HARBOUR
SYDNEY CONVENTION AND EXHIBITION CENTRE

Capacities:	Convention Centre	3,840
	Exhibition Hall 1	9,000
	Exhibition Hall 2	9,000
	Exhibition Hall 3	10,000
	Exhibition Hall 4	5,000
	Exhibition Hall 5	5,000
Events:	16-26 Sept	Weightlifting
	24-27 Sept	Wrestling – Greco-Roman
	28 Sept - 1 Oct	Wrestling – Freestyle
	16 Sept - 1 Oct	Boxing
	16-24 Sept	Fencing

Stretching almost the length of one side of the Darling Harbour area are the Sydney Convention and Exhibition Halls which will be used to stage a variety of Olympic events including boxing, fencing, judo, wrestling and weightlifting.

SYDNEY ENTERTAINMENT CENTRE
Capacity	11,000	
Events:	16 Sept-1 Oct	Volleyball

Located at the Chinatown end of Darling Harbour, the SEC has undergone a major refurbishment in the lead up to the Games. It has been Sydney's premier entertainment venue for 17 years but will come under pressure to maintain that role after the Olympics – although its downtown location will ensure it will be central to shows and concerts. Despite being host for the Sydney Kings basketball games, it will only be staging volleyball, sharing the qualifying games with Pavilion 4 at Homebush Bay but hosting all medal matches.

SYDNEY – OTHER VENUES
BONDI BEACH VOLLEYBALL CENTRE
Capacity: 10,000
Events: 16-26 Sept   Beach Volleyball

Can there be any better venue in the world to watch beach volleyball than the massive sweeping bay that provides the setting for Bondi Beach? In fact this will be the first time that beach volleyball has been played on an actual beach in the Games – the Atlanta venue was a man-made beach a long way from any real coastal sand!

A 10,000-seat grandstand has been built on the beach directly opposite the Pavilions. This will form the main temporary area that will include the one match court. External to this are several warm-up and practice courts. Beyond the Pavilions, the main street Campbell Parade has been totally re-furbished and provides home to some of the best places to catch a burger and beer in the area, while watching the surfers take their final runs of the day.

DUNC GRAY VELODROME
Capacity: 6,000
Events: 16-21 Sept   Cycling

Located in the cosmopolitan western suburbs of Sydney, the Dunc Gray Velodrome cost some £15 million to build and is named after the Olympian who won Australia's first ever gold medal for cycling – at the 1932 Games in Los Angeles.

The Velodrome contains a pine-constructed 250-metre track underneath its distinctive roof, which makes it stand out amidst the countryside. Its 6,000 capacity includes 3,000 seats, which are arranged to leave the competitors thinking they are competing in a Greek-style amphitheatre.

SYDNEY INTERNATIONAL EQUESTRIAN CENTRE
Capacity: 50,000
Events: 25-27 Sept Dressage
29-30 Sept Dressage
21, 24-25, 28 Sept, 1 October Jumping
16-21 Sept Three-day Event

Built at a cost of £17 million, the International Equestrian Centre is spread over 90 hectares of parkland and is rightly hailed as one of the best, if not the best, equestrian centre in the world. It comprises more than seven miles of courses for both training purposes and the three-day event and this dovetails with show jumping and dressage arenas, not to mention some 340 stables and associated changing facilities.

PENRITH WHITEWATER STADIUM
Capacity: 12,500
Events: 17-22 Sept Sport canoe/kayak

Brisbane Waters and the Woy Woy rip are as close as you will get to white water rapids in and around the Sydney area so hosting the canoe and kayak events was always going to be a bit problematic. However, take Penrith Lakes and with the injection of around £2.5 million plus some ingenuity you have a man-made rapids. Located some 40 miles from the city centre, the 200-metre course is actually located on the northern shores of the Sydney International Regatta Centre.

The water is moved at frothing speed by five large pumps that shift 14 cubic metres of water each and every second. The main drag is an average of 10 metres wide and around one metre deep along its whole length, and in its 200 metres it drops 5.5 metres. To make things as easy as possible a conveyor belt is there to take the competitors' boats back to the start.

SYDNEY INTERNATIONAL REGATTA CENTRE
Capacity: 27,000
Events: 17-24 Sept Rowing
26-31 Sept Canoe/kayak sprint

Finished in late 1997 at a cost of £15 million, the Regatta Centre evolved from the remains of a sand and gravel quarry in the Sydney hinterland. The result is Penrith Lakes and a breathtaking setting at the centre of which is a 2,300-metre competition course that is amongst the best in the world for rowing. The Centre also houses Penrith Whitewater Stadium which will be used for canoeing and kayak.

The banks are specially designed to absorb any waves created by competitors and the course itself is five metres deep across its entire length. It is said to contain 25,000 native underwater plants and 12,000 bass.

RYDE AQUATIC LEISURE CENTRE
Capacity: 4,000
Events: 23-30 Sept   Water Polo

Located in one of the more up-market areas of north west Sydney, the Ryde Aquatic Leisure Centre will host all the men's and women's preliminary matches and the women's bronze medal encounter. The local Ryde swimming pool has undergone a major renovation and facelift and now boasts a 51-metre pool.

SYDNEY INTERNATIONAL SHOOTING CENTRE
Capacity: 7,000
Events: 16-23 Sept   Shooting

Located at Cecil Park and built at a cost of over £12 million, this is the most advanced shooting facility of its kind in the world. It includes three Olympic shooting ranges including an indoor range, a 25-metre range and a 50-metre range.

BLACKTOWN OLYMPIC CENTRE
Capacity: 8,000 (softball), 4,000 (baseball)
17-24 Sept   Baseball
17-26 Sept   Softball

Some £8 million has been spent constructing the prime softball venue for the Olympic Games, located in the suburb of Blacktown. The venue includes one competition field, and two training fields. The centre also includes a moderately sized baseball centre where the preliminary round matches will be played as well as acting as a practice area for teams. The baseball centre includes three diamonds to international standards.

SYDNEY FOOTBALL STADIUM
Capacity: 42,000
Events: 16-29 Sept   Football

Moore Park until recently was very much the centre of Sydney sporting life. Located within walking distance of the city centre, the Sydney Football Stadium (SFS) sits alongside the Sydney Cricket Ground and also used to be home to the Showgrounds. The latter have relocated to Homebush Bay and the SFS will be competing with the likes of Stadium Australia for events in the post Olympic brush-down.

The SFS will host many of the football matches to be played in Sydney and will also be the site for the start of some of the cycling events. The stadium itself is very distinctive with its saddle roof design and has a very low profile due to the fact that the main playing area is well below the surrounding street level. It can provide a great atmosphere when full to its 42,000 capacity.

OTHER VENUES
BRISBANE CRICKET GROUND
Capacity: 37,500
Events: 13-23 Sept   Football

There can be few better ways to spend an evening than walking along South Bank as the Brisbane River meanders its way through the Queensland capital. A 10-hour drive from Sydney, its choice as a venue is more an attempt to spread a few of the games around the cities. As far as venues go there are few better places than the world-famous 'Gabba' to hold football matches. Given the poor season of the local team, the Brisbane Strikers – who play at a different venue in Brisbane, Lang Park – locals will be looking to see some of the brightest young names in world soccer in their own back yard.

Located in the Woolloongabba area of the city – from where it gets its nickname – the Gabba staged its first International Test cricket match on 27 November 1931, when Australia played South Africa and more recently it has become home to the Brisbane Lions Australian Rules football team.

Brisbane will host six preliminary matches and then a quarter-final match on 23 September.

BRUCE STADIUM, CANBERRA
Capacity: 25,000
Events: 3-24 Sept   Football

Located in the Australian Capital Territory (ACT) next to the Australian Institute of Sport, the brilliantly named Bruce Stadium rose from the ground in 1977 as a venue for the Pan Pacific Games. The Olympic football tournament has provided the impetus for some much needed redevelopment that includes a new three-mast roof over the east stand.

The venue isn't unknown to football because Australia's national women's football team – the Matildas – play their games here! During the rest of the year the facility is home to both the ACT Brumbies in the Rugby Union Super 12 series and the Canberra Raiders in the National Rugby League.

HINDMARSH STADIUM, ADELAIDE
Capacity: 20,000
Events: 13-23 Sept   Football

Hindmarsh Stadium is no stranger to football – the local ASF team Adelaide Force have their home there. As part of a £10million upgrade the stadium is being made into an all-seater – with its capacity increasing from 12,000 to 15,000 – and with the old single tier main stand being replaced by a more modern one, this time on three tiers. However, an extra 5,000 will be able to attend the Olympic preliminary matches there thanks to the addition of temporary seating. Games here start two days before the official opening of the Games and Hindmarsh will host six preliminary matches and one men's quarter-final.

MELBOURNE CRICKET GROUND
Capacity: 90,000
Events: 13-26 Sept   Football

Before the arrival of Stadium Australia, the famous MCG was Australia's biggest stadium. Not just the home of cricket, it welcomes spectators to Victoria's national pastime Aussie Rules, hosting the AFL Grand Final every year with almost 98,000 people turning up for that event alone. For the Olympics the capacity has been reduced and the men's and women's football preliminaries will not be the first Olympic events to be hosted in the facility – it was the centre stage for the 1956 Olympics staged in Melbourne.

The last major renovation work carried out on the MCG was in 1992 when £60 million was spent adding the Great Southern Stand and improving spectator facilities throughout. In addition to the preliminary matches it will also host a semi-final.

GB – All-Time Medals

Listed in the following pages are the names and details of all competitors who have won a medal for Great Britain. The listings are arranged by Games and by the medal type – gold first, then silver then bronze. Within the medal category winners are listed roughly in order of sport – thus medals won in Archery will appear at the front and those for Weightlifting towards the end.

1996

Name	Event	Medal
Matthew Pinsent	Rowing Coxless Pairs	Gold
Steve Redgrave	Rowing Coxless Pairs	Gold
Roger Black	400 Metres	Silver
Jamie Baulch	4 x 400m Relay	Silver
Roger Black	4 x 400m Relay	Silver
Iwan Thomas	4 x 400m Relay	Silver
Mark Richardson	4 x 400m Relay	Silver
Steve Backley	Javelin	Silver
Jonathan Edwards	Triple Jump	Silver
Paul Palmer	400 Metre Freestyle	Silver
Neil Broad	Tennis Doubles	Silver
Tim Henman	Tennis Doubles	Silver
Ben Ainslie	Yachting Open Laser	Silver
John Merricks & Ian Walker	Yachting 470	Silver
Denise Lewis	Heptathlon	Bronze
Steve Smith	High Jump	Bronze
Chris Boardman	Cycling Road Time Trial	Bronze
Max Sciandri	Cycling Road Race	Bronze
Tim Foster	Rowing Coxless Fours	Bronze
Rupert Obholzer	Rowing Coxless Fours	Bronze
Greg Searle	Rowing Coxless Fours	Bronze
Jonny Searle	Rowing Coxless Fours	Bronze
Graeme Smith	1500 Metre Freestyle	Bronze

1992

Name	Event	Medal
Linford Christie	100 Metres	Gold
Sally Gunnell	400 Metre Hurdles	Gold
Chris Boardman	Cycling Individual 4000m	Gold

Garry Herbert	Rowing Coxed Pairs	Gold
Matthew Pinsent	Rowing Coxless Pairs	Gold
Stephen Redgrave	Rowing Coxless Pairs	Gold
Greg Searle	Rowing Coxed Pairs	Gold
Johnathan Searle	Rowing Coxed Pairs	Gold
Gareth Marriott	Canoeing Canadian 1	Silver
Nicola Fairbrother	Judo 65kg	Silver
Raymond Stevens	Judo 95kg	Silver
Steven Holland	Archery Team	Bronze
Richard Priestman	Archery Team	Bronze
Leroy Watson	Archery Team	Bronze
Simon Terry	Archery Individual	Bronze
Tony Jarrett	110 Metre Hurdles	Bronze
Kriss Akabusi	400 Metre Hurdles	Bronze
Kriss Akabusi	4 x 400 Metre Relay	Bronze
Roger Black	4 x 400 Metre Relay	Bronze
David Grindley	4 x 400 Metre Relay	Bronze
John Regis	4 x 400 Metre Relay	Bronze
Sally Gunnell	Women's 4 x 400 Metre Relay	Bronze
Sandra Douglas	Women's 4 x 400 Metre Relay	Bronze
Phylis Smith	Women's 4 x 400 Metre Relay	Bronze
Jennifer Stoute	Women's 4 x 400 Metre Relay	Bronze
Steve Backley	Javelin	Bronze
Robin Reid	Boxing Light Middleweight	Bronze
Gillian Atkins	Women's Hockey	Bronze
Lisa Bayliss	Women's Hockey	Bronze
Victoria Dixon	Women's Hockey	Bronze
Wendy Fraser	Women's Hockey	Bronze
Susan Fraser	Women's Hockey	Bronze
Kathryn Johnson	Women's Hockey	Bronze
Sandra Lister	Women's Hockey	Bronze
Jackie McWilliams	Women's Hockey	Bronze
Tammy Miller	Women's Hockey	Bronze
Helen Morgan	Women's Hockey	Bronze
Mary Nevill	Women's Hockey	Bronze
Mandy Nicholls	Women's Hockey	Bronze
Alison Ramsay	Women's Hockey	Bronze
Jane Sixsmith	Women's Hockey	Bronze
Joanne Thompson	Women's Hockey	Bronze
Kate Howey	Judo 66kg	Bronze
Sharon Rendle	Judo 52kg	Bronze
Nicholas Gillingham	200 Metre Breaststroke	Bronze

1988

Name	Event	Medal
Paul Barber	Men's Hockey	Gold
Stephen Batchelor	Men's Hockey	Gold
Kulbir Bhaura	Men's Hockey	Gold
Robert Clift	Men's Hockey	Gold
Richard Dodds	Men's Hockey	Gold
David Faulkner	Men's Hockey	Gold
Russell Garcia	Men's Hockey	Gold
Martyn Grimley	Men's Hockey	Gold
Sean Kerly	Men's Hockey	Gold
James Kirkwood	Men's Hockey	Gold
Richard Leman	Men's Hockey	Gold
Stephen Martin	Men's Hockey	Gold
Veryan Pappin	Men's Hockey	Gold
Johnathan Potter	Men's Hockey	Gold
Imran Sherwani	Men's Hockey	Gold
Ian Taylor	Men's Hockey	Gold
Andrew Holmes	Rowing Coxless Pairs	Gold
Stephen Redgrave	Rowing Coxless Pairs	Gold
Malcolm Cooper	Small Bore Rifle (3P)	Gold
Adrian Moorhouse	100 Metre Breaststroke	Gold
Michael McIntyre	Yachting International Star	Gold
Bryn Vaile	Yachting International Star	Gold
Linford Christie	100 Metres	Silver
Peter Elliott	1500 Metres	Silver
Colin Jackson	110 Metre Hurdles	Silver
Elliott Bunney	4 x 100 Metre Relay	Silver
Linford Christie	4 x 100 Metre Relay	Silver
Mike MacFarlane	4 x 100 Metre Relay	Silver
John Regis	4 x 100 Metre Relay	Silver
Liz McColgan	Women's 10000 Metres	Silver
Fatima Whitbread	Women's Javelin	Silver
Ian Stark	Equestrian Individual Three Day	Silver
Virginia Leng	Equestrian Three Day Event Team	Silver
Mark Phillips	Equestrian Three Day Event Team	Silver
Ian Stark	Equestrian Three Day Event Team	Silver
Karen Straker	Equestrian Three Day Event Team	Silver
Alister Allan	Small Bore Rifle (3P)	Silver
Nicholas Gillingham	200 Metre Breaststroke	Silver
Steven Hallard	Archery Team	Bronze
Richard Priestman	Archery Team	Bronze
Leroy Watson	Archery Team	Bronze
Yvonne Murray	Women's 3000 Metres	Bronze

Mark Rowland	3000 Metre Steeplechase	Bronze
Richard Woodhall	Boxing Light Middleweight	Bronze
Virginia Leng	Equestrian Individual Three Day	Bronze
Dennis Stewart	Judo 95kg	Bronze
Graham Brookhouse	Modern Pentathlon	Bronze
Dominic Mahoney	Modern Pentathlon	Bronze
Richard Phelps	Modern Pentathlon	Bronze
Andrew Holmes	Coxed Pairs	Bronze
Stephen Redgrave	Coxed Pairs	Bronze
Patrick Sweeney	Coxed Pairs	Bronze
Andrew Jameson	100 Metre Butterfly	Bronze

1984

Name	Event	Medal
Sebastian Coe	1500 Metres	Gold
Tessa Sanderson	Javelin	Gold
Daley Thompson	Decathlon	Gold
Richard Budgett	Rowing Coxed Fours	Gold
Martin Cross	Rowing Coxed Fours	Gold
Adrian Ellison	Rowing Coxed Fours	Gold
Andrew Holmes	Rowing Coxed Fours	Gold
Stephen Redgrave	Rowing Coxed Fours	Gold
Malcolm Cooper	Small Bore Rifle (3P)	Gold
Sebastian Coe	800 Metres	Silver
Steve Cram	1500 Metres	Silver
Mike McLeod	10000 Metres	Silver
Kriss Akabusi	4 x 400 Metre Relay	Silver
Todd Bennett	4 x 400 Metre Relay	Silver
Phil Brown	4 x 400 Metre Relay	Silver
Garry Cook	4 x 400 Metre Relay	Silver
Shirley Strong	100 Metres Hurdles	Silver
Wendy Sly	3000 Metres	Silver
David Ottley	Javelin	Silver
Diana Clapham	Equestrian Three Day Event Team	Silver
Lucinda Green	Equestrian Three Day Event Team	Silver
Virginia Holgate	Equestrian Three Day Event Team	Silver
Ian Stark	Equestrian Three Day Event Team	Silver
Tim Grubb	Equestrian Team Jumping	Silver
Steven Smith	Equestrian Team Jumping	Silver
John Whitaker	Equestrian Team Jumping	Silver
Michael Whitaker	Equestrian Team Jumping	Silver
Neil Adams	Judo 71kg	Silver
Sarah Hardcastle	Women's 400 Metre Freestyle	Silver

Name	Event	Medal
Kathryn Cook	400 Metres	Bronze
Beverly Callender	4 x 100 Metre Relay	Bronze
Kathryn Cook	4 x 100 Metre Relay	Bronze
Simone Jacobs	4 x 100 Metre Relay	Bronze
Heather Oakes	4 x 100 Metre Relay	Bronze
Charles Spedding	Marathon	Bronze
Keith Connor	Triple Jump	Bronze
Susan Hearnshaw	Long Jump	Bronze
Fatima Whitbread	Javelin	Bronze
Robert Wells	Boxing Super Heavyweight	Bronze
Virginia Holgate	Equestrian Individual Three Day Event	Bronze
Paul Barber	Men's Hockey Team	Bronze
Stephen Batchelor	Men's Hockey Team	Bronze
Kulbir Bhaura	Men's Hockey Team	Bronze
Robert Cattrall	Men's Hockey Team	Bronze
Richard Dodds	Men's Hockey Team	Bronze
James Dutchie	Men's Hockey Team	Bronze
Norman Hughes	Men's Hockey Team	Bronze
Sean Kerly	Men's Hockey Team	Bronze
Richard Leman	Men's Hockey Team	Bronze
Stephen Martin	Men's Hockey Team	Bronze
William McConnell	Men's Hockey Team	Bronze
Veryan Pappin	Men's Hockey Team	Bronze
Johnathan Potter	Men's Hockey Team	Bronze
Mark Precious	Men's Hockey Team	Bronze
Ian Taylor	Men's Hockey Team	Bronze
David Westcott	Men's Hockey Team	Bronze
Neil Eckersley	Judo 60kg	Bronze
Alister Allan	Small Bore Rifle (3P)	Bronze
Barry Dagger	Air Rifle	Bronze
Michael Sullivan	Small Bore Rifle (Prone)	Bronze
Neil Cochrane	200 Metre Individual Medley	Bronze
Andrew Astbury	4 x 200 Metre Freestyle Relay	Bronze
Neil Cochrane	4 x 200 Metre Freestyle Relay	Bronze
Paul Easter	4 x 200 Metre Freestyle Relay	Bronze
Paul Howe	4 x 200 Metre Freestyle Relay	Bronze
June Croft	Women's 400 Metre Freestyle	Bronze
Sarah Hardcastle	Women's 800 Metre Freestyle	Bronze
David Mercer	Weightlifting Middle Heavyweight	Bronze
Noel Loban	Wrestling Freestyle Light Heavyweight	Bronze
Peter Allam	Yachting Flying Dutchman	Bronze
Jo Richards	Yachting Flying Duchman	Bronze

1980

Name	Event	Medal
Allan Wells	100 Metre	Gold
Steven Ovett	800 Metres	Gold
Sebastian Coe	1500 Metres	Gold
Daley Thompson	Decathlon	Gold
Duncan Goodhew	100 Metre Breaststroke	Gold
Allan Wells	200 Metre	Silver
Sebastian Coe	800 Metres	Silver
Neil Adams	Judo 71kg	Silver
Henry Clay	Rowing Eights	Silver
Andrew Justice	Rowing Eights	Silver
Chris Mahoney	Rowing Eights	Silver
Duncan McDougall	Rowing Eights	Silver
Malcolm McGowan	Rowing Eights	Silver
Colin Moynihan	Rowing Eights	Silver
John Pritchard	Rowing Eights	Silver
Richard Stanhope	Rowing Eights	Silver
Allan Whitwell	Rowing Eights	Silver
Sharron Davies	400 Metre Individual Medley	Silver
Phillip Hubble	200 Metre Butterfly	Silver
June Croft	4 x 100 Metre Medley Relay	Silver
Helen Jameson	4 x 100 Metre Medley Relay	Silver
Margaret Kelly	4 x 100 Metre Medley Relay	Silver
Ann Osgerby	4 x 100 Metre Medley Relay	Silver
Steven Ovett	1500 Metres	Bronze
Gary Oakes	400 Metre Hurdles	Bronze
Heather Hunte	Women's 4 x 100 Metre Relay	Bronze
Beverly Goodard	Women's 4 x 100 Metre Relay	Bronze
Sonia Lannaman	Women's 4 x 100 Metre Relay	Bronze
Kathryn Smallwood	Women's 4 x 100 Metre Relay	Bronze
Donna Hartley	Women's 4 x 400 Metre Relay	Bronze
Josyln Hoyte-Smith	Women's 4 x 400 Metre Relay	Bronze
Linsey MacDonald	Women's 4 x 400 Metre Relay	Bronze
Michelle Probert	Women's 4 x 400 Metre Relay	Bronze
Anthony Willis	Boxing Light Welterweight	Bronze
Arthur Mapp	Judo Open Category	Bronze
Malcolm Carmichael	Rowing Coxless Pairs	Bronze
Charles Wiggin	Rowing Coxless Pairs	Bronze
John Beattie	Rowing Coxless Fours	Bronze
Martin Cross	Rowing Coxless Fours	Bronze
Ian McNuff	Rowing Coxless Fours	Bronze
David Townsend	Rowing Coxless Fours	Bronze
Gary Abraham	4 x 100 Metre Medley Relay	Bronze

Duncan Goodhew	4 x 100 Metre Medley Relay	Bronze
David Lowe	4 x 100 Metre Medley Relay	Bronze
Martin Smith	4 x 100 Metre Medley Relay	Bronze

1976

Name	Event	Medal
Jeremy Fox	Modern Pentathlon Team	Gold
Adrian Parker	Modern Pentathlon Team	Gold
Robert Nightingale	Modern Pentathlon Team	Gold
David Wilkie	200 Metre Breaststroke	Gold
Reginald White	Yachting International Tornado	Gold
Keith Remfrey	Judo Open Category	Silver
Christopher Baillieu	Rowing Double Sculls	Silver
Michael Hart	Rowing Double Sculls	Silver
James Clark	Rowing Eights	Silver
Timothy Crooks	Rowing Eights	Silver
Richard Lester	Rowing Eights	Silver
H.Mattheson	Rowing Eights	Silver
David Maxwell	Rowing Eights	Silver
Len Robertson	Rowing Eights	Silver
Fred Smallbone	Rowing Eights	Silver
Patrick Sweeney	Rowing Eights	Silver
John Yallop	Rowing Eights	Silver
David Wilkie	100 Metre Breastsroke	Silver
Rodney Pattison	Yachting Flying Dutchman	Silver
Brendan Foster	10000 Metres	Bronze
Pat Cowdell	Boxing Bantamweight	Bronze
Ian Banbury	Cycling 4000 Metre Team Pursuit	Bronze
Michael Bennett	Cycling 4000 Metre Team Pursuit	Bronze
Robin Croker	Cycling 4000 Metre Team Pursuit	Bronze
Ian Hallam	Cycling 4000 Metre Team Pursuit	Bronze
David Starbrook	Judo 93kg	Bronze
Brian Brinkley	4 x 200 Metre Freestyle Relay	Bronze
Gordon Downie	4 x 200 Metre Freestyle Relay	Bronze
David Dunne	4 x 200 Metre Freestyle Relay	Bronze
Alan McClatchey	4 x 200 Metre Freestyle Relay	Bronze

1972

Name	Event	Medal
Mary Peters	Women's Modern Pentathlon	Gold
Richard Meade	Equestrian Individual Three Day	Gold
Mary Gordon-Watson	Equestrian Three Day Team	Gold
Richard Meade	Equestrian Three Day Team	Gold

Bridget Parker	Equestrian Three Day Team	Gold
Mark Phillips	Equestrian Three Day Team	Gold
David Hemery	4 x 400 Metre Relay	Silver
David Jenkins	4 x 400 Metre Relay	Silver
Alan Pascoe	4 x 400 Metre Relay	Silver
Martin Reynolds	4 x 400 Metre Relay	Silver
David Starbrook	Judo 80kg - 93kg	Silver
Ann Moore	Equestrian Individual Grand Prix Jumping	Silver
David Hemery	400 Metre Hurdles	Bronze
Ian Stewart	5000 Metres	Bronze
Ralph Evans	Boxing Light-Flyweight	Bronze
Alan Minter	Boxing Light-Middleweight	Bronze
George Turpin	Boxing Bantamweight	Bronze
Michael Bennett	Cycling 4000 Metre Team Pursuit	Bronze
Ian Hallam	Cycling 4000 Metre Team Pursuit	Bronze
Ronald Keeble	Cycling 4000 Metre Team Pursuit	Bronze
William Moore	Cycling 4000 Metre Team Pursuit	Bronze
Brian Jacks	Judo 70kg - 80kg	Bronze
Angelo Parisi	Judo Open Category	Bronze
John Kynoch	Shooting Running Game Target	Bronze

1968

Name	Event	Medal
David Hemery	400 Metre Hurdles	Gold
Christopher Finnegan	Boxing Middleweight	Gold
Derek Allhusen	Equestrian Three Day Team	Gold
Reuben Jones	Equestrian Three Day Team	Gold
Richard Meade	Equestrian Three Day Team	Gold
Robert Braithwaite	Shooting Olympic Trap	Gold
Iain MacDonald-Smith	Yachting Flying Dutchman	Gold
Rodney Pattison	Yachting Flying Dutchman	Gold
Lilian Board	Women's 400 Metres	Silver
Sheila Sherwood	Women's Long Jump	Silver
Derek Allhusen	Equestrian Individual Three Day	Silver
Marian Coakes	Equestrian Individual Grand Prix Jumping	Silver
Martyn Woodroffe	200 Metre Butterfly	Silver
John Sherwood	400 Metre Hurdles	Bronze
David Broome	Equestrian Individual Grand Prix Jumping	Bronze
Paul Anderson	Yachting 5.5 Metre Class	Bronze
Adrian Jardine	Yachting 5.5 Metre Class	Bronze

1964

Name	Event	Medal
Lynn Davies	Long Jump	Gold
Ken Matthews	20 Kilometre Walk	Gold
Ann Packer	Women's 800 Metres	Gold
Mary Rand	Women's Long Jump	Gold
John Cooper	400 Metre Hurdles	Silver
Ann Packer	Women's 400 Metres	Silver
Robert Brightwell	4 x 400 Metre Relay	Silver
John Cooper	4 x 400 Metre Relay	Silver
Tim Graham	4 x 400 Metre Relay	Silver
Adrian Metcalf	4 x 400 Metre Relay	Silver
Maurice Herriott	3000 Metre Steeplechase	Silver
Basil Heatley	Marathon	Silver
Paul Nihill	50 Kilometre Walk	Silver
William Hoskyns	Fencing Individual Epee	Silver
Mary Rand	Modern Pentathlon	Silver
Robbie McGregor	100 Metre Freestyle	Silver
Daphne Arden	Women's 4 x 100 Metre Relay	Bronze
Dorothy Hyman	Women's 4 x 100 Metre Relay	Bronze
Mary Rand	Women's 4 x 100 Metre Relay	Bronze
Janet Simpson	Women's 4 x 100 Metre Relay	Bronze
Peter Robeson	Equestrian Individual Grand Prix Jumping	Bronze

1960

Name	Event	Medal
Don Thompson	50 Kilometre Walk	Gold
Dorothy Hyman	Women's 80 Metres Hurdles	Silver
Carol Quinton	Women's High Jump	Silver
Allan Jay	Fencing, Epee Individual	Silver
Allan Jay	Fencing, Epee Team	Silver
Michael Howard	Fencing, Epee Team	Silver
John Pelling	Fencing, Epee Team	Silver
Henry Hoskyns	Fencing, Epee Team	Silver
Raymond Harrison	Fencing, Epee Team	Silver
Michael Alexander	Fencing, Epee Team	Silver
Peter Radford	100 Metres	Bronze
Dorothy Hyman	Women's 100 Metres	Bronze
David Jones	4 x 100 Metres Relay	Bronze
Peter Radford	4 x 100 Metres Relay	Bronze
Dave Segal	4 x 100 Metres Relay	Bronze
Nick Whitehead	4 x 100 Metres Relay	Bronze

Stan Vickers	20 Kilometre Walk	Bronze
Richard McTaggart	Boxing Lightweight	Bronze
James Lloyd	Boxing Welterweight	Bronze
William Fisher	Boxing Light Middleweight	Bronze
Brian Phelps	Diving, Platform	Bronze
David Broome	Showjumping Individual	Bronze
Louis Martin	Weightlifting, 90kg	Bronze

1956

Name	Event	Medal
Chris Brasher	3000 Metre Steeplechase	Gold
Richard McTaggart	Boxing Lightweight	Gold
Terence Spinks	Boxing Flyweight	Gold
Albert Hill	Equestrian Three Day Team	Gold
Arthur Rook	Equestrian Three Day Team	Gold
Frank Weldon	Equestrian Three Day Team	Gold
Gillian Sheen	Fencing Women's Foil	Gold
Judy Grinham	Women's 100 Metre Backstroke	Gold
Derek Johnson	800 Metres	Silver
Gordon Pirie	5000 Metres	Silver
Heather Armitage	Women's 4 x 100 Metre Relay	Silver
Ann Pashley	Women's 4 x 100 Metre Relay	Silver
June Paul	Women's 4 x 100 Metre Relay	Silver
Jean Scrivens	Women's 4 x 100 Metre Relay	Silver
Thelma Hopkins	Women's High Jump	Silver
Thomas Nicholls	Boxing Featherweight	Silver
Arthur Brittain	Cycling Team Road Race	Silver
Alan Jackson	Cycling Team Road Race	Silver
Trevor Simpson	Cycling Team Road Race	Silver
David Bowker	Yachting 5.5 Metre Class	Silver
N.A.Kennedy Cochran-Patrick	Yachting 5.5 Metre Class	Silver
J.D.Dillon	Yachting 5.5 Metre Class	Silver
Stanley Perry	Yachting 5.5 Metre Class	Silver
Derek Ibbotson	5000 Metres	Bronze
Peter Higgins	4 x 400 Metre Relay	Bronze
Derek Johnson	4 x 400 Metre Relay	Bronze
John Salisbury	4 x 400 Metre Relay	Bronze
Michael.Wheeler	4 x 400 Metre Relay	Bronze
Nicholas Gargano	Boxing Welterweight	Bronze
John McCormack	Boxing Light Middleweight	Bronze
Donald Burgess	Cycling 4000 Metre Team Pursuit	Bronze
Michael Cambrill	Cycling 4000 Metre Team Pursuit	Bronze
John Geddes	Cycling 4000 Metre Team Pursuit	Bronze

Alan Jackson	Cycling Individual Road Race	Bronze
Thomas Simpson	Cycling 4000 Metre Team Pursuit	Bronze
Peter Robeson	Equestrian Team Jumping	Bronze
Pat Smythe	Equestrian Team Jumping	Bronze
Frank Weldon	Equestrian Individual Three Day	Bronze
Wilfred White	Equestrian Team Jumping	Bronze
Margaret Edwards	Women's 100 Metre Backstroke	Bronze
Ronald Backus	Yachting Dragon Class	Bronze
Johnathan Janson	Yachting Dragon Class	Bronze
Graham Mann	Yachting Dragon Class	Bronze

1952

Name	Event	Medal
Lt.Col.Henry.M.Llewellyn	Equestrian Team Jumping	Gold
Lt.Col.Douglas Stewart	Equestrian Team Jumping	Gold
Wilfred.H.White	Equestrian Team Jumping	Gold
Sheila Lerwill	Women's High Jump	Silver
Charles.N.Currey	Yachting Olympic Monotype Class	Silver
Emmanuel McDonald Bailey	100 Metres	Bronze
Heather.J.Armitage	Women's 4 x 100 Metre Relay	Bronze
Slyvia Cheeseman	Women's 4 x 100 Metre Relay	Bronze
Jean.C.Desforges	Women's 4 x 100 Metre Relay	Bronze
June Foulds	Women's 4 x 100 Metre Relay	Bronze
John.I.Disley	3000 Metre Steeplechase	Bronze
Shirley Cawley	Women's Long Jump	Bronze
Donald.C.Burgess	Cycling 4000 Metre Team Pursuit	Bronze
G.A.Newberry	Cycling 4000 Metre Team Pursuit	Bronze
Alan Newton	Cycling 4000 Metre Team Pursuit	Bronze
Ronald.C.Stretton	Cycling 4000 Metre Team Pursuit	Bronze
Denys J.Carnill	Hockey	Bronze
John.A.Cockett	Hockey	Bronze
John.V.Conroy	Hockey	Bronze
Graham Dadds	Hockey	Bronze
Derek Day	Hockey	Bronze
Dennis Eagan	Hockey	Bronze
Robin.A.Fletcher	Hockey	Bronze
Roger.K.Midgley	Hockey	Bronze
R.O.A.Norris	Hockey	Bronze
Anthony.S.Nunn	Hockey	Bronze
Anthony.J.Robinson	Hockey	Bronze
J.P.Taylor	Hockey	Bronze
Helen.O.Gordon	200 Metre Breaststroke	Bronze
Kenneth Richmond	Wrestling Freestyle Heavyweight	Bronze

1948

Name	Event	Medal
Bertie Bushnell	Rowing Double Sculls	Gold
Richard Burnell	Rowing Double Sculls	Gold
William Laurie	Rowing Coxless Pairs	Gold
John Wilson	Rowing Coxless Pairs	Gold
David Bond	Yachting Swallow Class	Gold
Stewart Morris	Yachting Swallow Class	Gold
Dorothy Manley	Women's 100 Metres	Silver
Audrey Williamson	Women's 200 Metres	Silver
Maureen Gardner	Women's 80 Metre Hurdles	Silver
Alister McCorquodale	4 x 100 Metre Relay	Silver
John Archer	4 x 100 Metre Relay	Silver
Jack Gregory	4 x 100 Metre Relay	Silver
K.J.Jones	4 x 100 Metre Relay	Silver
Tom Richards	Marathon	Silver
Dorothy Tyler	Women's High Jump	Silver
Donald Scott	Boxing Light Heavyweight	Silver
John Wright	Boxing Middleweight	Silver
Alan Bannister	Cycling 2000 Metre Tandem	Silver
Reginald Harris	Cycling 1000 Metre Sprint	Silver
Reginald Harris	Cycling 2000 Metre Tandem	Silver
Robert. Maitland	Cycling Team Road Race	Silver
C.S.Ian Scott	Cycling Team Road Race	Silver
Gordon Thomas	Cycling Team Road Race	Silver
R.E.Adlard	Men's Hockey Team	Silver
Norman Borrett	Men's Hockey Team	Silver
David Brodie	Men's Hockey Team	Silver
William Griffiths	Men's Hockey Team	Silver
Frederick Lindsay	Men's Hockey Team	Silver
Robin Lindsay	Men's Hockey Team	Silver
John Peake	Men's Hockey Team	Silver
Frank Reynolds	Men's Hockey Team	Silver
George Sime	Men's Hockey Team	Silver
Michael Walford	Men's Hockey Team	Silver
Neil White	Men's Hockey Team	Silver
Christopher Barton	Rowing Eights	Silver
E.A.Paul Bircher	Rowing Eights	Silver
J.G.Dearlove	Rowing Eights	Silver
Michael Lapage	Rowing Eights	Silver
Charles Lloyd	Rowing Eights	Silver
Paul Massey	Rowing Eights	Silver
A.Paul Mellows	Rowing Eights	Silver
David Meyrick	Rowing Eights	Silver

G.Richardson	Rowing Eights	Silver
Julian Creus	Weightlifting Bantamweight	Silver
Terence Johnson	50 Kilometre Walk	Bronze
R.Gerald	Cycling 4000 Metre Team Pursuit	Bronze
Thomas Godwin	Cycling 1000 Metre Time Trial	Bronze
Thomas Godwin	Cycling 4000 Metre Team Pursuit	Bronze
David Ricketts	Cycling 4000 Metre Team Pursuit	Bronze
Wilfred Waters	4000 Metre Team Pursuit	Bronze
A.Carr	Equestrian Team Jumping	Bronze
Lt.Col. Henry Llewellyn	Equestrian Team Jumping	Bronze
Henry Nicoll	Equestrian Team Jumping	Bronze
Cathy Gibson	Women's 400 Metre Freestyle	Bronze
James Halliday	Weightlifting Lightweight	Bronze

1936

Name	Event	Medal
Arthur Brown	4 x 400 Metre Relay	Gold
Godfrey Rampling	4 x 400 Metre Relay	Gold
William Roberts	4 x 400 Metre Relay	Gold
Frederick Wolff	4 x 400 Metre Relay	Gold
Harold Whitlock	50 Kilometre Road Walk	Gold
Leslie Southwood	Rowing Double Sculls	Gold
Jack Beresford	Rowing Double Sculls	Gold
Miles Bellville	Yachting 6 Metre Class	Gold
Christopher Boardman	Yachting 6 Metre Class	Gold
Russell Harmer	Yachting 6 Metre Class	Gold
Charles Leaf	Yachting 6 Metre Class	Gold
Leonard Martin	Yachting 6 Metre Class	Gold
Donald Finlay	110 Metre Hurdles	Silver
Godfrey Brown	400 Metre Hurdles	Silver
Audrey Brown	Women's 4 x 100 Metre Relay	Silver
Barbara Burke	Women's 4 x 100 Metre Relay	Silver
Eileen Hisock	Women's 4 x 100 Metre Relay	Silver
Violet Olney	Women's 4 x 100 Metre Relay	Silver
Ernest Harper	Marathon	Silver
Dorothy Odam	High Jump	Silver
Capt.D.Dawnay	Polo Team	Silver
Capt.B.J.Fowler	Polo Team	Silver
Capt.H.P.Guiness	Polo Team	Silver
Capt.W.R.N.Hinde	Polo Team	Silver
Alan Barrett	Rowing Coxless Fours	Silver
Thomas Bristow	Rowing Coxless Fours	Silver
Peter Jackson	Rowing Coxless Fours	Silver
John Sturrock	Rowing Coxless Fours	Silver

Harry Hill	Cycling 4000 Metre Team Pursuit	Bronze
Ernest Johnson	Cycling 4000 Metre Team Pursuit	Bronze
Charles King	Cycling 4000 Metre Team Pursuit	Bronze
E.V.Mills	Cycling 4000 Metre Team Pursuit	Bronze
Capt.R.G.Fanshawe	Equestrian Three Day Event Team	Bronze
Lieut.E.D. Howard-Vyse	Equestrian Three Day Event Team	Bronze
Capt.A.B.J.Scott	Equestrian Three Day Event Team	Bronze
Peter Scott	Yachting Olympic Monotype	Bronze

1932

Name	Event	Medal
Thomas Hampson	800 Metres	Gold
Thomas Green	50 Kilometre Walk	Gold
John Badcock	Rowing Coxless Fours	Gold
Jack Beresford	Rowing Coxless Fours	Gold
Thomas Tyler	Rowing Coxless Fours	Gold
Rowland George	Rowing Coxless Fours	Gold
Clive Lewis	Rowing Coxless Pairs	Gold
Hugh Edwards	Rowing Coxless Pairs	Gold
John Cornes	1500 Metres	Silver
Thomas Evenson	3000 Metre Steeplechase	Silver
Samuel Ferris	Marathon	Silver
Lord David Burghley	4 x 400 Metre Relay	Silver
Thomas Hampson	4 x 400 Metre Relay	Silver
Godfrey Rampling	4 x 400 Metre Relay	Silver
Crew Stonley	4 x 400 Metre Relay	Silver
Ernest Chambers	Cycling 2000 Metre Tandem	Silver
Stanley Chambers	Cycling 2000 Metre Tandem	Silver
Judy Guiness	Fencing Women's Foil	Silver
Peter Jaffe	Yachting International Star	Silver
Colin Ratsey	Yachting International Star	Silver
Donald Finlay	110 Metre Hurdles	Bronze
Nellie Halstead	Women's 4 x 100 Metre Relay	Bronze
Ethel Johnson	Women's 4 x 100 Metre Relay	Bronze
Gwendoline Porter	Women's 4 x 100 Metre Relay	Bronze
Violet Webb	Women's 4 x 100 Metre Relay	Bronze
William Harvell	Cycling 4000 Metre Team Pursuit	Bronze
Charles Holland	Cycling 4000 Metre Team Pursuit	Bronze
Ernest Johnson	Cycling 4000 Metre Team Pursuit	Bronze
Frank Southall	Cycling 4000 Metre Team Pursuit	Bronze
Edna Valerie Davies	100 Metre Backstroke	Bronze
Edna Valerie Davies	4 x 100 Metre Freestyle Relay	Bronze

Phylis Harding	4 x 100 Metre Freestyle Relay	Bronze
Edna Hughes	4 x 100 Metre Freestyle Relay	Bronze
M.Joyce-Cooper	4 x 100 Metre Freestyle Relay	Bronze

1928

Name	*Event*	*Medal*
Douglas Lowe	800 Metres	Gold
Lord David Burghley	400 Metre Hurdles	Gold
Michael Warriner	Rowing Coxless Fours	Gold
Richard Beesley	Rowing Coxless Fours	Gold
Edward Bevan	Rowing Coxless Fours	Gold
John Lander	Rowing Coxless Fours	Gold
Jack London	100 Metres	Silver
Walter Rangeley	200 Metres	Silver
Ernest Chambers	Cycling 2000 Metre Tandem	Silver
Jack Lauterwasser	Cycling Team Road Race	Silver
C.Marshall	Cycling Team Road Race	Silver
Jack Middleton	Cycling Team Road Race	Silver
J.E.Sibbit	Cycling 2000 Metre Tandem	Silver
Frank Southall	Cycling Team Road Race	Silver
Frank Southall	Cycling Individual Road Race	Silver
Muriel Freeman	Fencing Women's Foil	Silver
J.C.Badcock	Rowing Eights	Silver
Jack Beresford	Rowing Eights	Silver
Donald Gollan	Rowing Eights	Silver
James Hamilton	Rowing Eights	Silver
Gordon Killick	Rowing Eights	Silver
Harold Lane	Rowing Eights	Silver
Guy Nickalls	Rowing Eights	Silver
Robert Nisbet	Coxless Pairs	Silver
Terence O'Brien	Coxless Pairs	Silver
Arthur Sulley	Rowing Eights	Silver
Harold West	Rowing Eights	Silver
Ellen King	100 Metre Backstroke	Silver
M.Joyce Cooper	4 x 100 Metre Freestyle Relay	Silver
Ellen King	4 x 100 Metre Freestyle Relay	Silver
Sarah Stewart	4 x 100 Metre Freestyle Relay	Silver
Vera Tanner	4 x 100 Metre Freestyle Relay	Silver
Jack London	4 x 100 Metre Relay	Bronze
Cyril Gill	4 x 100 Metre Relay	Bronze
Walter Rangeley	4 x 100 Metre Relay	Bronze
Edward Smouha	4 x 100 Metre Relay	Bronze
Montford Southall	Cycling 4000 Metre Team Pursuit	Bronze
Frederick Wyld	Cycling 4000 Metre Team Pursuit	Bronze

L.A.Wyld	Cycling 4000 Metre Team Pursuit	Bronze
P.Wyld	Cycling 4000 Metre Team Pursuit	Bronze
A. Broadbent	Gymnastics Women's Team	Bronze
Lucy Desmond	Gymnastics Women's Team	Bronze
M.B. Hartley	Gymnastics Women's Team	Bronze
A.C. Jagger	Gymnastics Women's Team	Bronze
I.M.R. Judd	Gymnastics Women's Team	Bronze
J.T. Kite	Gymnastics Women's Team	Bronze
M. Moreman	Gymnastics Women's Team	Bronze
E.C. Pickles	Gymnastics Women's Team	Bronze
E. Seymour	Gymnastics Women's Team	Bronze
A. Smith	Gymnastics Women's Team	Bronze
T.David Collett	Rowing Single Sculls	Bronze
M.Joyce Cooper	100 Metre Freestyle	Bronze
M.Joyce Cooper	100 Metre Backstroke	Bronze
Samuel Rabin	Wrestling Freestyle Middleweight	Bronze

1924

Name	Event	Medal
Harold Abrahams	100 metres	Gold
Eric Liddell	400 metres	Gold
Douglas Lowe	800 metres	Gold
Harry Mallin	Boxing Middleweight	Gold
Harry Mitchell	Boxing Light Heavyweight	Gold
Jack Beresford	Rowing Single Sculls	Gold
Charles Eley	Rowing Coxless Fours	Gold
James McNabb	Rowing Coxless Fours	Gold
Robert Morrison	Rowing Coxless Fours	Gold
Terence Sanders	Rowing Coxless Fours	Gold
Cyril Mackworth-Praed	Shooting Running Deer Team	Gold
Philip Neame	Shooting Running Deer Team	Gold
Herbert Perry	Shooting Running Deer Team	Gold
Allen Whitty	Shooting Running Deer Team	Gold
Lucy Morton	200 Metre Breaststroke	Gold
Harold Abrahams	4 x 100 Metre Relay	Silver
William Nichol	4 x 100 Metre Relay	Silver
Walter Rangeley	4 x 100 Metre Relay	Silver
Lancelot Royle	4 x 100 Metre Relay	Silver
Gordon Goodwin	10,000 Metre Walk	Silver
Harry Johnston	3,000 Metres Team	Silver
Bernard McDonald	3,000 Metres Team	Silver
George Webber	3,000 Metres Team	Silver
John Elliott	Boxing Middleweight	Silver
James McKenzie	Boxing Flyweight	Silver
Cyril Alden	Cycling 50km Track	Silver

Gladys Davis	Women's Fencing Foil	Silver
Cyril Mackworth-Praed	Shooting Running Deer (Single)	Silver
Cyril Mackworth-Praed	Shooting Running Deer (Double)	Silver
Phyllis Harding	100 Metre Backstroke	Silver
F.Barker	4 x 100 Metre Freestyle Relay	Silver
C.M.Jeans	4 x 100 Metre Freestyle Relay	Silver
Grace McKenzie	4 x 100 Metre Freestyle Relay	Silver
Vera Tanner	4 x 100 Metre Freestyle Relay	Silver
Mrs Covell	Tennis Women's Doubles	Silver
Kathleen McKane	Tennis Women's Doubles	Silver
T. Riggs	Sailing 8-metre	Silver
W Riggs	Sailing 8-metre	Silver
Mr Jacob	Sailing 8-metre	Silver
Mr Roney	Sailing 8-metre	Silver
Mr Fowler	Sailing 8-metre	Silver
Eric Liddell	200 metres	Bronze
Guy Butler	400 Metres	Bronze
Henry Stallard	1500 metres	Bronze
Malcolm Noakes	Hammer	Bronze
Frank Wylede	Cycling 50km Track	Bronze
Gladys Carson	200 Metre Breaststroke	Bronze
E.L.Coyler	Tennis Women's Doubles	Bronze
Kathleen McKane	Tennis Women's Singles	Bronze
Miss Shepherd-Barron	Tennis Women's Doubles	Bronze
Andrew McDonald	Wrestling Freestyle Heavyweight	Bronze

1920

Name	Event	Medal
Albert Hill	800 Metres	Gold
Albert Hill	1500 Metres	Gold
Percy Hodge	3000 Metre Steeplechase	Gold
John Ainsworth-Davies	4 x 400 Metre Relay	Gold
Guy Butler	4 x 400 Metre Relay	Gold
Cecil Griffiths	4 x 400 Metre Relay	Gold
Robert Lindsay	4 x 400 Metre Relay	Gold
George Canning	Tug Of War	Gold
Frederick Holmes	Tug Of War	Gold
Frederick Humphreys	Tug Of War	Gold
Edwin Mills	Tug Of War	Gold
John Sewell	Tug Of War	Gold
John Shepherd	Tug Of War	Gold
Harry Stiff	Tug Of War	Gold
Ernest Thorn	Tug Of War	Gold
Harry Mallin	Boxing Middleweight	Gold
Ronald Rawson	Boxing Heavyweight	Gold

Thomas Lance	Cycling 2000 Metre Tandem	Gold
Harry Ryan	Cycling 2000 Metre Tandem	Gold
Charles Atkins	Men's Hockey Team	Gold
John Bennett	Men's Hockey Team	Gold
Harold Cassels	Men's Hockey Team	Gold
Harold Cooke	Men's Hockey Team	Gold
Eric Crockford	Men's Hockey Team	Gold
Reginald Crummack	Men's Hockey Team	Gold
Harry Haslam	Men's Hockey Team	Gold
Arthur Leighton	Men's Hockey Team	Gold
John McBryan	Men's Hockey Team	Gold
George McGrath	Men's Hockey Team	Gold
Charles Marcon	Men's Hockey Team	Gold
Stanley Shoveller	Men's Hockey Team	Gold
William Smith	Men's Hockey Team	Gold
Cyril Wilkinson	Men's Hockey Team	Gold
Frederick Barrett	Polo Team	Gold
Vivian Lockett	Polo Team	Gold
Teignmouth Melvill	Polo Team	Gold
Lord John Wodehouse	Polo Team	Gold
Kathleen McKane	Tennis Women's Doubles	Gold
Winifred.M.McNair	Tennis Women's Doubles	Gold
Oswald Turnball	Tennis Men's Doubles	Gold
Maxwell Woosnam	Tennis Men's Doubles	Gold
Charles Bugbee	Water Polo Team	Gold
William Dean	Water Polo Team	Gold
Christopher Jones	Water Polo Team	Gold
William Peacock	Water Polo Team	Gold
Noel Purcell	Water Polo Team	Gold
Paul Radmilovic	Water Polo Team	Gold
Charles Smith	Water Polo Team	Gold
Robert Coleman	Yachting 7 Metre Class	Gold
W.J.Maddison	Yachting 7 Metre Class	Gold
Dorothy Wright	Yachting 7 Metre Class	Gold
Cyril Wright	Yachting 7 Metre Class	Gold
T.Hedberg	Yachting Olympic Monotype	Gold
F.A.Richards	Yachting Olympic Monotype	Gold
Guy Butler	400 Metres	Silver
Philip Baker	1500 Metres	Silver
Arthur Nichols	Team Cross Country	Silver
Frank Hegarty	Team Cross Country	Silver
James Wilson	Team Cross Country	Silver
Charles Blewitt	3000 Metre Team Race	Silver
Albert Hill	3000 Metre Team Race	Silver
William Seagrove	3000 Metre Team Race	Silver

Alexander Ireland	Boxing Welterweight	Silver
Cyril Alden	Cycling 50 Kilometre Track	Silver
H Thomas Johnson	Cycling 1000 Metre Sprint	Silver
Eileen Armstrong	Diving Women's Highboard	Silver
Jack Beresford	Rowing Single Sculls	Silver
Leander Club	Rowing Eights	Silver
Miss Birkenhead	4 x 100 Metre Freestyle Relay	Silver
C.M.Jeans	4 x 100 Metre Freestyle Relay	Silver
G.McKenzie	4 x 100 Metre Freestyle Relay	Silver
Miss Ratcliffe	4 x 100 Metre Freestyle Relay	Silver
Dorothy Holman	Tennis Women's Singles	Silver
Mrs Beamish	Tennis Women's Doubles	Silver
Dorothy Holman	Tennis Women's Doubles	Silver
Kathleen McKane	Tennis Mixed Doubles	Silver
Maxwell Woosnam	Tennis Mixed Doubles	Silver
Harry Edward	100 Metres	Bronze
Harry Edward	200 Metres	Bronze
James Wilson	10000 Metres	Bronze
Charles Gunn	10 Kilometre Walk	Bronze
William Cuthbertson	Boxing Flyweight	Bronze
H.Franks	Boxing Light Heavyweight	Bronze
James McKenzie	Boxing Bantamweight	Bronze
Harry Ryan	Cycling 1000 Metre Sprint	Bronze
Johnson	Skating Pairs	Bronze
Williams	Skating Pairs	Bronze
H.E.Annison	4 x 200 Metre Freestyle Relay	Bronze
P.Peters	4 x 200 Metre Freestyle Relay	Bronze
L.Savage	4 x 200 Metre Freestyle Relay	Bronze
Henry Taylor	4 x 200 Metre Freestyle Relay	Bronze
Kathleen McKane	Tennis Women's Singles	Bronze
P.W.Bernard	Wrestling Freestyle Featherweight	Bronze
Peter Wright	Wrestling Freestyle Lightweight	Bronze

1912

Name	Event	Medal
Arnold Jackson	1500 Metres	Gold
William Applegarth	4 x 100 Metre Relay	Gold
Victor D'Arcy	4 x 100 Metre Relay	Gold
David Jacobs	4 x 100 Metre Relay	Gold
Henry MacIntosh	4 x 100 Metre Relay	Gold
William Kinnear	Rowing Single Sculls	Gold
Philip Fleming	Rowing Eights	Gold
Arthur Garton	Rowing Eights	Gold
James Gillian	Rowing Eights	Gold

Ewart Horsfall	Rowing Eights	Gold
Alister Kirby	Rowing Eights	Gold
Edgar. Burgess	Rowing Eights	Gold
Sidney Swann	Rowing Eights	Gold
Henry Wells	Rowing Eights	Gold
Leslie Wormald	Rowing Eights	Gold
Edward Lessimore	Shooting Small Bore Team (50m)	Gold
Robert Murray	Shooting Small Bore Team (50m)	Gold
Joseph Pepe	Shooting Small Bore Team (50m)	Gold
William Pimm	Shooting Small Bore Team (50m)	Gold
Ronald Brebner	Football Team	Gold
Arthur Berry	Football Team	Gold
Thomas Burn	Football Team	Gold
Joseph Dines	Football Team	Gold
Gordon Hoare	Football Team	Gold
Arthur Knight	Football Team	Gold
Henry Littlewort	Football Team	Gold
Douglas McWhirter	Football Team	Gold
Ivan Sharpe	Football Team	Gold
Harold Walden	Football Team	Gold
Vivian Woodward	Football Team	Gold
Jennie Fletcher	4 x 100 Metre Freestyle Relay	Gold
Isabella Moore	4 x 100 Metre Freestyle Relay	Gold
Annie Speirs	4 x 100 Metre Freestyle Relay	Gold
Irene Steer	4 x 100 Metre Freestyle Relay	Gold
Isaac Bentham	Water Polo Team	Gold
Charles Bugbee	Water Polo Team	Gold
George Cornet	Water Polo Team	Gold
Arthur Hill	Water Polo Team	Gold
Paul Radmilovic	Water Polo Team	Gold
Charles Smith	Water Polo Team	Gold
George Wilkinson	Water Polo Team	Gold
Charles Dixon	Tennis Mixed Doubles (Indoor)	Gold
Edith Hannam	Tennis Mixed Doubles (Indoor)	Gold
Edith Hannam	Tennis Women's Singles (Indoor)	Gold
W.Chaffe	Tug Of War	Silver
J.Dowler	Tug Of War	Silver
Frederick Humphreys	Tug Of War	Silver
M.Hynes	Tug Of War	Silver
Edwin Mills	Tug Of War	Silver
A.Munro	Tug Of War	Silver
John Shepherd	Tug Of War	Silver
Ernest Webb	10 Kilometre Walk	Silver
Frederick Grubb	Cycling Team Road Race	Silver
Frederick Grubb	Cycling Individual Road Race	Silver

Meredith Moss	Cycling Team Road Race	Silver
Jack Beresford	Rowing Coxed Fours	Silver
Geoffrey Carr	Rowing Coxed Fours	Silver
Charles Rough	Rowing Coxed Fours	Silver
Karl Vernon	Rowing Coxed Fours	Silver
H.G.Burr	Shooting Military Rifle Team	Silver
A.G.Fulton	Shooting Military Rifle Team	Silver
H.Ommundsen	Shooting Military Rifle Team	Silver
E.L.Parnell	Shooting Military Rifle Team	Silver
J.Reid	Shooting Military Rifle Team	Silver
E.Skilton	Shooting Military Rifle Team	Silver
John Butt	Shooting Clay Pigeon Team	Silver
William Grosvenor	Shooting Clay Pigeon Team	Silver
Harry Humby	Shooting Clay Pigeon Team	Silver
Alexander Maunder	Shooting Clay Pigeon Team	Silver
Charles Palmer	Shooting Clay Pigeon Team	Silver
George Whitaker	Shooting Clay Pigeon Team	Silver
William Milne	Shooting Small Bore Rifle (Prone)	Silver
William Milne	Shooting Small Bore Rifle (25m)	Silver
Joseph Pepe	Shooting Small Bore Team (25m)	Silver
William Pimm	Shooting Small Bore Team (25m)	Silver
W.K.Styles	Shooting Small Bore Team (25m)	Silver
John Hatfield	400 Metre Freestyle	Silver
John Hatfield	1500 Metre Freestyle	Silver
Charles Dixon	Tennis Men's Singles (Indoor)	Silver
Miss Aitchison	Tennis Mixed Doubles (Indoor)	Silver
H.Roper-Barrett	Tennis Mixed Doubles (Indoor)	Silver
William Applegarth	200 Metres	Bronze
Gordon Hutson	5000 Metres	Bronze
W.Cotrill	3000 Metre Team Race	Bronze
Gordon Hutson	3000 Metre Team Race	Bronze
W.C.Moore	3000 Metre Team Race	Bronze
C.H.A.Porter	3000 Metre Team Race	Bronze
E.J.Henley	4 x 400 Metre Relay	Bronze
G.Nicol	4 x 400 Metre Relay	Bronze
C.N.Seedhouse	4 x 400 Metre Relay	Bronze
J.T.Soutter	4 x 400 Metre Relay	Bronze
E.Glover	Cross Country Team	Bronze
F.N.Hibbins	Cross Country Team	Bronze
T.Humphreys	Cross Country Team	Bronze
Isabelle White	Diving Women Springboard	Bronze
Harry Burt	Shooting Small Bore Rifle (Prone)	Bronze
Charles Stewart	Shooting Free Pistol (50m)	Bronze
H.Durant	Shooting Team (Over 50m)	Bronze
A.J.Kempster	Shooting Team (Over 50m)	Bronze

H.O.Poulter	Shooting Team (Over 50m)	Bronze
Charles Stewart	Shooting Team (Over 50m)	Bronze
H.Durant	Shooting Team (Over 30m)	Bronze
A.J.Kempster	Shooting Team (Over 30m)	Bronze
H.O.Poulter	Shooting Team (Over 30m)	Bronze
Charles Stewart	Shooting Team (Over 30m)	Bronze
Jennie Fletcher	100 Metre Freestyle	Bronze
Percy Courtman	400 Metre Breaststroke	Bronze
Thomas Battersby	4 x 200 Metre Freestyle Relay	Bronze
William Foster	4 x 200 Metre Freestyle Relay	Bronze
John Hatfield	4 x 200 Metre Freestyle Relay	Bronze
Henry Taylor	4 x 200 Metre Freestyle Relay	Bronze
E.A.Beamish	Tennis Men's Doubles (Indoor)	Bronze
Charles Dixon	Tennis Men's Doubles (Indoor)	Bronze
Mabel Parton	Tennis Women's Singles (Indoor)	Bronze

1908

Name	Event	Medal
William Dod	Archery Men's Singles	Gold
Queenie Newall	Archery Women's Singles	Gold
Wyndham Halswelle	400 Metres	Gold
Arthur Russell	3000 Metre Steeplechase	Gold
William Coales	3 Miles Team Race	Gold
Joseph Deakin	3 Miles Team Race	Gold
Arthur Robertson	3 Miles Team Race	Gold
Emil Voigt	5 Mile Race	Gold
George Larner	3500 Metre Walk	Gold
George Larner	10 Mile Walk	Gold
Tim Ahearne	Triple Jump	Gold
Edward Barrett	Tug Of War	Gold
Frederick Goodfellow	Tug Of War	Gold
William Hirons	Tug Of War	Gold
Frederick Humphreys	Tug Of War	Gold
Albert Ireton	Tug Of War	Gold
Frederick Merriman	Tug Of War	Gold
Edwin Mills	Tug Of War	Gold
John Shepherd	Tug Of War	Gold
John Douglas	Boxing Middleweight	Gold
Frederick Grace	Boxing Lightweight	Gold
Albert Oldham	Boxing Heavyweight	Gold
Henry Thomas	Boxing Bantamweight	Gold
Richard Gunn	Boxing Featherweight	Gold
Victor Johnson	Cycling 660 Yards Track	Gold
Clarence Brickwood-Kingsbury	Cycling 4000 Metre Team Pursuit	Gold

Name	Event	Medal
Benjamin Jones	Cycling 4000 Metre Team Pursuit	Gold
Lewis Leon Meredith	Cycling 4000 Metre Team Pursuit	Gold
Ernest Payne	Cycling 4000 Metre Team Pursuit	Gold
Benjamin Jones	Cycling 5000 Metre Track	Gold
Clarence Brickwood-Kingsbury	Cycling 20 Kilometre Track	Gold
Charles Bartlett	Cycling 100 Kilometre Track	Gold
Louis Baillon	Men's Hockey Team	Gold
Harry Freeman	Men's Hockey Team	Gold
Eric Green	Men's Hockey Team	Gold
Gerald Logan	Men's Hockey Team	Gold
Alan Noble	Men's Hockey Team	Gold
Edgar Page	Men's Hockey Team	Gold
Reginald Pridmore	Men's Hockey Team	Gold
John Robinson	Men's Hockey Team	Gold
Percy Rees	Men's Hockey Team	Gold
Stanley Shoveller	Men's Hockey Team	Gold
Harvey Wood	Men's Hockey Team	Gold
John Fields-Richards	Motor Boating 60ft Class	Gold
Bernard Redwood	Motor Boating 60ft Class	Gold
Isaac Thornycroft	Motor Boating 60ft Class	Gold
John Fields-Richards	Motor Boating 8 Metre Class	Gold
John Fields-Richards	Motor Boating 8 Metre Class	Gold
John Fields-Richards	Motor Boating 8 Metre Class	Gold
Charles Miller	Polo Team	Gold
George Miller	Polo Team	Gold
Patteson Nickalls	Polo Team	Gold
Hernet Wilson	Polo Team	Gold
Evan Noel	Rackets Men's Singles	Gold
Vane Pennell	Rackets Team	Gold
John Jacob Aster	Rackets Team	Gold
Harry Blackstaffe	Rowing Single Sculls	Gold
John Fenning	Rowing Coxless Pairs	Gold
Gordon Thomson	Rowing Coxless Pairs	Gold
Duncan Mackinnon	Rowing Coxless Fours	Gold
Robert Cudmore	Rowing Coxless Fours	Gold
John Fenning	Rowing Coxless Fours	Gold
James Gillian	Rowing Coxless Fours	Gold
Henry Bucknall	Rowing Eights	Gold
Charles Burnell	Rowing Eights	Gold
Raymond Etherington-Smith	Rowing Eights	Gold
Albert Gladstone	Rowing Eights	Gold
Frederick Kelly	Rowing Eights	Gold
Banner Johnstone	Rowing Eights	Gold
Gilchrist Maclagen	Rowing Eights	Gold

Ronald Sanderson	Rowing Eights	Gold
Edward Amoore	Shooting Small Bore Team	Gold
Harry Humby	Shooting Small Bore Team	Gold
M.K.Matthews	Shooting Small Bore Team	Gold
William Pimm	Shooting Small Bore Team	Gold
Arthur Carnell	Shooting Small Bore (Prone)	Gold
John Fleming	Shooting Small Bore (Moving)	Gold
Col.Jerry Millner	Shooting Free Rifle (+1000 yards)	Gold
P.Easte	Shooting Clay Pigeon Team	Gold
Alexander Maunder	Shooting Clay Pigeon Team	Gold
F.W.Moore	Shooting Clay Pigeon Team	Gold
Charles Palmer	Shooting Clay Pigeon Team	Gold
J.F.Pike	Shooting Clay Pigeon Team	Gold
J.M.Postans	Shooting Clay Pigeon Team	Gold
William Styles	Shooting Small Bore Rifle	Gold
Florence Syers	Skating Women's Singles	Gold
Horace Bailey	Soccer Team	Gold
Arthur Berry	Soccer Team	Gold
Frederick Chapman	Soccer Team	Gold
Walter Corbett	Soccer Team	Gold
Harold Hardman	Soccer Team	Gold
Robert Hawkes	Soccer Team	Gold
Keith Hunt	Soccer Team	Gold
Clyde.H.Purnell	Soccer Team	Gold
Herbert Smith	Soccer Team	Gold
Henry Stapley	Soccer Team	Gold
Vivian Woodward	Soccer Team	Gold
Frederick Holman	200 Metre Breaststroke	Gold
Henry Taylor	400 Metre Freestyle	Gold
Henry Taylor	1500 Metre Freestyle	Gold
John Derbyshire	4 x 200 Metre Freestyle Relay	Gold
William Foster	4 x 200 Metre Freestyle Relay	Gold
Paul Radmilovic	4 x 200 Metre Freestyle Relay	Gold
Henry Taylor	4 x 200 Metre Freestyle Relay	Gold
Herbert.R.Barrett	Men's Doubles (Indoor)	Gold
Reginald Doherty	Men's Doubles	Gold
Dorothea Chambers	Tennis Women's Singles	Gold
Gwen EastLake-Smith	Tennis Women's Singles (Indoor)	Gold
Arthur Gore	Tennis Men's Singles (Indoor)	Gold
Arthur Gore	Tennis Men's Doubles (Indoor)	Gold
George Hillyard	Tennis Men's Doubles	Gold
George Cornet	Water Polo Team	Gold
Charles Forsyth	Water Polo Team	Gold
George Nevinson	Water Polo Team	Gold
Paul Radmilovic	Water Polo Team	Gold
Charles Smith	Water Polo Team	Gold

Thomas Thould	Water Polo Team	Gold
George Wilkinson	Water Polo Team	Gold
George O'Kelly	Wrestling Freestyle Heavyweight	Gold
George de Relwyskow	Wrestling Freestyle Lightweight	Gold
Stanley Bacon	Wrestling Freestyle Middleweight	Gold
Charles Crichton	Yachting 6 Metre Class	Gold
Gilbert Laws	Yachting 6 Metre Class	Gold
Thomas McMeekin	Yachting 6 Metre Class	Gold
S.S.N.Bingley	Yachting 7 Metre Class	Gold
Richard Dixon	Yachting 7 Metre Class	Gold
Charles Rivett-Carnac	Yachting 7 Metre Class	Gold
Francis Rivett-Carnac	Yachting 7 Metre Class	Gold
Charles Campbell	Yachting 8 Metre Class	Gold
Blair Onslow Cochrane	Yachting 8 Metre Class	Gold
John Rhodes	Yachting 8 Metre Class	Gold
Henry Sutton	Yachting 8 Metre Class	Gold
Arthur Wood	Yachting 8 Metre Class	Gold
T.C.Glen-Coats	Yachting 12 Metre Class	Gold
R.B.Brooks King	Archery Men's Singles	Silver
Charlotte Dod	Archery Women's Singles	Silver
Harold Wilson	1500 Metres	Silver
Arthur Robertson	3000 Metre Steeplechase	Silver
Edward Owen	5 miles	Silver
Ernest Webb	3500 Metre Walk	Silver
Ernest Webb	10 Mile Walk	Silver
Dennis Horgan	Shot Put	Silver
Cornelius Leahy	High Jump	Silver
T.Butler	Tug Of War	Silver
J.M.Clarke	Tug Of War	Silver
C.Foden	Tug Of War	Silver
W.Greggan	Tug Of War	Silver
A.Kidd	Tug Of War	Silver
D.McDonald Lowey	Tug Of War	Silver
P.Philbin	Tug Of War	Silver
G.Smith	Tug Of War	Silver
T.Swindlehurst	Tug Of War	Silver
S C H Evans	Boxing Heavyweight	Silver
John Gordon	Boxing Bantamweight	Silver
C W Morris	Boxing Featherweight	Silver
Frederick Spiller	Boxing Lightweight	Silver
Charles Denny	Cycling 100 Kilometre Track	Silver
F.G.Hamlin	Cycling 2000 Metre Tandem	Silver
H.T.Johnson	Cycling 2000 Metre Tandem	Silver
E.M.Amphlett	Fencing Epee Team	Silver
E.Castle	Fencing Epee Team	Silver

C.L.Daniell	Fencing Epee Team	Silver
C.H.Haig	Fencing Epee Team	Silver
R.C.L.Montgomerie	Fencing Epee Team	Silver
Eustace Miles	Jeu de Paume	Silver
G.Alexander	Lacrosse Team	Silver
G.Buckland	Lacrosse Team	Silver
E.O.Dutton	Lacrosse Team	Silver
S.Hayes	Lacrosse Team	Silver
W.A.Johnson	Lacrosse Team	Silver
E.P.Jones	Lacrosse Team	Silver
R.G.Martin	Lacrosse Team	Silver
G.Mason	Lacrosse Team	Silver
J.Parker-Smith	Lacrosse Team	Silver
H.W.Ramsey	Lacrosse Team	Silver
N.H.P.Whitley	Lacrosse Team	Silver
S.W.Tysal	Individual Combined Exercises	Silver
Alexander McCulloch	Rowing Single Sculls	Silver
W.S.Buckmaster	Polo Team	Silver
F.M.Freake	Polo Team	Silver
W.H.Jones	Polo Team	Silver
Lord John Wodehouse	Polo Team	Silver
Henry Leaf	Rackets Men's Singles	Silver
J.Davey	Rugby Union Team	Silver
F.Dean	Rugby Union Team	Silver
E.J.Jackett	Rugby Union Team	Silver
R.Jackett	Rugby Union Team	Silver
E.J.Jones	Rugby Union Team	Silver
J.T.Jose	Rugby Union Team	Silver
A.Laurey	Rugby Union Team	Silver
J.Marshall	Rugby Union Team	Silver
B.Solomon	Rugby Union Team	Silver
N.Tregurtha	Rugby Union Team	Silver
J.Trevaskis	Rugby Union Team	Silver
J.Willocks	Rugby Union Team	Silver
A.J.Wilson	Rugby Union Team	Silver
W.Ellicott	Shooting Running Deer Team	Silver
A.G.Fulton	Shooting Military Rifle Team	Silver
H.I.Hawkins	Shooting Small Bore (Dis)	Silver
Harry Humby	Shooting Small Bore (Prone)	Silver
W.R.Lane-Joynt	Shooting Running Deer Team	Silver
Ar-Sgt. Martin	Shooting Military Rifle Team	Silver
M.K.Matthews	Shooting Small Bore (Moving)	Silver
Sgt.H.Ommundsen	Shooting Military Rifle Team	Silver
C.J.A.Nix	Shooting Running Deer Team	Silver
S.Padgett	Shooting Military Rifle Team	Silver
Ted Ranken	Shooting Running Deer (Single)	Silver

Ted Ranken	Shooting Running Deer (Double)	Silver
Ted Ranken	Shooting Running Deer Team	Silver
Major Richardson	Shooting Military Rifle Team	Silver
Major Varley	Shooting Military Rifle Team	Silver
Arthur Cumming	Skating Men's Singles	Silver
Mrs Johnson	Skating Pairs	Silver
Mr Johnson	Skating Pairs	Silver
Sydney Battersby	1500 Metre Freestyle	Silver
William Robinson	200 Metre Breaststroke	Silver
Dorothy Boothby	Women's Singles	Silver
George Caridia	Tennis Men's Singles (Indoor)	Silver
George Caridia	Tennis Men's Doubles (Indoor)	Silver
G.M.Simond	Tennis Men's Doubles (Indoor)	Silver
Angela Greene	Tennis Women's Singles (Indoor)	Silver
J.C.Parke	Tennis Men's Doubles	Silver
Josiah Ritchie	Tennis Men's Doubles	Silver
William Press	Wrestling Freestyle Bantamweight	Silver
George de Relwyskow	Wrestling Freestyle Middleweight	Silver
James Slim	Wrestling Freestyle Featherweight	Silver
C.MacIver	Yachting 12 Metre Class	Silver
Hill-Lowe	Archery Women's Singles	Bronze
Norman Hallows	1500 Metres	Bronze
Leonard Tremeer	400 Metre Hurdles	Bronze
Edward Spencer	10 Mile Walk	Bronze
W.Chaffe	Tug Of War	Bronze
J.Dowler	Tug Of War	Bronze
E.W.Ebbage	Tug Of War	Bronze
T.Homewood	Tug Of War	Bronze
A.Munro	Tug Of War	Bronze
W.Slade	Tug Of War	Bronze
W.B.Tammas	Tug Of War	Bronze
T.J.Williams	Tug Of War	Bronze
J.Woodget	Tug Of War	Bronze
H H Johnson	Boxing Lightweight	Bronze
Frederick Parks	Boxing Heavyweight	Bronze
W Philo	Boxing Middleweight	Bronze
Hugh Roddin	Boxing Featherweight	Bronze
W Webb	Boxing Bantamweight	Bronze
C.Brooks	Cycling 2000 Metre Tandem	Bronze
W.H.T.Isaacs	Cycling 2000 Metre Tandem	Bronze
Benjamin Jones	Cycling 20 Kilometre Track	Bronze
Neville Lytton	Jeu de Paume	Bronze
John Jacob Aster	Rackets Men's Singles	Bronze
Edward Amoore	Shooting Small Bore (Distance target)	Bronze
George Barnes	Shooting Small Bore (Prone)	Bronze

Maurice Blood	Shooting Free Rifle (Over 1000 yards)	Bronze
G.H.Coles	Shooting Team	Bronze
W.Ellicott	Shooting Team	Bronze
Capt.H.G.Lynch-Staunton	Shooting Team	Bronze
W.B.Marsden	Shooting Small Bore (Moving)	Bronze
Alexander Maunder	Shooting Olympic Trap	Bronze
Alexander Rogers	Shooting Running Deer (Single)	Bronze
Sgt.Maj Wallingford	Shooting Team	Bronze
Dorothy Greenhough-Smith	Skating Women's Singles	Bronze
George Hall-Say	Skating Men's Singles	Bronze
Florence Syers	Skating Pairs	Bronze
E.Syers	Skating Pairs	Bronze
Herbert Haresnape	100 Metre Backstroke	Bronze
C.H.L.Cazarlet	Tennis Men's Doubles	Bronze
Charles Dixon	Tennis Men's Doubles	Bronze
Wilberforce Eves	Tennis Men's Singles	Bronze
Josiah Ritchie	Tennis Men's Singles (Indoor)	Bronze
Joan Winch	Tennis Women's Singles	Bronze
Edmond Barrett	Wrestling Freestyle Heavyweight	Bronze
Frederick Beck	Wrestling Freestyle Middleweight	Bronze
Albert Gingell	Wrestling Freestyle Lightweight	Bronze
William McKie	Wrestling Freestyle Featherweight	Bronze

1906

Name	Event	Medal
Henry Hantrey	10000 Metres	Gold
Cornelius Leahy	High Jump	Gold
Peter O'Connor	Triple Jump	Gold
Thomas Matthews	Cycling 2000 Metre Tandem	Gold
Arthur Rushen	Cycling 2000 Metre Tandem	Gold
William Pett	Cycling 20 Kilometre Track	Gold
Wyndham Halswelle	400 Metres	Silver
Alfred Healey	110 Metre Hurdles	Silver
John McGough	1500 Metres	Silver
Cornelius Leahy	Triple Jump	Silver
Peter O'Connor	Long Jump	Silver
H.C.Bouffler	Cycling 1000 Metre Sprint	Silver
Herbert Crowther	Cycling 1000 Metre Time Trial	Silver
Herbert Crowther	Cycling 5000 Metre Track	Silver
Wyndham Halswelle	800 Metres	Bronze

1904

Name	Event	Medal
Thomas Kiely	Decathlon	Gold
John Daly	2500 Metres Steeplechase	Silver

1900

Name	Event	Medal
Alfred Tysoe	800 Metres	Gold
Charles Bennett	1500 Metres	Gold
Charles Bennett	5000 Metre Team Road Race	Gold
John Rimmer	4000 Metres Steeplechase	Gold
John Rimmer	5000 Metre Team Road Race	Gold
Sidney Robinson	5000 Metre Team Road Race	Gold
Stanley Rowley	5000 Metres Team Road Race	Gold
Alfred Tysoe	5000 Metre Team Road Race	Gold
J.E.Barridge	Football Team	Gold
Claude Buckenham	Football Team	Gold
Alfred Chalk	Football Team	Gold
William Gosling	Football Team	Gold
Harold Hardman	Football Team	Gold
A.Haslam	Football Team	Gold
J.H.Jones	Football Team	Gold
J.Nicholas	Football Team	Gold
William Quash	Football Team	Gold
F.G.Spackman	Football Team	Gold
R.R.Turner	Football Team	Gold
James Zealey	Football Team	Gold
John Jarvis	1000 Metres Freestyle	Gold
John Jarvis	4000 Metre Freestyle	Gold
Charlotte Cooper	Tennis Women's Singles	Gold
Charlotte Cooper	Tennis Mixed Doubles	Gold
Hugh Doherty	Tennis Men's Singles	Gold
Hugh Doherty	Tennis Men's Doubles	Gold
Reginald Doherty	Tennis Men's Doubles	Gold
Reginald Doherty	Tennis Mixed Doubles	Gold
Thomas Coe	Water Polo Team	Gold
Peter Kemp	Water Polo Team	Gold
William .H.Lister	Water Polo Team	Gold
Paul Radmilovic	Water Polo Team	Gold
Arthur Robertson	Water Polo Team	Gold
Eric Robinson	Water Polo Team	Gold
George Wilkinson	Water Polo Team	Gold
Lorne Currie	Yachting 1/2 - 1 Ton Class	Gold
William Exshaw	Yachting 2 - 3 Ton Class	Gold
John Gretton	Yachting 1/2 - 1 Ton Class	Gold
John Gretton	Yachting Open Class	Gold

Algernon Maudslay	Yachting 1/2 - 1 Ton Class	Gold
Algernon Maudslay	Yachting Open Class	Gold
Sidney Robinson	2500 Metres	Silver
Charles Bennett	4000 Metres Steeplechase	Silver
Patrick Leahy	High Jump	Silver
Walter Rutherford	Golf Men's Singles	Silver
Harold Mahoney	Tennis Men's Singles	Silver
Peter Kemp	200 Metre Obstacle	Bronze
Sidney Robinson	4000 Metres Steeplechase	Bronze
Patrick Leahy	Long Jump	Bronze
David Robertson	Golf Men's Singles	Bronze
St. George Ashe	Rowing Single Sculls	Bronze
Crittenden Robinson	Shooting Live Pigeon	Bronze
Reginald Doherty	Tennis Men's Singles	Bronze
A.B.Norris	Tennis Men's Singles	Bronze

1896

Name	Event	Medal
John Boland	Tennis Men's Singles	Gold
Launceston Elliott	Weightlifting Heavyweight (One Hand)	Gold
Grantley Goulding	110 Metres Hurdles	Silver
F Keeping	Cycling 12 Hours Track	Silver
Launceston Elliott	Weightlifting Heavyweight (Two Hand)	Silver
F Battel	Cycling Individual Road Race	Bronze

Archery

Introduced: 1900 (revived 1972)
Scheduled: 17-22 September
Venue: Sydney International Archery Park
Events: Men: Individual and Team
Women: Individual and Team

Introduction

The most important characteristics of an archer are steady hands, strong arms and a keen eye. Archery equipment looks hi-tech but the bow is a simple device that hasn't changed the essential character of the sport over many years. Competitors usually use a recurve bow coated in fibreglass. The arrows are made of aluminium or carbon graphite.

Archery was a feature of the Olympic Games several times from 1900 to 1920, but then disappeared for more than 50 years. It reappeared at Munich in 1972 and has remained a fixture ever since.

There are four archery events at the Olympics, consisting of male individual and male team, and female individual and female team competitions.

Archers, or teams, compete in head-to-head matches in single elimination after being ranked from one to 64. The semi-finals winners decide the gold and silver medals in the final, and the semi-finals losers shoot for the bronze.

The US men have been the most successful Olympic archers and have won six gold medals since 1972, including both individual and team gold at the Atlanta Games in 1996. Justin Huish, who at 21 won the individual competition in Atlanta and led the US to victory in the team event, will be competing again in Sydney. Alison Williamson, ranked second in the world, is Britain's best medal hope.

South Korea is the outstanding women's team. Its members have won seven gold medals since 1972, including both individual and team gold at each of the past three Games. Kim Kyung-Wook, the star of the show in Atlanta, is not expected to be in Sydney. Runners-up last time West Germany will be looking to break the Korean domination.

Atlanta 1996

	Gold	*Silver*
MS	Justin Huish, USA	Magnus Petersson, Swe
MT	USA	South Korea
WS	Kim Kyung-Wook	He Ying, Chn
WT	South Korea	Germany

American Justin Huish from California took individual and team gold and was a big hit with the crowds for the way he played to them during the events – watch out for that in Sydney. Huish secured gold when he scored 112 to beat Magnus Petersson, who scored 107 and had to settle for the silver. Oh Kyo-moon, from South Korea, who entered the Olympics as the number one ranked archer in the world, had to settle for the bronze.

In the men's team competition the US team of White, Johnson and Huish beat South Korea by just two points while Italy beat Australia to grab the bronze position.

In the women's individual Kim Kyung-Wook (South Korea) beat He Ying from China to capture the gold medal. The Ukraine's Olena Sadovnycha won the bronze. In the 70m team competition South Korea scored 245 to beat Germany with 239. The bronze went to Poland, who beat Turkey in the play-off by 244 to 239.

Outline rules

There are sixty-four competitors in each competition. When these have shot a 72-arrow open round, the best 32 go on to the knock-out phase, as in tennis. Scores from the open round determine the results of the team competition, with three competitors counting from each country.

Archers fire at targets 70 metres away. The target is 1.22 metres in diameter and marked with 10 concentric rings. The centre ring, or bullseye, measures 12.2 centimetres in diameter. It counts as 10 points, the outer ring counts as one, and the rings in between increase by one point in value as they near the centre.

Did you know?

- The arrows can travel at a speed of more than 240km per hour.
- You can score a 'Robin Hood' in archery by splitting the shaft of an arrow already in the target with another arrow. It does happen!

Jargon buster

Blind	A dugout where scoring judges, the archers' representatives and a spotter sit.
Bow hand	The hand that holds the bow.
Bowshot	The distance a bow sends an arrow.
Bowsight	A mechanical device placed on the bow to help the archer aim; also called the 'sight'.
Bullseye	The central spot on the target.
Draw	To pull back the bowstring and arrow in preparation to shoot.
End	A group of arrows, usually three, shot in one sequence before the archer goes to the target to retrieve them.
Flight	The real or artificial feathers at the back of an arrow designed to make it fly straight; also called the 'fletching'.
Group	The pattern of arrows on a target, or to shoot three arrows on a target.
Riser	The handle of the bow.
Scoring hit	Any arrow that hits the target and counts for points.
Spotter	A person who identifies each archer's score with a telescope and enters the score.
Stabiliser	A weight mounted on the bow to stabilise it during and after a shot.
X	A mark denoting an arrow that strikes the inner circle, or X10, within the bullseye on a target.

Athletics

Introduced: 1896 and various
Scheduled: September 22-October 1
Venue: Olympic Stadium
Events: Women: Individual sprint, middle distance, long distance, hurdling, road, throwing, jumping, combined. Team sprint relays.
Men: Individual sprint, middle distance, long distance, hurdling, road, throwing, jumping, combined. Team sprint relays.

Introduction

Athletics (or track and field) is split into the disciplines of running, jumping and throwing and a fourth type of event combines these. Out of those simple skills come a wide range of competitions, from the 100 metres sprint to determine the fastest person in the world to the 26 mile marathon to determine the most enduring. The events also call for a variety of athletic prowess, from the heavyweight hammer throwers to the sprung coils of the triple jumpers. About 2000 Olympians will compete for medals in athletics in Sydney and the best-known names always seem to come from the track. The track events include sprints (100m, 200m, 400m), middle-distance running (800m and 1500m) and long-distance running (5000m and 10000m), hurdling (100m and 400m for women, 110m and 400m for men), relays (4 x 100m and 4 x 400m) and the men's 3000m steeplechase.

Field events, for both men and women, include the long jump, triple jump, high jump, pole vault, shot put, discus, javelin and hammer throw. Road events consist of the men's and women's marathons, the men's 20km and 50km race walks and the women's 10km race walk.

There are two combined events which are becoming more well-known and which, in reality, produce the best all-round athletes of the Games. The heptathlon is for women and the decathlon for the men. Points are awarded based upon their performances in each event, and the person with the most points wins.

At Sydney the United States' Marion Jones is aiming for an unprecedented five gold medals in the women's 100m, 200m, 4 x 100m and 4 x 400m relays, and the long jump. The shortest but most exciting event is the men's 100-metre final, which is expected to pit defending Olympic champion Donovan Bailey of Canada, against current world record holder Maurice Greene of the United States and Trinidad's Ato Boldon. This showdown is sure to be one of the highlights of the Games.

In the women's 400m France's defending Olympic gold medallist Marie-Jose Perec takes on Australia's dual world champion, Cathy Freeman, who can expect massive home support in Stadium Australia – will the Aussie girl get the gold or will the pressure take its toll?

Other big names expected to compete in Sydney include Australian pole vaulter Emma George, Moroccan middle-distance runner Hicham El Guerrouj, Ethiopian long-distance runner Haile Gebrselassie, Brazilian marathoner Ronaldo da Costa, and 200m and 400m Olympic champion Michael Johnson of the United States with his unique running style.

Athletes qualify for the track and field events by meeting a minimum entry standard. This standard must be met in an official competition with International Amateur Athletic Federation rules between 1 January 1999 and midnight 11 September 2000, 10 days before the athletics competition begins in Sydney. Most athletes will surely not have left it this late!

Atlanta 1996

Men's Event	Gold	Silver
100m	Donovan Bailey, Can	Frankie Fredericks, Nam
200m	Michael Johnson, USA	Frankie Fredericks, Nam
400m	Michael Johnson, USA	Roger Black, GBR
800m	Vebjorn Rodal, Nor	Hezekiel Sepeng, SA
1500m	Noureddine Morceli, Alg	Fermin Cacho, Esp
5000m	Venuste Niyongabo, Bur	Paul Bitok, Ken
10000m	Haile Gebrselassie, Eth	Paul Tergat, Ken
Marathon	Josiah Thugwane, SA	Lee Bong-Ju, Kor
110m hurdles	Allen Johnson, USA	Mark Crear, USA
400m hurdles	Derrick Adkins, USA	Samuel Matete, Zam
3000m s'chase	Joseph Keter, Ken	Moses Kiptanui, Ken
4 x 100m	Canada	USA
4 x 400m	USA	GBR
High jump	Charles Austin, USA	Artur Partyka, Pol

Pole vault	Jean Galfione, Fra	Igor Trandenkov, Rus
Long jump	Carl Lewis, USA	James Beckford, Jam
Triple jump	Kenny Harrison, USA	Jonathan Edwards, GBR
Javelin	Jan Zelezny, Cze	Steve Backley, GBR
Discus	Lars Riedel, Ger	Vladimir Dubrovshchik, Bel
Hammer	Balazs Kiss, Hun	Lance Deal, USA
Shot	Randy Barnes, USA	John Godina, USA
Decathlon	Dan O'Brien, USA	Frank Busemann, Ger
20km walk	Jefferson Perez, Ecu	Ilja Markov, Rus
50km walk	Robert Korzeniowski, Pol	Mikhail Shchennikov, Rus

Women's Event	*Gold*	*Silver*
100m	Gail Devers, USA	Merlene Ottey, Jam
200m	Marie-Jose Perec, Fra	Merlene Ottey, Jam
400m	Marie-Jose Perec, Fra	Cathy Freeman, Aus
800m	Svetlana Masterkova, Rus	Ana Fidelia Quirot, Cub
1500m	Svetlana Masterkova, Rus	Gabriela Szabo, Rom
5000m	Wang Junxia, Chn	Pauline Konga, Ken
10000m	Fernanda Ribeiro, Por	Wang Junxia, Chn
Marathon	Fatuma Roba, Eth	Valentina Yegorova, Rus
100m hurdles	Lyudmila Engquist, Swe	Brigita Bukovec, Slo
400m hurdles	Deon Hemmings, Jam	Kim Batten, USA
4 x 100m	USA	Bahamas, Jam
4 x 400m	USA	Nigeria, Ger
High jump	Stefka Kostadinova, Bul	Niki Bakogianni, Gre
Long jump	Chioma Ajunwa, Nig	Fiona May, Ita
Triple jump	Inessa Kravets, Ukr	Inna Lasovskaya, Rus
Shot	Astrid Kumbernuss, Ger	Sun Xinmei, Chn
Discus	Ilke Wyludda, Ger	Natalya Sadova, Rus
Javelin	Heli Rantanen, Fin	Louise McPaul, Aus
Heptathlon	Ghada Shouaa, Syr	Natasha Sazanovich, Bel
10km walk	Yelena Nikolayeva, Rus	Elisabeta Perrone, Ita

The medals for track and field went to a wider selection of nations than ever before and Caribbean and African athletes fared particularly well. Josiah Thugwane became the first black South African to collect an Olympic gold medal when he won the closest Olympic marathon in history just three seconds ahead of South Korean Lee Bong-Ju, while

Eric Wainaina, of Kenya, was only eight seconds behind the winner. He was also the first South African since Kenneth McArthur, at Stockholm in 1912, to win the Olympic marathon and the first South African since women's high jumper Esther Brand, at Helsinki in 1952, to win an athletics gold medal. Earlier in the Games, 800m runner Hezekiel Sepeng had won a silver for South Africa. The women's marathon also went to an African runner, Fatuma Roba, of Ethiopia.

There were tears and sympathy as 100m defending champion, Linford Christie, was disqualified for two false starts. His successor, Canada's Donovan Bailey, won in a world record time of 9.84s. Noureddine Morceli won the 1500 Olympic title but unfortunately his main opponent the Moroccan Hicham El Guerroudj dropped out of the race after being 'spiked'. This left to fend off only the last-lap challenge from the defending champion, Fermin Cacho, of Spain.

Venuste Niyongabo gave Burundi their first Olympic medal as he made a stunning championship debut in the 5000m. Niyongabo opted for the longer distance that he had raced only twice prior to the Games, because he believed that it offered a more realistic chance of success than his usual 1500m. He took the lead with 450 metres remaining. Olympic 10000m champion, Haile Gebrselassie, of Ethiopia had withdrawn from a double-gold opportunity with injured feet.

Britain's Steve Backley came back from a nine week injury break to get the silver medal in the javelin, one better than his Barcelona performance. Backley typically threw very long with his first throw but arch rival Jan Zelezny responded with a second round golden effort of 88.16m.

Svetlana Masterkova delighted the crowd with her running skills as the Russian became the second woman in Olympic history to complete the 800 and 1500 metres double. In the 1500m the Russian's acceleration eased her away from Gabriela Szabo, of Romania, to win in eight tenths of a second more than four minutes.

The American women crowned the home team's performances with wins in both the 4 x 100m and 4 x 400m relays, although in the 400 Nigeria and Germany, second and third respectively, came close to snatching victory. In the 4 x 100 the Bahamas were second while Jamaica's bronze medal enabled Merlene Ottey to equal the women's all-time record of seven Olympic medals.

Britain's 4 x 400m squad set European record time of 2m 56.60s and earned a silver medal. The USA dug deep to win the gold but Michael Johnson had to withdraw so couldn't get a third gold. Johnson had previously run the 200 metres in 19.32s and won his favourite 400m in one of the sport's all-time achievements. Frenchwoman Marie-Jose Perec did not get the same acclaim although she achieved the same feat in the women's 200m/400m.

History was also made in the marathon by badly injured Abdul-Basar Wasiqi, of Afghanistan, who struggled home in 4h 24m 17s, the slowest ever time. In true Olympic spirit – it's the taking part not the winning – the workers in the stadium moved tarpaulins to give him the honour of completing in the stadium.

Outline Rules

Track Races: The running events are held on an oval track measuring 400m in its inside lane. A kerb five centimetres high borders the inside of the track. Each of the lanes is 1.25m wide and they are numbered 1 to 8 from the inside. Races run anticlockwise and runners placed first or second in each heat of the early qualifying rounds progress to the next stage, along with the third-place finishers or fastest finishers.

After the first round the lane draw is based on the runner's finish and time in each previous round. When possible, athletes from the same nation run in different heats.

Runners stay in lanes for the sprints, the 110m hurdles and the 4 x 100m relay. Sprinters start from a crouched start and a false start is declared if an athlete leaves the blocks before the starter's gun is fired. Two false starts result in disqualification. The 800m and the 4 x 400m relay begin in lanes until they pass the breakline, at which point they compete for position on the inside of the track. In the 800 and 1500 especially, it can get pretty rough.

The winner of a race is the first athlete whose torso reaches the plane of the finish line. If two athletes vying for a spot in the next round tie to 0.001 of a second, both advance to the next round. Judges make their decisions on the evidence of the photo-finish camera.

In relays runners carry a baton which they must pass on to the next runner within a 20m take-over zone. A runner may recover a baton he has dropped but for practical purposes any drop results in failure in the race.

Road Races: In the road events the race begins 'en masse' at the sound of the starter's pistol. Water, other refreshments and sponges are provided at designated spots along the route. In the walking races a walker must have at least one foot on the ground at all times. Also the advancing leg must not be bent at the knee. Judges may warn a walker if he is in danger of breaking this rule. Three warnings mean disqualification.

Field Events: All the jumps and throws have a qualifying round, which reduces the field to (usually) twelve athletes. The medals are decided only by performances in the final.

Throwing Events: Javelin throwers take a run up to a line, which they must not cross, before releasing. Hammer throwers hold the grip that is attached to a head (ball) via a wire. They pivot at speed to propel the hammer out of a safety cage. Speed, correct angle and direction all play a part. A similar technique is used in the discus but the disc is held in the hand and pulled from behind the athlete's back as the thrower acts as a kind of coiled spring. The shot-putter explodes in a small space to put energy into the shot, which is held on one hand under the chin with the elbow bent. The more energy imparted, the greater the distance on the throw.

After three rounds in all the throwing events, the top eight advance to the final three rounds, where they compete in reverse order of the rankings at that point. Ties are resolved by taking second-best performances into account.

In hammer and shot-put the athlete enters and leaves the throwing circle at the back and must not fall from the circle during the throw. If a throw goes wrong, sometimes the athlete will walk from the circle deliberately to cause a 'no throw' that is not measured.

Jumping Events: The high jump and pole vault finals are straight elimination events, while the long jump and triple jump finals consist of six rounds each.

High-jumpers have to get over the bar without dislodging it – rattling the bar and getting away with it is part of the fun – and must take off on one foot. The level take-off area is at least 20 metres long. Jumpers can enter at a height of their choice and miss out (pass) heights. A jumper stays in the competition until they fail to clear the bar three straight times. If two people tie with their highest jumps, the winner is the jumper with the fewest failures. If the tie remains, the athletes are awarded the same placing unless a gold medal is at stake, in which case a jump-off is held.

The pole vault competition follows the same format. Vaulters approach on a level runway at least 40 metres long and take off by placing their poles in a metre-long box sunk into the runway.

Combined Events: In the combined events decathletes and heptathletes score points based on their performances in each event and the points are biased towards a strong finish in every event rather than a win in any one. Both the heptathlon and decathlon are held over two days. In running events except the 1500m and 800m, the athletes are placed in heats based on their personal bests. In the 1500m and 800m runs – the final events – the final heat is contrived to contain all the leading competitors in with a chance of a medal. For the field events, athletes are divided into two pools, based upon their personal bests in those events. Decathletes and heptathletes are disqualified after three false starts. The maximum allowable wind strength for recognition of new world or Olympic records is four metres a second instead of two.

Long and triple jumpers jump as far as possible into the landing area. The runway for both events is at least 40 metres long. They must not cross the front of the take-off board. The triple jump involves a hop from the board, a step in the middle and a final jump. Only a jumper's best performance counts. After three rounds, the top eight advance to the final three rounds. They then compete in reverse order of the rankings from the first three rounds. If there is a tie for a medal, the second-best jump is taken into account. If the tie remains and a gold medal is at stake then the athletes continue competing until there is a clear winner.

Did you know?

- Bob Beamon's world-record long-jump of 1968 was not matched for almost a quarter of a century and remains the Olympic record.
- The Marathon run of legend was 25 miles. In the first modern Games it was set at 26 miles. In London in 1908 the race was extended to 26 miles, 385 yards (42.195km) so that the royal party could see the start and finish in front of them. The distance stuck.
- Abebe Bikila won consecutive gold medals in the marathon in 1960 and 1964, first barefoot, then with shoes!
- Only two men have won the decathlon twice. The first was Bob Mathias of the United States, who won at age 17 in 1948 and then again in 1952. Daley Thompson, from Great Britain, was the second, winning in 1980 and 1984.
- The first sisters to win gold medals at the Olympics were Irina and Tamara Press of the Soviet Union, who in 1969 won the 80m hurdles and shot-put respectively. Irina returned four years later to

win the first women's pentathlon. Between them, they set 26 world records and won five gold medals, as well as a silver.
- Josiah Thugwane became the first black South African to collect an Olympic gold medal when he won the closest Olympic marathon in history just three seconds ahead of South Korean Lee Bong-Ju at the Atlanta Games in 1996.

Jargon buster

Anchor	Last runner in a relay race.
Baton	A smooth, hollow metal or wooden tube used in relay races.
Breakline	An arc painted across the track denoting where runners may leave their original lane and use any part of the track.
Broad jump	Former name for the long jump.
Changeover	Passing of the baton from one runner to the next.
Countback	A process used to determine the winner if two high jumpers or pole vaulters reach equal heights.
Hurdles	The lightweight bars which are the obstacles in a 'hurdles race'.
Kick	When an athlete sprints in the final stretch of a race.
Lap	Once around the 400m track and 'to lap' when an athlete in the long distance races catches and passes another runner.
Middle distance	Refers to the 800 and 1500 metres.
Road race	A race run on established roads or footpaths. The Olympic road races usually finish on the track in the stadium.
Starting blocks	A pair of angled supports temporarily attached to the track and onto which the runners set the soles of their feet ready to push off at the start.
Take-off board	A rectangular board, usually made of wood, from which the jumpers leap. Plasticine on its far edge detects a foul jump.

Badminton

Introduced: 1992 (Mixed in 1996)
Scheduled: September 16-23
Venue: Ross Pavilion (Pavilion 2)
Events: Men and Women: Singles and Doubles. Mixed Doubles

Introduction

With agility and quickness of wrist being a key component for a badminton player it is perhaps not surprising that countries such as Indonesia and China have dominated the sport in recent times. Indeed the biggest problem for both these nations may be in selecting who will represent then – such is the depth of talent available to them. A look at the medals tables for the previous two Olympic Games tells its own story, and in Atlanta 1996 badminton players from Asian countries won no less than 14 of the 15 medals up for grabs. The one exception then was the men's singles gold which was won by Denmark's Hoyer-Larsen, and expect Denmark to be a contender again this time around, not just in the men's event but the women's as well.

There will be 172 players taking part in the badminton competitions. For qualification purposes these will be composed of 29 men's and 29 women's singles players plus 19 pairs each for the men's, women's and mixed doubles. However, the caveat here is once a player has qualified for one of these events they may compete in the other events. The top eight ranked in each competition are seeded. For the singles competitions a base of 32 players will form the first round draw. If there are more than 32 players then the unseeded players go into a draw for the number of elimination matches required to leave 32 players. For the doubles, the first round figure is 16 teams and the elimination option applies here as well.

Players qualified for the Olympic Games based on their world rankings as of 1st May 2000, but no country can have more than three players or pairs in any one event if they are ranked in the top 16; two if ranked 17th-64th and one if ranked below 64th.

Atlanta 1996

Event	Gold	Silver
Men's Singles	P-E Hoyer Larsen, Den	Jiong Dong, Chn
Women's Singles	Bang Soo-Hyun, Kor	Mia Audina, Ind
Men Doubles	Indonesia	Malaysia
Women Doubles	China	South Korea
Mixed Doubles	South Korea	South Korea

Asia dominated the Atlanta badminton tournament. Of the 15 medals up for grabs that continent took all but one. However, it was a red-ribbon event that slipped from their hands as Denmark's Poul-Erik Hoyer-Larsen beat China's Jiong Dong 15-12, 15-10 in the men's singles final. Hoyer-Larsen made his four inch height advantage pay while his ability to catch the corners of the court and follow up with nudged drop shots over the net had Jiong Dong not knowing what to expect. Having taken the first game 15-12, the Dane rushed out to a 5-0 lead in the second and from that point never looked like losing.

In the women's singles final South Korea's Bang Soo-Hyun easily overcame the aspirations of Indonesia's 16-year-old Mia Audina, 11-6, 11-7. Bang, a silver medallist at Barcelona, was the favourite after she ousted defending champion Susi Susanti in the semi-finals. In fact Bang was the dominant player throughout the tournament, not losing a single game and even winning one game 11-0, 11-0 inside ten minutes! Bang trailed in the second set, 7-5, but then won six points on the trot to secure the coveted gold.

The winners of the men's doubles had found themselves a game down and staring defeat in the face, but a change in tactics at a vital point turned matters and with Indonesia's Rexy Mainaky and Ricky Subagja starting to drive home smashes, they came back to beat Malaysia's Cheah Soon Kit and Yap Kim Hock, 5-15, 15-13, 15-12 to win the title. That opening game loss was Subagja and Mainaky's first dropped game of the tournament.

Ge Fei and Gu Jun of China captured the women's doubles gold, beating South Korea's Gil Young-ah and Jang Hye-ock, 15-5, 15-5. It was the seventh time the finalists had met in finals in 12 months.

The mixed doubles final was an all-China affair with Liu Jianjun and Sun Man getting the better of Chen Xingdong and Peng Xingyong 13-15, 17-15, 15-4.

Outline rules

Badminton is played as a game between two people (singles) or four people (doubles – two per side). Singles are played between like sexes whilst doubles may be of like or mixed sex. There are five events in the Olympic games: men's singles and doubles; women's singles and doubles and mixed doubles. The game takes place, indoors, on a rectangular court between contestants who hit a shuttlecock, with a racket, over a central net. The aim is to try and hit the shuttlecock so that it touches the floor, within the bounds of the court, on the opposition's side of the court. Points can only be won on serve and if a play is won on the opposition's serve then serve is transferred. Thus, only the serving team can score a point, while the receiving side is trying to win the right to serve the following point.

The match consists of a best-of-three series – the first to win two games. Games are started with a coin toss with the winner deciding whether to serve or receive first or which end of the court to start at. In men's matches, games are played to 15 points and 11 points in women's games. However, if games are ties at 14-14 (men) or 10-10 (women) the side that reached 14 or 10 first can choose how the game will finish. They can choose to 'set' – in which case the first side to score 17 (men) or 13 (women) is the winner. However, if they choose not to set than it is the first to 15 (men) or 11 (women), ie, the next scoring point wins the game.

The shuttle or shuttlecock has a round cork base covered by leather, with 16 goose feathers attached to the base. The feathers can vary in length from shuttle to shuttle – within the bounds 64mm to 70mm – but in any one shuttle, all feathers must be of equal length. Shuttles are light, weighing between 4.74 and 5.5 grams. The racket used to hit the shuttle may be up to 68cm long and 23cm wide, with a head up to 29cm long.

The badminton court is a rectangle 13.4 metres long and 5.18 metres wide for singles with the full court for doubles being 42 centimetres (18 inches) wider on each side. The net is hung across the centre and is 1.55m high at the posts on either end and 1.524m in the centre. The back corner of each side contains a service court into which the serve must be placed.

On serve the server aims to place the shuttle within the receiver's service court. In singles, the server serves from the left-hand service court if his or her point total is an odd number, and the right-hand service court if the total is even. The serve then serves to the diagonally opposite service court. In doubles, the player who serves first serves from the right-hand service court and alternates sides each time a point is won. When the team loses a rally, the serve passes to the team-mate, who serves from the other service court. When both players on one side have lost their services, the other team serves and follows the same process.

A point or service is won by a player hitting the shuttle to the floor on the opponent's side of the net or if the opponent fails to keep the shuttle in play. It is declared out of play if it fails to go over the net, lands outside the court or hits the ceiling. If a player touches the net during play the point is automatically lost.

Did you know?

- Players can cover up to six kilometres in a single match.
- When hit hard the shuttle can travel at speeds of 260 kph.
- The average match lasts 1 hour 16 minutes, during which the shuttle is in play for an average of 37 minutes.
- There are nearly 2,000 strokes played in each match with an average of 13 strokes per rally.

Jargon buster

Alley	The 'tramline' area on each side of the court which is ued in doubles.
Back alley	The area between the back boundary line and the long service line used in doubles.
Baseline	The boundary line at the back of the court, parallel to the net.
Baulk	A deceptive 'feint' movement that disconcerts an opponent before or during the serve.
Forecourt	The front third of the court, between the net and the start of the service line.
Kill	A fast, powerful shot hit down into the opponent's court so it cannot be returned.
Set	To choose to extend a game beyond its normal ending score if the score is tied with one point to go.

Baseball

Introduced:	1912
Scheduled:	September 17-27
Venues:	Baseball Stadium, Sydney Olympic Park
	Baseball Centre, Aquilina Reserve
Events:	Men's: Team

Introduction

In Sydney 2000, for the first time baseball will follow Olympic sports such as basketball and cycling in opening the doors to professionals. This change could challenge the position of the usually powerful (amateur) Cubans, who won baseball's first two Olympic gold medals in 1992 and 1996 and have won every World Championship since 1974. However, US major-league players will be involved in the climax of their season, so the US team will not be at its strongest.

Eight teams will compete in the Sydney 2000 Games. Each team will play the other seven once, and the top four teams will advance to the semi-finals. The first-placed team then plays the fourth-placed team, and second plays the third. The winners of those semi-finals meet to decide the gold and silver medals, with the two losing teams playing for the bronze.

The teams have qualified for the Games through regional competitions.

When Japan beat Cuba in the 1997 Intercontinental Cup, it marked Cuba's first tournament loss in 23 years. However, Cuba remains the team to beat but the Japanese will expect to be strong with the open format. Many of the Hispanic nations will look to improve – after all many of the top stars playing in the USA in Major League Baseball come from places such as Venezuela and Puerto Rico.

The arrival of professional baseball players in the Olympic Games means the departure of the aluminium bats. The Sydney 2000 Games will allow only wooden bats.

Atlanta 1996

	Gold	Silver	Bronze
Men	Cuba	Japan	USA

After the Olympic Games was finished the Olympic Stadium was converted into what is now Turner Field, the home of the Atlanta Braves. But it was just across the road at Fulton County Stadium, what was then the Braves' base, that the majority of the baseball games at the Atlanta Olympics were played. The USA kicked off the tournament with a 4-1 win over Nicaragua. Cuba set their stall out with a 19-8 victory over Australia.

The US kept winning and so did the Cubans. Japan beat Holland, who then beat Australia. Nicaragua came back with a 8-3 win over South Korea and Australia surprised Japan 8-6. Cuba defeated the US 10-8 and Japan continued to get stronger. In the first semi-final Cuba easily beat Nicaragua 8-1 to set up a final with Japan.

The power-hitting star of the Games was Cuba's Orestes Kindelan. He set a Games record with nine home runs in nine games in Atlanta. He also hit a 159m (521ft) home run. The question remains whether the aluminium bats, batters or pitchers were the prime reason for the power display.

Omar Linares hit three homers in Cuba's 13-9 gold medal victory over Japan and promptly said he would like to play there. Ninety per cent of the salary of players signing for Japanese clubs would go to the Cuban government. In the bronze medal playoff the US secured victory by 10-3 over Nicaragua.

Outline rules

A baseball game consists of nine innings with the two teams contesting the game taking turns at batting and fielding. The aim is to score runs and the team with the most runs at the end of nine innings is the winner. It the scores are equal at the end of nine innings additional innings are played until one side has taken the lead after both sides have taken the same number of extra innings.

An innings lasts three outs. That is, when the fielding team has retired or 'got-out' three batting players, the teams swap roles. Players on the batting team take turns at batting in order and continue to do so until three of them are out. If a batter hits the ball then he must run (unless it is a foul ball as described below).

The batter stands at 'home-plate' and to score a run he must run and touch the three bases spread out in a diamond shape – with home plate forming the fourth base of the diamond. The batter must touch each base with hand or foot. The most spectacular run is called the 'home-run'. Here the batter hits the ball beyond the boundary and automatically advances around all bases to score. However, a batter can also score by advancing around the bases by being aided by other batters. For instance, a batter might only hit the ball well enough to reach first base. Once there, he can stop. The next batter comes into play and when he has hit the ball, the first batter can attempt to run home or to any of the bases between the base he is on and home.

A batter can be given out in a variety of ways. If he hits the ball and it is caught before hitting the ground it is out. If the batter hits the ball or is running between bases a fielder can gather the ball and touch the player with the ball for an out – this is called 'tagging'. A player can also be given out if the ball is thrown to the base where he is running to. However, if there is no player running to the base behind him, he can attempt to run back to the originating bases (but not home plate) to be safe. In this instance the fielders will aim to run in and touch the ball on the runner. Watch out for players trying to steal bases. Crafty players try to run from one base to another quite often before the pitcher bowls the ball. Providing the ball isn't hit foul, this is quite legal but the player faces getting out. If the ball is foul the player is allowed back to their previous base.

A player can also be promoted to first base from home plate by drawing a 'walk'. The ball pitcher has to throw the ball at the batter so that it arrives across the wide of the home plate base and at a height between shoulders and knees. If it does this and the hitter fails to hit the ball then it is called a 'strike'. If the batter faces three strikes she is out. If the ball is pitched outside this 'strike-zone' it is deemed a 'ball'. If the pitcher bowls four balls to an individual batter the batter automatically walks to first base. If a member of the batting side is already on first base they are promoted to second base. Equally a player on second base would be walked onto third and if someone was also on third they would be promoted home to score a run.

If a player hits the ball in the air – called an air-ball – and it is caught then any players already on bases can only run after the ball is caught. If they run before the ball is caught they must get back to their previous bases – but could be run-out in the process!

Extending from home plate either side of the batter are single lines. This is the foul-line. If a batter hits the ball and it falls behind the foul line then it is called a foul ball and counts as a strike against the batter. However if the ball is caught behind the foul line the batter is out. A player cannot commit a third strike on a foul ball and so in these cases the ball is simply re-pitched.

Baseball is played on a field of grass and dirt – or artificial turf – called a diamond because the infield, the area enclosed by home plate and the three bases, forms a diamond. The bases lie 27.43m (90ft) apart and form a square turned on a 45-degree angle. The pitcher stands in the middle of the infield on a 25.4cm (10in) mound, pitching to the batter 18.34m (60ft, 6in) away. The distance from home plate to the nearest part of the outfield fence must be at least 98.4m (321ft), but many baseball fields are larger. The fence usually arcs to more than 120m (about 400ft) from home plate.

Did you know?

- Baseball first appeared in the United States in the mid-1800s and probably evolved from an English game called rounders. It now is played in more than 60 countries.
- The first official game of baseball was between the Knickerbockers and the New York Nine in Hoboken, New Jersey, in 1846.
- Baseball is played in more than 120 countries.
- The hardest-throwing baseball pitchers throw the ball up to 160km per hour.
- Baseball's all-time home-run champion is a man named Sadaharu Oh, who hit 868 during a fabled career in Japan.
- Jim Thorpe, the American Indian who won the decathlon and pentathlon in the 1912 Stockholm Games, also led a makeshift United States baseball team to victory over Sweden in an exhibition that year. However, he later lost his medals for allegedly receiving $30 a month in a brief baseball career in his youth. In 1983 the IOC reinstated the medals.
- Baseball was an official demonstration sport at the Olympic Games seven times from 1912 to 1988 before admission as a medal sport.

Jargon buster

Ball	A pitch outside the strike zone that the batter does not try to hit.
Base	One of the three safe stations for the batter or baserunner.
Baseline	The direct line between each base, along which the baserunner generally must run.
Baserunner	A batter who has reached base safely.
Bases loaded	Bases are said to be loaded when there is a baserunner on each base.
Batter	The player trying to hit the pitch.
Bunt	An attempt by the batter to tap the ball instead of swinging at it.
Catcher	The fielder positioned behind home plate who catches the pitches.
Curveball	A pitch thrown with a rotation that makes the ball curve – the technique is to try and make the ball curve late.
Double play	A play in which two outs are made with one pitch.
Flyball	A ball hit in the air to the outfield.
Foul ball	A ball hit outside the foul lines.
Grand slam	A home run with a baserunner on each base, scoring four runs.
Home plate	The five-sided slab of whitened rubber, 17 inches wide, the batter stands beside to hit the pitch.
Home run	A hit by a batter, which usually goes over the outfield fence, that enables him to run around all the bases safely.
Pitcher	The player who throws the ball to the batter.
Sacrifice	A bunt that allows a baserunner to move to the next base while the batter gets out.
Single	A hit that allows a batter to reach first base.
Steal	A baserunner's successful advance from one base to the next on his own, usually during a pitch that is not hit.
Strike zone	The area over home plate between the batter's armpits and the top of his knees, where a pitch is called a strike even if he does not swing the bat.
Strikeout	An out where the batter gets three strikes.
Walk	An automatic advance to first base for the batter after the pitcher throws four balls.

Basketball

Introduced: 1936
Scheduled: 16 September - October 1
Venues: The Dome and SuperDome, Sydney Olympic Park
Events: Men and Women: Team

Introduction

The basketball final at the Games has provided some of the most dramatic moments of Olympic history – no one who saw it will forget the 1972 matchup between the USA and the USSR. The gold medal has become the exclusive domain of the USA team, ever since the introduction of professional players was allowed. Stars of the men's games such as Michael Jordan and Scottie Pippen can count Olympic gold alongside their NBA titles. Such is the golden nature of the USA team they are referred to as the 'Dream Team'.

The Sydney 2000 Games will include 12 men's and 12 women's basketball teams. They are divided into two pools of six for the preliminary rounds, in which every team plays the other five in its group in a round-robin series, with the top four teams in each pool advancing to the quarter-finals. From there, the tournament follows a knockout format. The winning semi-finalists meet to decide the gold and silver medals, and the losing semi-finalists play for the bronze.

The winner of the 1998 World Championships and Australia, as host nation, receive automatic entries and teams are seeded on their performnaces in this and other competitions.

The USA are firm favourites for the gold medal and four-time runner-up Yugoslavia will lead the challenge to the USA, followed by 1992 and 1996 bronze medallist Lithuania. Croatia is another European improver to watch out for. Australia, after improving performances in recent Games, and with the home crowd, will be challenging in both competitions.

Until the Soviet Union finally toppled the US team in that controversial 1972 game, the USA dominated the amateur days of the game which they invented. The sport opened to professionals in Barcelona in 1992, with a squad featuring some of the world's best-known athletes — Michael Jordan, Magic Johnson and Larry Bird —

the gold-medal winning US 'Dream Team' gave a magnificent exhibition of basketball.

The women's competition, established in 1976, is far more open. The US team is favourite and is reigning Olympic Games gold medallist and world champion. Strong challenges however will come from China, Brazil, Russia and Australia.

Atlanta 1996

	Gold	Silver	Bronze
Men	USA	Yugoslavia	Lithuania
Women	USA	Brazil	Australia

The 80-1 on Dream Team, the nucleus of which was Barkley, David Robinson, Scottie Pippen, Olajuwon and Shaquille O'Neal, represented the USA. At the Georgia Dome they cruised to a 96-68 victory over Argentina, crushed little Angola 87-54 and won a high-scoring 104-82 clash with Lithuania. Australia also started well and kept the momentum with a big win over Greece. The rest of the teams were pretty equally matched. Out of the pack emerged Yugoslavia and Lithuania. Lithuania won through to the semi-finals and Yugoslavia made it all the way to the final, in which the US ran out 95-69 winners.

In the women's preliminaries the US began with a 101-84 win over Cuba. Eventual finalists Brazil also started with a win, over Canada 69-56. Zaire suffered 107-47 at the hands of the US team, who dominated the round-robin competition. South Korea was next in line. Meanwhile eventual bronze winners Australia lost to Ukraine.

In the quarter-finals USA (108-93) beat Japan, Australia (74-70) beat Russia, Ukraine (59-50) beat Italy and Brazil (101-69) beat Cuba. Australia took the bronze with a 66-56 win over Ukraine. In the final the US completed an impressive overall performance to win gold with 111 points to Brazil's 87.

Outline rules

The basket in basketball stands 3.05m (10 feet) off the floor. The rim, made of iron, is 45cm (17.5 inches) in diameter and attached to a rigid, transparent backboard. A net hangs from the rim. The court is 28m (94 feet) by 15m (50 feet), measured from the inside edges of the boundary lines. The ceiling must be at least seven metres high.

Two teams of five players each try to score points by shooting the ball into the opposing team's basket. If they do so from within the large semi circle they score two-points. If they shoot successfully from outside the semi-circle they score three points.

Players advance the ball by bouncing it, called dribbling, or by passing it to a team-mate. The defending team tries to take away the ball before the attacking team can attempt a shot.

A player can only dribble with one hand at a time and can continue for any length of time, but once the ball comes to rest in the player's hand or hands, he or she can't start dribbling again. It is a foul if they do.

Once stopped the player must keep one foot fixed to the floor (the pivot foot) but may move the other. He or she has five seconds to pass or shoot or the other team gets the ball. If a player is attacking the basket, he or she can take two steps after ending the dribble before shooting.

Basketball in the Olympic Games consists of two 20-minute halves, with the game clock stopping whenever the referee blows the whistle to indicate a dead ball. If the game is tied at the end, the teams play five-minute overtimes until a winner is decided.

When the offence (attacking team) makes a basket, a defensive player takes the ball out of bounds at the end of the court and passes it in-bounds to a team-mate to restart the game.

The attacking team has 10 seconds from the time of taking possession before it must cross the centre line. It loses possession if it fails to do so or if it takes the ball back behind the centre line after crossing over. The attacking team has 30 seconds from the time it takes possession until it must shoot.

In theory basketball is a non-contact sport. However, as anyone who has played it will tell you, it is one of the most physically demanding sports in the world. If an illegal contact is made then a personal foul is awarded – one of the on-court referees determines if a foul has taken place. If a player has five fouls in the game then he is 'fouled-out' and can take no further part in the game. For example, a foul would be awarded if a player tried to steal the ball from an opponent but accidentally hit him on the arm. Fouls are the most difficult aspect of the game to understand.

A player fouled while shooting gets two or three (depending on where he or she was shooting from) free throws worth one point each. If a player makes a basket while being fouled, the basket counts, and the player is awarded one extra free throw. After a team commits seven fouls in a half, the other team is awarded free throws for any further foul in that half, regardless whether the player was shooting.

If a team sends the ball out of bounds or offends in a non shooting situation, the other team throws in from out of bounds. The 30-second shot clock does not restart if the offensive team retains possession after a defensive player touches the ball. A player may not touch the ball on its downward arc to the basket nor put a hand inside the rim to prevent the ball from going into the basket. A goal scored as playing time ends counts if the ball was in the air when time expired.

Did you know?

- When Dr James Naismith nailed up two peach baskets on a YMCA balcony in the United States in January 1892 (or December 1891, some accounts say), he was inventing a game.
- There are more than 100 million registered players in 208 countries around the world.
- Basketball appeared as a demonstration sport at the 1904 Olympic Games in St Louis, but did not arrive as a medal sport until 1936 in Berlin, when it was played outdoors.
- The Olympic's top scorer is Brazilian Oscar Schmidt. He has played 38 games over the last five Olympics, scoring 1,093 points at an average of 28.8 points a game.

Jargon buster

Assist	A pass that leads directly to a basket by a team-mate.
Back court	The half of the court that a team is defending.
Backboard	The rigid rectangular board behind the rim.
Block	To intercept a player's shot, preventing the ball from continuing on its path towards the basket.
Dunk	To force the ball down into the basket with one or both hands. Also called a Jam.
Lay-up	A shot by a moving player who jumps very close to the basket and shoots while in the air.
Press	To extend defensive pressure beyond its usual area.
Rebound	To grab the ball in the air after a player has missed a shot.
Steal	To take the ball from an opposing player.

Beach Volleyball

Introduced: 1996
Scheduled: September 16-26
Venue: Bondi Beach
Events: Men and Women: Team

Introduction

Despite being some way from the sea the biggest new event for the Atlanta Olympics was without doubt the introduction of beach volleyball. The competition literally stole the 1996 show and it is sure to be a big puller in Sydney not least for the fact that it will be set on the sands of Bondi Beach – one of the world's most glamorous settings.

Apart from being played on sand or in a sand pit, the biggest difference you will notice from the indoor game is that teams are composed of just two players. Games are played using rules more akin to the original indoor game with sets being played to 15 points.

The game itself is quite old, originating on the beaches of Santa Monica and being played through the rest of Southern California in the 1920s. Appropriately the USA won the first men's Olympic Gold medal in Atlanta with a team that included Karch Kiraly, who also has two indoors gold medals in his locker. Brazil won the ladies' gold medal and you can expect both these teams to be in the running again this time around. The Aussies will be strong on home silica while Cuba and Argentina will also provide stern tests for whomever they encounter.

The Sydney 2000 competition will include 24 teams for both the men's and women's competitions. Teams qualified via their world rankings up to August 2000. The format is seeded so that the number one seeded team plays the team seeded 24th, the number two seeded team plays the 23rd seeded team and so on. The 12 teams that lose in the first round of games go forward to a repechage to play two further elimination rounds to leave four survivors who rejoin the first round winners in a final 16, which then becomes a straight knock-out tournament – lose and you go home!

Atlanta 1996

	Gold	*Silver*	*Bronze*
Men	USA	USA	Canada
Women	Brazil	Brazil	Australia

For the inaugural beach volleyball competition the USA was guaranteed the gold medal when its two entrants both made it through to the final. Equally it was no real surprise when volleyball great Karch Kiraly and partner Kent Steffes defeated Mike Dodd and Mike Whitmarsh 12-5, 12-8. John Child and Mark Heese helped Canada win the bronze medal – the Torontonians beating the Portuguese in two sets 12-5, 12-8.

The women's final mirrored the men's in that it was a one nation affair – this time battled out by the Brazilian ladies with Sandra Pires and Jackie Cruz beating the Brazil II team of Rodrigues and Ramos 12-11, 11-6. The bronze went to Australia with Cook and Pottharst seeing off the Americans Fontana Harris and Hanley.

Outline rules

There are just two players per team and they can line-up anywhere in their half of the court. The object of the game is to score points by touching the ball into the opponent's side of the court. To enable a team to do this they can touch the ball three times on their side of the net without it touching the sand on their side of the court. They cannot, however, hold the ball nor can the same player touch it twice in a row. A team wins the point if they get the ball to touch the sand on the opponent's side of the court, but within the bounds of the court, or if the other team fails to get the ball back over the net or if the other team hits the ball out of court without it first touching in the court. A team can also lose the point if a player touches the net with his or her body.

Service may be over or under arm and must be from behind the end line, but the player may land within the court after the serve. The serve can be to anywhere inside the opponent's half and it continues until the server's team loses a point. When the service is lost, it transfers to the opposition and to the player on that side who did not serve last time the team had service.

A team can only score a point on its own serve. If the serving team loses the point then there is no score but the serve is transferred to the other team. In other words a team can only score a point when it is serving. Each set is played to 15 points, providing the winning team has a clear margin of two points or reaches 17 points first. Games are best of three sets. However, for matches where a medal is at stake the rules change slightly. Games are played to the best of three sets with sets played to 12 points. If the game goes to a decisive third set then points are scored regardless of who serves and the first team to reach 12 points and have a margin of two points wins the decisive set. If a two point margin is not achieved at this stage then the winner is the first team to gain a two point margin, regardless of the score.

No substitutions are allowed in beach volleyball and only two 30-second time-outs per match are allowed per team. A hard game.

A beach volleyball court is identical in size to an indoor court. It is 18 metres long by nine metres wide and is separated in half by a net which is 2.43m high for men and 2.24m high for women. The boundary lines are included in the court.

Did you know?

- One rule change for 2000 that will please some. The women must now wear two-piece bikinis...
- In Beach Volleyball teams swap sides of the court throughout a match after every five points.

Jargon buster

Ace	This is a clean serve that lands in the opponent's court without being touched.
Block	When a front player jumps at the net to stop an opposing player spiking the ball.
Chuck	When the ball is pushed or thrown rather than hit.
Dig	When both arms are placed together to push a hard-hit ball back into the air – digging-out.
Fault	An error which results in the loss of the rally, ie, serving the ball out of court.
Heater	A hard-hit shot or spike.
Kong	A one-handed block.
Spike	The process of performing an over-arm smash of the ball into the opponent's half of the court.

Boxing

Introduced: 1904
Scheduled: September 16 - 1 October
Venue: Sydney Exhibition Centre, Darling Harbour
Events: Men: 12 weight divisions

Introduction

Some of the geatest boxers in history have made their mark in the Olympic Games – remember Cassius Clay, Joe Frazier, George Foreman, Lennox Lewis and Evander Holyfield? All fought as Olympians!

Around 312 boxers will have travelled to Sydney all looking for a medal and the stepping stone to the big money of the top of the professional ranks. Qualification for the Games has not been as clear cut as in many sports and in some cases has been biased according to the strength of different regions at different weight divisions.

For the Games there is no seeding in the 12 weight divisions – boxers are paired off at random and the winner of each bout advances to the next round and the loser drops out of the competition. Winning boxers progress to the quarter-finals and semi-finals. The two semi-finals winners fight for the gold and silver medals, while both losing semi-finalists receive bronze medals.

At the Sydney 2000 Games, each bout will consist of four two-minute rounds, with one-minute intervals. The Olympic format in 1996 at Atlanta still consisted of three three-minute rounds.

The four-time World Champion heavyweight Felix Savon of Cuba could join Teofilo Stevenson and Laszlo Papp of Hungary as three-time modern Olympic boxing champions if he wins in Sydney Middleweight Ariel Hernandez, a fellow Cuban, also would be looking at his third straight gold if he returns.

Cuba is the team to watch again after dominating in Atlanta. The Cubans have won 42 titles at World Championships, the most success of any team. The United States leads in gold medals with 46 champions in the 19 modern Olympic Games.

Atlanta 1996

Weight	Gold	Silver
Light Flyweight	Daniel Petrov, Bul	M Valesco, Phil
Flyweight	Maikro Romero, Cub	B Dzumadilov, Kaz
Bantamweight	Istvan Kovacs, Hun	A Mesa, Cub
Featherweight	Somluck Kamsing, Thai	S Todorov, Bul
Lightweight	Hocine Soltani, Alg	T Tontchev, Bul
Light Welterweight	Hector Vinent, Cub	J Hernandez, Cub
Welterweight	Oleg Saitov, Rus	O Urkal, Ger
Light Middleweight	David Reid, USA	A Duvergel, Cub
Middleweight	Ariel Hernandez, Cub	M Beyleroglu, Tur
Light Heavyweight	Vasilii Jirov, Kaz	Lee Seung-Bae, S Kor
Heavyweight	Felix Savon, Cub	D Defiagbon, Can
Super Heavyweight	Vladimir Klichko, Ukr	P Wolfgram, Ton

The Cubans suffered from defections from the camp as Ramon Garbey and Jose Casamayor sought political asylum. Garbey, a former double world champion, was the last man to beat Olympic favourite Antonio Tarver, from America, and Casamayor, the Olympic champion, was seen as the best amateur in the world. It also emerged that Mariano Leiva, a top Cuban coach, arrived in Miami seeking political asylum. In the end it didn't stop Cuba finishing with five golds and two silvers!

As the finals approached the top Cubans, Russians, Germans and Bulgarians started to dominate. The American boxers struggled, with the exception of reigning world light heavyweight champion and pre-Olympic favourite Antonio Tarver, and David Reid, who gave the United States their only boxing gold medal by knocking out Cuban Alfredo Duvergel in the light middleweight final. The technical nature of the sport didn't always suit the US boxers, or the partisan crowd.

Cuba's heavyweight, Felix Savon, won his second title. If Cuba had not boycotted Los Angeles and Seoul, Savon would probably have collected his fourth gold in Atlanta. His main contender French heavyweight Christophe, was disqualified in an earlier round for delivering a low punch.

US boxer David Reid needed a knockout to get a gold medal against Cuban Alfredo Duvergel as he trailed on points but that punch made sure the US won at least one boxing gold. American boxers also got five bronze medals, and the total of six medals doubled the total they won in Barcelona.

In the middleweight semi-final Magee (Ireland) lost on points to come away with a bronze.

Maiko Romero got the first Cuban gold on the final day when he rallied in the third round for a 12-11 decision over Bulat Dzumadilov of Kazakhstan, and Hector Vinent, a 1992 Olympic and two-time world champion, outpointed European champion Oktay Urkal of Germany.

In the featherweight section Somluck Kamsing promised after his quarterfinal win that if he won a gold, he would give it to King Bhumibol Adulyadej of Thailand. Kamsing did win it, 8-5 over Serafim Todorov of Bulgaria. After the decision was announced, Kamsing ran around the ring, holding high a plaque with the king's picture on it. Vasilii Jirov of Kazakstan, outpointed Lee Seung-Bae of South Korea 17-4 at 178 pounds, and Vladimir Klichko of Ukraine outpointed Paea Wolfgram of Tonga 7-3 at super heavyweight.

Outline rules

Two men exchange punches in a square ring measuring 6.1 metres on each side. The floor of the ring consists of canvas stretched over a soft underlay, and it extends 45.72 centimetres outside the ropes. Each side of the ring has four ropes running parallel to it. The lowest one runs 40.66cm above the ground, and the ropes are 30.48cm apart.

The corners of the ring are distinguished by colours. The corners occupied by the boxers are coloured red and blue, and the other two corners, called 'neutral' corners, are white. In Sydney, a bout will consist of four two-minute rounds, with a one-minute interval between each round. Previously, Olympic bouts involved three three-minute rounds, but medical advice suggests boxers will suffer less punishment under the new system.

Each boxer can score points by landing blows on the opponent or can win by injuring him so that he can't continue. The boxers wear boxing gloves and may hit each other only on the side or front above the waist with clenched fists.

A clean hit with force gains a point. Punches to an opponent's arms or without force, do not score points.

A panel of five judges decides which hits are scoring hits, and an electronic scoring system ensures no point is awarded for a hit unless three of the five judges agree. The judges each have two buttons before them, one for each boxer, and they press the appropriate button when they believe a boxer delivers a scoring hit. No score is registered unless at least three judges press the button within a second of each other. When two boxers trade blows in a flurry, the judges wait until the end of the exchange and award a point to the boxer who got the better of it.

The boxer awarded the most points is declared the winner. If two boxers end up with the same number of points, the judges decide a winner by aggression and style, with defence a further tie-breaker.

A boxer is considered down if, as a result of being hit, he touches the floor with any part of his body besides his feet, or is partly outside the ropes or if he still is standing but is judged to be unable to continue. The count is timed electronically, with a beep sounding for each number. The referee signals the count to the downed boxer by holding a hand in front of him and counting with his fingers. If the boxer is still down after the 10 seconds, the opponent wins on a knockout.

The boxer is obliged to take a mandatory eight-count if he falls. A boxer who is down and being counted can be saved by the bell only in the final round of the final. In all other rounds and bouts, the count continues after the bell sounds. If both boxers go down at the same time, counting continues as long as one remains down. If both remain down at 10, the boxer with the most points is declared the winner.

Boxers can withdraw or be withdrawn by their corner and the referee can stop the fight. When a boxer commits a foul, he faces a caution. Two cautions for a particular offence mean an automatic warning, and three warnings of any kind mean disqualification.

Some of the more common fouls include hitting below the belt, holding, pressing an arm or elbow into the opponent's face, pressing the opponent's head back over the ropes, hitting with an open glove, hitting with the inside of the glove and hitting the opponent on the back of the head, neck or body. Others include passive defence, not stepping back when ordered to break, speaking offensively to the referee and trying to hit the opponent immediately after the order to break.

If any boxer takes three counts in one round or four counts in the bout, the referee will stop the fight. Similarly if a boxer has suffered a cut eye or a similar injury in the first round. If an injury occurs later then the judges' point tallies up to that time determine the winner.

Before every bout, a medical examiner must declare the boxers fit. Three doctors then sit at ringside, and each can stop a bout if medical reasons appear to necessitate it. Olympic boxers must be at least 17 years old and no older than 34. Beards are prohibited, and moustaches must not be longer than the upper lip.

Jargon buster

Apron	The part of the ring canvas outside the ropes.
Belt	An imaginary line from the navel to the top of the hips, below which opposing boxers are not allowed to hit.
Bout	A boxing contest; also called a 'match.'
Break	A referee's order for boxers to step back and separate if they are in a clinch.
Clinch	The act of one or both boxers holding the other in a way that hinders the other's punches.
Hold	To clutch the opposing boxer so he cannot punch.
Infighting	Fighting at close quarters so blows using the full reach of the arm cannot be delivered.
Knockout	A ruling where the referee stops the bout and declares a boxer the winner if his opponent has been down for the count of 10.
Out for the count	Knocked out for the referee's count of 10.
Reach	The distance between the fingertips of the outstretched arm across the chest to the fingertips of the other arm outstretched.
Second	A boxer's assistant.
Southpaw	A left-handed boxer.

Canoe and Kayak Slalom

Introduced: 1972
Scheduled: September 16-20
Venue: Penrith Whitewater Stadium
Events: Men and Women: Individual and Pair

Introduction

The Sydney 2000 Games include four slalom events. The K1, C1 and C2 are the men's events with the K1, or single-person kayak, the lone women's event. The letters denote canoe or kayak and the numbers denote one or two paddlers. Each event includes a qualification and a final. The number of competitors in the qualification and finals varies with each event.

The sport was introduced in the 1972 Olympics with great success but cost kept it out until Barcelona in 1992. The slalom was again removed from the Olympic programme after Atlanta but a unique deal between a local council, the International Canoe Federation and the state government has managed to get it reinstated into the Sydney 2000 Games. Penrith Whitewater Stadium, the site of the slalom, has had to be specially constructed (See Venues section).

Paddlers qualified for the Sydney 2000 Games through the 1999 World Championships in Spain. The qualifiers include 18 women for K1, 22 men for K1, 15 men for C1 and 10 crews for C2. Australia, as host nation, is allowed an automatic entry in each event.

A top contender to watch out for is Slovakia's Michal Martikan. Martikan was 16 years old when he won the bronze medal in the C1 slalom at the 1995 World Championships. He won Olympic gold at Atlanta in 1996, then at the World Championships in 1997.

Atlanta 1996

Event	Gold	Silver
Men K1	Oliver Fix, Ger	Andraz Vehovar, Slo
Men C1	Michal Martikan, Svk	Lukas Pollert, Cze
Men C2	France	Czech Republic
Women K1	Stepanka Hilgertova, Cze	Dana Chladek, USA

Atlanta found a rugged course along the Ocoee River in Tennessee, in an Appalachian Mountain gorge more than 200 kilometres from the city. The course had artificial enhancements, but looked like a real whitewater experience.

More than 14,000 spectators sitting on bleachers along a narrow river bank watched Germany's Oliver Fix and the Czech Republic's Stepanka Hilgertova win the kayak singles titles. In canoe, Slovakia's 17-year-old Michal Martikan overtook Pollert for gold, winning by a 0.14 second margin. Europeans dominated, but the river came out top when all three 1992 women's medallists were among the dozen or more paddlers who capsized.

Outline rules

Slalom boats are light and short and stubby for negotiating the twists and turns. They are decked, or enclosed around the waist. Paddlers wear spray skirts which seal them into the boat to prevent water from entering. In kayaks the paddler sits and in canoes the paddler kneels to paddle. The kayak paddler uses a paddle which has two curved blades. The canoe paddler uses a paddle which only has one flat blade and which may not be fixed to the boat in any way.

Competitors go down the slalom course one at a time – the run. Each run requires the paddlers to negotiate 20 to 25 gates in turbulent water over a 300-metre course. Competitors aim to complete the course in the shortest time after penalties for hitting gates have been added.

The aim is to complete the course as quickly as possible (usually between 100 and 130 seconds) while going through all the gates and hitting none. In both runs of a qualification, the paddlers start in reverse order of their world rankings. In the final, they start in reverse order of how they performed in the qualification, then in reverse order of their time from that first run.

Each run starts automatically when the boat breaks a light beam across the water at the starting point. The timing ends when the boat breaks another light beam at the finish. A two-second penalty is added any time a competitors' boat, body or paddle hits a gate, and a 50-second penalty is added if a paddler misses a gate altogether. The paddler may go back and make a second attempt at a gate but the next competitor gets the right of way if they have caught up. Each competitior takes two runs at the course. The times of the two runs, plus any penalties, are added together in seconds, which equate to points. The person with the lowest total points wins.

A gate consists of two striped poles suspended just above the water from a wire stretched across the course. They are arranged so that paddlers negotiate a minimum of six of them upstream. Green-and-white striped poles identify the downstream gates, and red-and-white striped poles mark the upstream gates.

All rulings on gate penalties must be based on what judges see with the naked eye, so gates will not be wired electronically. At least one judge will man every gate, and up to three will position themselves on the rocks for a close view of the more difficult gates. Rudders are prohibited on all boats. Competitors must wear approved safety helmets and buoyancy jackets.

Did you know?

- In 1972, West Germany spent about US$4 million constructing an artificial river in Augsburg for the inaugural canoe/kayak slalom. East Germany built a replica and won all four events.
- The 300-metre artificial course in Sydney is a channel dropping five-and-a-half metres between two ponds, with seating or footpaths running the length of its U shape.
- The key penalty in canoe/kayak slalom competition, the time addition for touching a gate, has been reduced from five seconds to two seconds for the Sydney 2000 Games.

Jargon buster

Broach	To become caught in the current against an obstruction and turn sideways.
Chute	An area where a river suddenly is constricted, compressing and amplifying the current's energy into a narrow tongue of water.
Draw	A stroke pulling in toward the paddler at 90 degrees to the direction of travel, causing the bow of a canoe to turn in the direction of the drawing side when performed by the bowhand.
Eskimo roll	The rolling over, or capsizing, of a canoe, with the paddler remaining in place, and the subsequent righting of the canoe at the completion of the roll.

Canoe and Kayak Sprint

Introduced: 1936
Scheduled: September 26 - October 1
Venue: Sydney International Regatta Centre, Penrith Lakes
Events: Men and Women: Individual, Pair and Four

Introduction

Canoe/kayak racing in the sprint form was a demonstration sport at the 1924 Olympic Games before gaining full-medal status in 1936. Germany, Sweden and the athletes of the former Soviet bloc countries are usually somewhere in the frame.

Three women's and nine men's sprint events are scheduled for the Sydney 2000 Games in canoe/kayak. Women race in the 500-metre K1, K2 and K4 (denoting one, two or four paddlers in a kayak). Men compete in the 500m and 1000m K1 and K2, 1000m K4 and 500m and 1000m C1 and C2 (canoe). Races with more than nine entries include both heats and semi-finals.

The number of entrants in the sprint events at the Sydney 2000 Games, totalling no more than 275, varies from event to event. As a general rule, countries qualify boats by finishing near the top in the World Championships. Each country is allowed only one boat in each event.

In general, boats are seeded into heats based on their previous finish in the World Championships, with lots drawn to determine seeding for any boats not among the top 18 finishers. Officials use a formula aimed at distributing the strongest contenders evenly among the heats. The competition committee uses a random selection to determine how boats progress to later rounds.

Two of the leading names in canoe/kayak sprint today are Germany's Birgit Fischer and Norway's Knut Holmann. Fischer is the top women's medal-winner in Olympic history, and Holmann could win both the 500m and 1000m men's K1.

Atlanta 1996

Men	Gold	Silver
500m K1	Antonio Rossi, Ita	Knut Holmann, Nor
1000m K1	Knut Holmann, Nor	Beniamino Bonomi, Ita
500m K2	Germany	Italy
1000m K2	Italy	Germany
1000m K4	Germany	Hungary
500m C1	Martin Doktor, Cze	Slovomir Knazovicky, Slo
500m C2	Hungary	Germany
1000m C1	Martin Doktor, Cze	Ivan Klementyev, Lat
1000m C2	Germany	Romania

Women	Gold	Silver
500m K1	Rita Koban, Hun	Caroline Brunet, Can
500m K2	Sweden	Germany
500m K4	Germany	Switzerland

Knut Holman in the Kayak and Martin Doktor in the Canoe, both took two medals each. Holman (Norway) won his gold in the 1,000m kayak singles and a silver in the 500m kayak singles, losing out to Italy's Rossi by less than a second.

Doktor (Czech Rep) was first over 500m and 1,000m, beating Knazovicky (Slovakia) and Pulai (Hungary) into silver and bronze in the former, and Klementyev (Latvia) and Zala (Hungary) in the latter.

Hungary were one of the stronger canoeing nations and Rita Koban won the 500m kayak singles and Hungary won the 500m canadian pairs.

Germany however were the top sprint paddlers. They took gold in the 1,000m canadian pairs, 500m kayak pairs, 500m kayak fours and 1,000m kayak fours. Italy won the 1,000m kayak pairs, pushing Germany, for once, into silver position.

Sweden took its only gold, from Germany and Australia, in the 500m kayak pairs.

Outline rules

Races are held on a flat water course divided into the nine-metre lanes by buoys. The course includes nine lanes for the maximum number of competitors allowed in a heat. The boats are held in barriers which open automatically when the starter's gun fires. The canoeists sprint from start line to finish line.

Women compete only in kayaks, the closed boats paddled from a sitting position with a double-blade paddle. Men race in kayaks and canadian canoes. Canoes are open boats paddled from a kneeling position with a single-blade paddle.

A boat finishes a race when its bow crosses the finish line. However, competitors must be in their boat when it crosses the line. If paddlers capsize their boats at the line while lunging forward, they will lose their place. In case of a capsize earlier in the race, paddlers can continue a race, provided they get back into their boat without any help.

The five-metre rule means that no boat can get within five metres of another boat in a neighbouring lane. This prevents boats from riding the wash of other boats, or being pulled along in the water broken by another boat.

An umpire, who follows the competitors in a motorboat, will disqualify any boat breaking the rule. The lanes are nine metres wide, giving a boat room to manoeuvre away from the wash of another boat.

If the umpire has seen a breach of rules, he or she will show a red flag at the end of a race. If a white flag is shown, no violation has occurred, and the result stands.

Sprint canoes and kayaks are longer and narrower than the slalom versions. Sprint kayaks are the only boats in canoe/kayak fitted with steering rudders. Officials check the boats three days before competition and again after each race to make sure they comply with specifications.

Did you know?

- A flat-water paddler can achieve up to 125 strokes per minute.
- The straight bottom edge of a flat-water boat's keel enables the boat to follow a straight line.
- If a boat complies with the specified dimensions, it can be built from any material. Modern boats are usually made of a carbon-kevlar compound, although some are made of fibreglass and even good old timber.
- The most dramatic finish in the event was probably at the 1988 Games at Seoul. Australia's Grant Davies was declared the winner

in the one-man 1000m kayak, only to have officials announce 11 minutes later that he lost by five-thousandths of a second!

Jargon buster

Beam	The widest part of a canoe.
Blade	The wide part of a paddle, which passes through the water.
Cockpit	The enclosed space in a kayak or slalom canoe where the paddler or paddlers sit.
Deck	The closed-in area over the bow and/or stem of a canoe or kayak, intended to shed water and strengthen the gunwales.
Flat water	Lake water or a slow-moving river current with no rapids.
Grip	The end of a canoe paddle opposite from the blade.
Gunwale	The upper edge of a canoe's side (pronounced 'gunnel').
Hull	The frame or body of a boat.
J stroke	A paddle stroke that ends with a rudder manoeuvre.
Keel	The ridge running the length of a canoe on the bottom.
Shaft	The narrow part of a paddle, gripped by the paddler.
Stem	The forward part of a boat.
Stern	The back end of a boat.
Thwart	A supporting member of a canoe's structure, extending across the canoe from side to side between the gunwales.
Wash	The rough or broken water left behind a moving boat.

Cycling: Mountain Bike

Introduced: 1996
Scheduled: September 23-24
Venue: Fairfield City Farm, Fairfield
Events: Men and Women: Individual

Introduction

Mountain biking debuted in 1996 at Atlanta and so these Games mark only the second appearance of mountain biking on the Olympic programme. As in Atlanta, there will be one men's and one women's event, racing on a technically demanding downhill course.

Men race between 40 and 50 kilometres, and women cover 30 to 40km. The exact distances are decided the night before the race, when officials ponder the weather. The course is set so men complete six to seven laps and women race five to six.

A total of 80 riders will compete in the mountain bike event, 50 in the men's field and 30 in the women's. Entry is based on the world rankings of individual competitors.

Australia's Cadel Evans is favoured in the men's event, although France's Miguel 'Mighty Mouse' Martinez is not to be dismissed. In the women's event, Canada's Alison Sydor is the frontrunner, with Australia's Mary Grigson among the challengers.

The mountain bike course for the Sydney 2000 Games is set out on a bush track around seven kilometres long, made up of mainly rough terrain. Competitors must negotiate 310m of steep gradient per lap, as well as gullies and other obstacles. There is a sign every kilometre along the course indicating the distance yet to be covered on the circuit.

Mountain biking was recognised by the International Cycling Union in 1990 and Purgatory, Colorado, hosted the inaugural World Championships in the same year.

Atlanta 1996

Event	Gold	Silver
Men's	Bart Brentjens, Hol	Thomas Frischknecht, Swi
Women's	Paola Pezzo, Ita	Alison Sydor, Can

Paola Pezzo (Italy) won this first cross country mountain biking event for women with a time of one hour 50 minutes, 51 seconds. Alison Sydor (Canada) took the silver, some eight seconds down and Susan de Mattei (US) won the bronze.

Europe dominated the men's mountain biking when Bart Brentjens (Holland) beat Thomas Frischknecht (Switzerland) into second place by nearly three minutes. Miguel Martinez (France) got the bronze but Foord (GB) was some 12 minutes off the winner.

Outline rules

Men race over a distance of between 40-50km (six to seven laps of the course), while women must cover between 30-40km (five to six laps). The number of laps of the 6.9km course is set to best achieve an optimum finishing time of two hours and 15 minutes for the winning man and two hours for the winning woman (plus or minus 15 minutes). The decision on the final race distance is made on the night before the race, taking into account weather conditions

After the starting gun is fired, riders complete a lap of the 1.8km start loop, which brings them back through the start/finish area to start the main course, which riders must follow according to the signs provided. The first rider across the finish line is the winner. Any objections must be made immediately after the race is completed.

Mountain bikers must not receive any kind of assistance and therefore carry their own repair kits. Pushing or leaning on other competitors or pulling their jerseys may lead to relegation down the ranking. The number of places lost is at the discretion of the race commissaire. Obstructing another rider in the final sprint may result in disqualification. Competitors are permitted to change their eye wear and receive food and liquids, but only at specified feeding zones.

Helmets must be worn in all cycle events and the rule seems especially appropriate in this discipline. Mountain bike frames are sturdy, fitted with fork-like front suspension and may also have shock absorbers in the rear. They are equipped with straight handlebars, powerful brakes, and up to 24 gear options. The chunky tyres have a large tread to give added grip. Attachments intended to decrease forward air resistance or artificially increase speed or acceleration are prohibited.

Did you know?

- Officials set the course distance for an optimum finishing time of two hours and 15 minutes for the top man, two hours for the top woman.
- Cyclists must allow faster riders to overtake without obstruction. A lapped rider is allowed to finish that lap but is then removed from the competition.

Jargon buster

Brodie	A locking up of the rear brake to force the rear end to skid around so as to make a sharp turn.
Bunny-hop	To jump the bike, without dismounting, over an obstacle.
Clunking	The original term for mountain biking, when the practice involved stripping down cruiser bicycles and racing them down fire roads, trails etc.
Hardtail	A mountain bike with no rear suspension.
Pixie gear	The smallest chainring on a mountain bike, combined with the biggest sprocket to make the lowest gear; also called granny gear or weenie gear.
Pushclimb	A section of a mountain biking trail with inadequate traction or too-steep a pitch, that forces cyclists to dismount and carry their bikes.

Cycling: Road Race

Introduced: 1896 men, 1984 women
Scheduled: September 26-30
Venue: Road Cycling Course, Centennial Parklands
Events: Men and Women: Individual and Time Trials

Introduction

The road races are some of the most spectacular Olympic events with their colourful mass starts, cat and mouse tactics and close sprints at the death. Competitors face gruelling distances and do everything they can to save their legs for the final dash.

A total of 212 athletes will compete in road cycling in Sydney. Competitors qualify as a nation rather than individual riders. The men's and women's road races and men's and women's time trials are the four events that make up the Olympic road-racing programme.

Teams are mainly selected according to the world rankings of their top riders, but placings at previous world championships are also taken into account.

One of the top medal hopes in both men's events is German Jan Ullrich, the 1999 time-trial world champion. The key challengers include Laurent Jalabert of France, 1999 road-race champion Oscar Freire Gomez of Spain and Australia's Stuart O'Grady.

Australia's Anna Wilson, silver medallist in both the time trial and road race at the 1999 World Championships, will be looking to go one better on her home soil. Other women to watch include Germany's Hanka Kupfernagel, the Netherlands' Leontien van Moorsel and Lithuania's Edita Pucinskaite.

No single rider has won the Olympic road race more than once, though the top placings have been consistently filled by Italians, Frenchmen and Swedes. In 1984 women entered the fray and at the 1996 Atlanta Games time trials were introduced. Australia and the US are now making inroads at the elite level, particularly in the women's competition.

Atlanta 1996

Men	Gold	Silver
Road Race	Pascal Richard, Sui	Ralf Sorensen, Den
Time Trial	Miguel Indurain, Esp	Abraham Olano, Esp
4000m IP	Andrea Collinelli, Ita	Philippe Ermenault, Fra
4000m TP	France	Russia Australia

Women	Gold	Silver
Time Trial	Zulfia Zabirova, Rus	Jeannie Longo-Ciprelli, Fra
Road Race	Jeannie Longo-Ciprelli, Fra	Imelda Chiappa, USA
3000m IP	Antonella Bellutti, Ita	Marion Clignet, Fra

IP=Individual Pursuit; TP=Team Pursuit.

In the individual time trial, Britain had a medal prospect in Chris Boardman, who eventually had to settle for the bronze as Tour de France star Miguel Indurain took Olympic gold. The eight-mile circuit around the leafiest and most elegant of Atlanta's suburbs saw the efforts of three top cyclists enduring temperatures in the high 80s. Olano finished 12 seconds behind Indurain but 19 better than the Briton.

In the road race, one of the Olympics' most gruelling events, Pascal Richard (Switzerland) won in a photo finish, after nearly five hours in the saddle, from Ralf Sorensen (Denmark). They were awarded the same time. Max Sciandri (GB) took bronze.

In the women's road race gold went to Frenchwoman Jeannie Longo-Ciprelli ahead of Imelda Chiappa (Italy) and Hughes (Canada). In the individual time trial Zulfia Zabirova (Russia) broke this axis but Jeannie Longo-Ciprelli (France) got her second medal, this time a silver and Canada's Hughes picked up another bronze. Britain's riders were just off the pace.

Outline rules

The road races, with a mass start are over 228km for men, 128km for women. The time trials are raced against the clock, with riders starting at intervals. In these, the men race over 46.8km, the women over 31.2km. There will be a single course used for both the road race and individual time trial events, though the length of the circuit will vary with each race. An 18km course will be used in the road race event, while the individual time trial will take place on a 14.8km course.

The road-race teams are positioned at the front of the pack on the starting line in accord with 1999 UCI rankings. Designated feeding stations around the course offer food, such as chocolate, sandwiches and bananas, as well as liquid refreshments. Riders of the same nationality are allowed to share food items as they travel along.

Official vehicles carry spare bicycles and wheels and repairs are allowed. Cyclists on the same national team may also assist each other by offering repair tools, but they can't push another cyclist.

In the individual time trial riders set out one by one at 90 second intervals. The fastest time around the course wins. Cyclists can seek assistance with repairs and replacement parts from a follow vehicle, which must be travelling at least 10 metres behind the rider. Competitors may not help each other during the race.

Road bikes can be constructed from lightweight steel, aluminium, titanium or carbon fibre. They have brakes and derailleurs, which provide up to eight gears. Road bikes weigh between eight and 10 kilograms. It is compulsory to wear a helmet

In the time trial event a cyclist is not allowed to lead or follow in the slipstream of another the cyclist. The rider who catches up must leave a lateral gap of two metres between them.

Did you know?

- In 1920 some cyclists were forced to rest at different railway crossings, six of which intersected the course, with timekeepers posted at each crossing to record delays.
- The longest Olympic road race was in Stockholm in 1912 Stockholm, which ran over 320km (199 miles) around the shores of Lake Malar.

Jargon buster

Attack A sudden acceleration to move ahead of another rider or group of riders.
Domestique A team rider who will sacrifice his/her standing to help a team-mate.
Draft To ride closely behind a competitor, saving energy by using that racer as a windbreak.

Cycling: Track

Introduced: 1996
Scheduled: September 16-21
Venue: Dunc Gray Velodrome, Bankstown
Events: Men and Women: Various

Introduction

Track cycling combines hi-tech equipment with flat-out power, one-on-one sprints and the cat-and-mouse racing skills. The races take place on a 250m track with a wooden surface. The track is banked for the whole of its length, although the banking is steeper at the bends (42 degrees) than in the straights (12.4 degrees). The aerodynamic bikes, and the riders' kit, are designed specifically to get every last bit of extra speed from the riders' legs. The track cycling programme will gain new races yet again at the Sydney 2000 Games. Women will compete in a 500-metre time trial, and men will add the keirin, Madison and Olympic races.

Qualification for Sydney was based on each nation performing well at the World Championships or at one of the four regional qualification tournaments held the year prior to the Games.

Women took to the track in 1988 when, in the 1000m sprint, German Christa Luding-Rothenburger, a Winter Olympic Games gold medallist, was narrowly defeated by Soviet Erika Salumae

Traditional powerhouse France again leads the world in cycling, with Germany, Australia and the United States chasing.

Technology has always played a part in cycling. The spokeless, carbon-fibre disc wheel appeared in 1984. Chris Boardman introduced the completely carbon-fibre bike, weighing less than nine kilograms, in 1992. The bike helped Boardman to win his country's first cycling gold medal since 1920.

Atlanta 1996

Men	Gold	Silver
Sprint	Jens Fiedler, Ger	Marthy Nothstein, USA
1000m Time Trial	Florian Rousseau, Fra	Erin Hartwell, USA
Individual Points Race	Silvio Martinello, Ita	Brian Walton, Can

Women	Gold	Silver
Sprint	Felicia Ballanger, Fra	Michelle Ferris, Aus
Points Race	Nathalie Lancien, Fra	Ingrid Haringa, Hol

Jens Fiedler (Germany) beat Marthy Nothstein (US) 2-0 in the final of the men's sprint. Harnett (Canada) won the bronze, from fourth-placed Neiwand (Australia) in another 2-0 win. In the individual points race Silvio Martinello (Italy) won with 37 points, from Walton (Canada) on 29 ponts and O'Grady (Australia) on 27. The individual pursuit was won by Andrea Collinelli from Italy and the team pursuit by France.

Florian Rousseau (France) took the men's 1km time trial from Erin Hartwell (US) and Takandu Jumonji (Japan).

In the women's sprint Felicia Ballanger (France) beat Ferris (Australia) 2-0. The bronze went to Ingrid Haringa (Holland). Another Frenchwoman won the individual ponts race. Nathalie Lancien scored 24 to push Ingrid Haringa into silver position on 23 points.

France and Italy continued to share the rostrum in the women's cycling events. The individual pursuit gold went to Italy's Antonella Bellutti with Marion Clignet (France) in silver position.

Outline rules

In the time trial, cyclists race one at a time against the clock. The rider with the fastest time is declared the winner. This event is a single-round competition, four laps (one kilometre) for men and two laps (500m) for women. Riders are held in starting blocks, which open after a 90-second countdown.

In the sprints, riders race one on one to a sprint finish. It is a tactical race over three laps. Riders race head to head in a best-of-three-heats series of match races. The winner of each race is the first to cross the finish line. Over the first two laps the riders manoeuvre for the best position to make the final sprint. The first lap must be ridden no slower than walking pace, but after that riders can try anything, from track standing to sprinting. The leading rider must leave room on the right to pass, and cannot cut off a competitor in the sprinter's lane unless they have a clear lead. There is a red line – the sprinter's line – that runs around the track, 80cm outside the pole line. In sprint events, once a rider moves inside the sprinter's line they cannot move out if it will cause interference to the other rider. In addition, if one rider is inside the sprinter's line, his or her opponent is not allowed to overtake on the inside. Lots are drawn to choose who leads the first lap from the pole position. The roles are reversed in the next heat. If a third heat is needed, lots are drawn again. If one competitor causes a fall, that rider must lead the first lap.

In the pursuit races the riders start on opposite sides of the track and race flat out to a finish. The team pursuit involves three team members who help eachother. The team finishes when the third rider crosses the line. The cyclists attempt to win a pursuit race by catching the other rider or recording the fastest time. The pursuit takes place over 4km in the men's event, and 3km in the women's. In the team pursuit there are four members but the race is over when the third team member's front wheel crosses the finishing line, or when the third rider from one team draws level with the third rider of the other.

The object of the points race is to accumulate the most points over the course of one 40km race (25km for women). Beginning with a mass start after one lap has been completed, competitors then jockey for position to score points. The first four riders across the finishing line every tenth lap score points – five for first, three for second, two for third and one for fourth. Double points are awarded in the final sprint.

The Madison – named after Madison Square Garden in New York – is a tactical team race for men over 60km (240 laps), with only one rider from each team competing at any one time. Teams of two riders try to accumulate the most points in intermediate sprints every 20 laps, and swap over with a sort of tag, called a 'handsling'.

The keirin (pronounced 'kay-rin') began as a betting race in 1940s Japan, and makes its Olympic debut in Sydney. Competitors ride behind a motorbike for the first five-and-a-half laps, initially at 25km/h, gradually accelerating to 45km/h. The motorbike leaves the track with two-and-a-half laps to go and the riders then sprint for the finish line.

The main requirement for bikes used in the track events is that they have a triangular frame and wheels that are the same size (either 66 or

68cm in diameter). They can be constructed from steel, aluminium, titanium or carbon fibre. Track bikes have a single 'fixed' gear so that riders must pedal any time they are moving.

Did you know?

- During the semi-final of the 1,000 metre sprint in Tokyo in 1964, Giovanni Pettenella of Italy and Pierre Trentin of France stood motionless for 21 minutes, 57 seconds, each waiting for the other to lead off. The length of this standoff set an Olympic record, and standing still was later limited to a maximum of three minutes.
- The first modern Games programme included a gruelling 12 hour ride which only two cyclists managed to complete!

Jargon buster

Neutralisation	In the event of a danger on the track, officials will tell all riders to go to the top of the track, ride at a steady pace and maintain their relative position.
Repechage	A round in which losers of previous heats race against each other to gain re-entry into the competition.
Sprinters' lane	The inner area on a cycling track bounded by the pole line and the sprinter's line.
Sprinters' line	A red line which marks the outside edge of the sprinters' lane.
Stand Still	A manoeuvre in which both riders remain (almost) motionless and balancing on the track for a maximum of three minutes.
Starting block	Holds the bicycle at the starting line until the starting signal.
Velodrome	A banked bicycle racing track.

Diving

Introduced: 1896 mens; 1912 womens; 2000 synchronised pairs
Scheduled: September 22-30
Venue: Sydney International Aquatic Centre
Events: Men and Women: Individual

Introduction

Diving is highly technical but offers spectators a brief spectacular glimpse of athleticism and grace between board and water. The spectacle is due to double up this year when for the first time there will be diving in pairs! The traditional men's and women's 10-metre platform and three-metre springboard diving events will be repeated for the synchronised portion, with judges assessing both individual dives and synchronisation.

An estimated 130 divers will compete in the eight Olympic diving events. Each country is limited to two divers per event. They must meet the A standard to qualify although a country's single entrant need only meet the B standard.

There was a number of qualifying events for diving but only the January 2000 Diving World Cup was a qualifying event for the synchronised diving.

Sweden and Germany dominated the early years of the sport, until the US emerged. US star Pat McCormick won the women's springboard and platform in 1952 and 1956, the latter just eight months after giving birth. Countryman Greg Louganis repeated the double in 1984 and 1988.

The United States has won 125 of the 225 medals awarded, including 46 of the 75 gold. But in a major turn-around, Chinese divers won three of the four gold medals at Atlanta in 1996 and are predicted to figure prominently in 2000.

China's Yu Zhuocheng, Sun Shuwei and Tian Liang will be pushed by Mexico's Fernando Platas, Germany's Andreas Wels and Russia's Dmitry Sautin. The top women include China's Xiaoqlao Liang and Xue Sang, Ukraine's Yulia Pakhalina and Olena Zhupina and Canadian Myriam Boileau. China, Russia, Germany, Australia, Mexico and Ukraine head the synchronised events.

Atlanta 1996

Event	Gold	Silver
Men's Springboard	Ni Xiong, Chn	Yu Zhuocheng, Chn
Men's Platform	Dmitri Sautin, Rus	Jan Hempel, Ger
Women's Springboard	Mingxia Fu, Chn	Irina Laschko, Rus
Women's Platform	Mingxia Fu, Chn	Annika Walter, Ger

The Chinese improvement in the diving competitions, which had started in the 1980s, was crowned with three out of four gold medals in Atlanta. Only in the men's high platform dive did the Chinese competitor, Hailiang Xiao, come in third. It was a case of gold and silver in the springboard diving so perhaps Hailiang was just making up the set.

One individual won gold in the women's event. Mingxia Fu beat Irina Laschko from Russia into second place in the springboard and defeated Germany's Annika Walter in the high diving. Both winning margins were significant. Mingxia, who at the age of 12 became the youngest diver to win a world title, won in Barcelona two years later, and at 17, she retained her title. The USA's Mary Ellen Clarke repeated her bronze medal performance of four years previously to become the oldest American diver, at 33, to win an Olympic medal. Britain's unknown Hayley Allen came ninth.

Outline rules

Divers perform a series of dives and are awarded points up to 10, depending upon their elegance and skill. The points then are adjusted for the degree of difficulty, based on the number and types of manoeuvres attempted, such as somersaults, pikes, tucks and twists. A reverse 1.5 somersault with 4.5 twists is one of the most difficult combinations.

A panel of seven judges traditionally scores a dive, judging such elements as approach, take-off, execution and entry into the water. Nine judges will assess synchronised diving, split between four judging the execution and five assessing the synchronisation.

The springboard is a flexible board with adjustable spring three metres above the water, and the platform is an unbending board 10 metres above the water. The springboard competition consists of five groups: front, back, reverse, inward and twisting. The platform competition includes one more, the armstand dive.

The dives involve several variables, which combined to form a degree of difficulty For example, a forward 2.5 somersault pike from the three-metre springboard carries a degree of difficulty of 2.4. A set formula means that divers can put together their own combinations and be confident about the points on offer. The judges work independently, evaluating each stage of a dive. They are looking for control and balance, lift from the take-off, correct mechanics, technique, form and grace. Entry to the water should create as little splash as possible, with the body straight as it hits the water.

Eight pairs of divers will compete in the synchronised diving events. The pairs of dives must include one set of forward facing dives, one set of backward facing dives and one set where the divers take off facing different ways. A preliminary round in the individual event will cut the field to 18 for the semi-finals, with 12 eventually moving into the finals. Only the semi-final and final scores determine the final results.

Divers have to give officials a list of all dives they intend to try and no points are awarded for dives which aren't on the list and only two points per judge are awarded for dives performed out of order. Other penalties are incurred when set style for dive types are not adhered to. A dive is considered finished when the body disappears completely under the surface of the water.

The springboard must be at least 4.8 metres long and a half-metre wide, with a non-slip surface. For platform, the board must be at least six metres long and two metres wide, with a non-slip surface. The front of the platform, where divers take off, projects at least 1.5m over the water. The pool must be at least 4.5 metres deep, with five metres preferred in competition.

Did you know?

- In 1988, Greg Louganis of the United States, arguably the greatest Olympic diver in history, cracked his head on the springboard while attempting a reverse 2.5 pike. After getting stitches, Louganis won gold in both men's events.
- Platform divers hit the water at about 55kph
- When divers tie for 18th place in the preliminary round or 12th place in the semi-finals, they both advance. In the finals, ties remain ties, even if a medal is involved.

Jargon buster

Approach	Three or more steps a diver takes before take-off.
Back dive	When a diver takes off with their back to the water.
Elevation	The height a diver achieves from a take-off.
Entry	The end of a dive when the diver enters the water.
Execution	The performance of a dive, judged on mechanics, technique, form and grace.
Free position	A combination of straight, pike or tuck positions used only in twisting dives.
Hurdle	The last part of a diver's approach when the final step starts from one foot and ends on two feet before leaving the board.
Inward dive	During the execution, the diver rotates toward the board.
Layout	A diving position where a diver's body and legs are straight, the feet are together, and the toes are pointed; also called 'straight'.
Pike	A diving position where the body is bent at the hips, the legs are straight, and the toes are pointed.
Reverse dive	A forward facing take-off where the diver jumps upward and outward, then rotates backward, to enter the water facing away from the board; also sometimes called 'gainers'.
Rip	The ideal entry that creates little splash, named for its ripping sound as the diver enters the water.
Somersault	The full rotation of the body on an imaginary horizontal axis through the hips.
Tuck	A diving position in which the body is bent at the waist and knees, with the thighs drawn tightly to the chest and the heels pulled close to the buttocks.

Equestrian: Dressage

Introduced: 1912
Scheduled: September 25-27
Venue: Equestrian Centre, Horsley Park
Events: Men and Women: Individual and Team

Introduction

Dressage is a kind of artistic gymnastics for horses, involving discipline and beauty. The term dressage comes from the French word 'dresser', meaning 'to train', and the discipline was originally developed on the battlefield and the parade ground. The horse performs set movements, or tests, in response to its rider's signals. In the first two rounds, horse and rider perform a set routine of dressage movements, including passages, pirouettes and piaffes in a walk, trot and canter. The third round is freestyle and performed to music.

Dressage, and the other two equestrian events, are among the few Olympic sports in which men and women compete against each other. Germany has the pedigree in this event, having won the team and individual golds at the past four Olympic Games.

Eight of the teams qualified at the 1998 World Championships, with another place going to a qualifying team from the European Championships and the last spot going to Australia, as host nation. The individual event is open to 50 riders. Besides the 40 in team competition, another 10 qualify because of their world rankings. The limit is two additional riders per nation.

The opening up of the competition in 1952 pitched men and women against each other. Lisa Hartel, a top horsewoman who had recovered from polio to take part, although she was still paralysed below the knees, won the silver and came back in 1956 to repeat the performance. Women have continued to perform well in dressage. In 1972 at Munich, Liselott Linsenhoff of Germany became the first female gold medallist. In 1988 at Seoul, all three medallists were women.

Atlanta 1996

Event	Gold	Silver
Individual	Isabell Werth, Ger	Anky van Grunsven, Ned
Team	Germany	Netherlands

The first stage of the dressage resulted in a team victory for Germany with Holland strong in second. Richard Davison, the only British rider to reach the second stage, was out of the top 13 who progressed to the final. Germany lost their reigning Olympic champion when Nicole Uphoff-Becker's Rembrandt failed to pass the horse inspection for the final. Anky van Grunsven from Holland, and horse Bonfire, led their old rivals, Isabell Werth and Gigolo, after the second round and looked likely winners with their favourite freestyle to come. But the depth of talent in Germany was demonstrated when Isabell Werth and Gigolo, triple European champions, came back to overtake the Dutch woman for the gold.

Outline rules

The event is held over three rounds during which horse and rider must perform a series of movements, testing the rider's control of the horse. A panel of judges marks them on execution. In the individual event, the rider with the highest score after the final round wins. The team event is decided after the first round – known as the grand prix – by adding the best three individual scores from each team.

In the grand prix, the riders follow a set routine of dressage movements, such as the pirouette, piaffe and passage, combined with changes between walk, trot and canter.

The top 25 individual performers progress to the second round, the grand prix special, a shorter but more concentrated version of the first round. The 15 leading competitors then progress to the third and final round, the grand prix freestyle test. In this final round the riders perform their own choreographed routine to music.

Riders are given a few minutes to familiarise their horse with the arena before a routine begins. The arena, 60 metres long and 20 metres wide, is flat and level with a mainly sand surface. There are 12 lettered markers positioned at specific points along the outside edge that serve as reference points for certain movements. A military style opening to each routine is traditional.

The five judges, positioned at specific locations around the arena, score each movement from zero (not executed) to 10 (excellent). Some of the more difficult movements earn scores that are doubled.

The rider can only use touch and pressure. Talking or making noise as a signal is prohibited and penalised severely. Time is only a factor in the grand prix freestyle, where each rider has six minutes to perform a routine. Comparing the scores of the third highest scorer from each team breaks a tie in the team event.

English-type saddles are used, and the horse must have a double bridle. The ring of the bit must be no bigger than eight centimetres in diameter. The spurs must be metal, but the arms of the spurs must be smooth. The horse's mane may be plaited, but any other decorations are prohibited.

Did you know?

- When the Olympic Games were held in Australia in 1956 in Melbourne, the host country's strict quarantine laws forced the equestrian events to Stockholm.

Jargon buster

Canter	An easy gait of a horse (between a trot and a gallop in speed) where, in the course of each stride, three legs are off the ground at once.
Flying change	A skipping movement at the canter where a horse changes its lead leg at every fourth, third, second and finally single stride.
Half pass	A forward and sideways movement at the trot or canter where the horse crosses its legs.
Movement	A single characteristic style of motion of a horse, several of which make up a dressage performance.
Passage	A suspended trot in slow motion where each diagonally opposite pair of feet is raised and returned to the ground alternately.
Piaffe	Majestic trot on the spot, with each diagonally opposite pair of feet raised and returned to the ground alternately while the horse's head ideally is vertical.
Pirouette	A rhythmic turning on the spot at the walk and canter where the inside hind foot is the pivot for the circle.

Equestrian: Jumping

Introduced: 1900
Scheduled: September 21, 24-25, 28, October 1
Venue: Equestrian Centre, Horsley Park
Events: Men and Women: Individual and Team

Introduction

Showjumping is a rather dated looking event. The essence of the event at the Games is that the horse and rider team have to complete a course of about 15 obstacles, such as triple bars, parallel rails, water jumps and simulated stone walls. If a horse knocks down a rail then it gets a points penalty. Additional penalties come from taking jumps in the wrong order, refusing a jump or exceeding a given time limit.

The individual event consists of three qualifying rounds and two finals rounds. The team event is decided in the second and third qualifying rounds.

Riders and horses qualify by country, not world ranking. The 16 nations in the team event will have three or four riders each with teams qualifying via various events in the lead-up to the Games, starting with the 1998 World Championships.

The riders in team competition are also part of the individual event, where a further 15 riders qualify through various international championships. The limit within those qualifiers is two per nation.

When equestrian events debuted at the Olympic Games in 1900, the programme included showjumping, the high jump and long jump. The high jump and long jump disappeared but showjumping has become a popular Olympic event.

In recent years, Germany has re-emerged as showjumping's best. The individual and team gold medals went to Germans in 1996, following an individual gold in 1992 and a team gold in 1988. They appear strong again for the Sydney 2000 Games. Germany is traditionally strong and won both the individual and team jumping events in Atlanta. Among the challengers in Sydney will be two-time world showjumping champion Rodrigo Pessoa of Brazil.

Atlanta 1996

Event	Gold	Silver
Individual	Ulrich Kirchhoff, Ger	Willi Melliger, Sui
Team	Germany	USA

In the team event, only seven of the 82 starters were able to come home clear inside the time, including two of the home team, Anne Kursinski with the Australian bred Eros and Leslie Burr-Howard with Extreme. Britain's Geoff Billington and It's Otto lay in eighth place. The top 45 qualified for the individual final.

None of the British could recover form for the second round of the team competition and the best of the trio, It's Otto, who had jumped a superb clear in the qualifier, backed off the water despite his rider's urgings, and collected additional faults at both the double and the last.

Germany's Franke Sloothaak, their reigning individual world champion, had a fall but Lars Nieberg came back with a gritty clear round on the stallion For Please. Ulrich Kirchhoff followed up by having Jus de Pommes perfectly placed at every fence to collect just 0.75 penalty points for being over the time.

Ireland's Peter Charles had the first of the few clears on Beneton. A one-error round from Eddie Macken on Schalkhaa left the Irish well in the running for a medal. The German team of Kirchhoff, Nieberg, Sloothaak and Beerbaum almost inevitably triumphed, followed by the US and Brazil.

Ludger Beerbaum couldn't defend the individual title he won in Barcelona as his mare Ratina suffered a pulled fetlock ligament. Of the British, Geoff Billington did best in sixth and it was another German Kirchhoff on Jus De Pommes who took the individual gold.

Outline rules

As there is a distinct advantage to be gained from watching the first few riders take the course, the order of participation is determined by a draw.

Once started, the horse and rider have to complete the course by jumping the designated sequence of numbered fences with the fewest penalties they can manage. The rider and team with the fewest penalties at the end of the competition win the gold medals.

Essentially penalty points are awarded for each error a jumper makes – the more serious the error the higher the penalty points The most common penalties are:

Fault	Penalty
Knocking down an obstacle	Four penalties
Baulking at a jump – first time	Three penalties
Baulking at a jump – second time	Six penalties
Baulking at a jump – third time	Elimination
Placing a foot in the water	Four penalties
Fall – horse or rider – first time	Eight penalties
Fall – horse or rider – second time	Elimination
Refusing a jump – first time	Three penalties
Refusing a jump – second time	Six penalties
Refusing a jump – third time	Elimination
Exceeding time limit in final jump-offs against the clock	One point per second

A tie for the lead is not uncommon in show jumping and this is resolved by a jump-off to determine the winner. The course is changed, and the obstacles are moved or raised. Jumping occupies the entire main arena of the equestrian centre, which runs 120 metres by 80 metres. The jumps are no higher than 1.7m, and the water jumps are no longer than 4.5m. The lath of the water jump is marked with plasticine to show if a horse's hoof touches it.

Did you know?

- In all equestrian events, riders must wear formal dress, which includes military attire, if appropriate.
- The story of the 1968 Games was Great Britain's Marion Coakes, who won a silver medal on her tiny pony Stroller, just 1.45 metres tall.

Jargon buster

Aid	A prompt, with hand or foot, that a rider gives to a horse to change gaits and make other manoeuvres.
Baulk	To stop before an obstacle.
Lath	The thin white strip that defines the water jump.
Oxer	A single fence consisting of two elements which make a spread jump.

Equestrian: Three-Day

Introduced: 1912
Scheduled: September 16-22
Venue: Equestrian Centre, Horsley Park
Events: Men and Women: Individual and Team

Introduction

The three-day event combines two of the main equestrian events – dressage and showjumping – and adds a third – cross country. The event is designed to test the all-around ability of both the horse and rider. As in the other equestrian events, men and women compete as equals in both individual and team competition. At the Sydney 2000 Olympic Games, they will compete over seven straight days – four for the team event, followed immediately by three for the individual event.

There are 16 teams in all – Australia as hosts and then 15 others who qualified through a variety of tournaments, including the World Championship. For the individual event there are 36 competitors who qualify through international and regional rankings within their countries.

The Australians enter the Sydney 2000 Games as two-time defending team champions. While European and US riders have traditionally dominated the three-day event, Australia and New Zealand have come out on top in more recent times, and will be hoping local knowledge helps them to continue their winning ways in Sydney.

Atlanta 1996

Event	Gold	Silver
Individual	Blyth Tait, Nzl	Sally Clark, Nzl
Team	Australia	USA

New Zealander Blyth Tait followed his superb cross-country ride with an equally inspired one in the show jumping to take the Olympic three-day event individual gold medal on the inexperienced Ready Teddy. The eight-year-old former racehorse was only brought in to the Games when Mark Todd had to drop out. Tait also won a team bronze medal on Chesterfield. After the speed and endurance day, with 56.8 points, they could not afford a mistake if they were to hold off the challenge of compatriot Sally Clark with Squirrel Hill (on 60.4 points).

They sailed inches clear over the first nine of the 12 fences and rattled the next two, but came home deservedly clear to triumph. The top three after the cross-country kept their positions, with Kerry Milliken and Out and About taking the bronze for the home team.

Outline rules

Competitors incur penalty points during each event. The winners are the rider and team with the fewest penalty points. A country may enter four riders in the team event, but only the best three scores are used, although four riders receive medals if the team wins one.

In dressage, each rider and horse are required to perform a prescribed set of some 20 movements within the arena. Judges award marks for each movement, ranging from zero to 10, and errors are penalised. The marks are converted into penalty points later to fit the scoring for the rest of the competition.

The second event was once known as the speed and endurance test and that was perhaps a better description than 'cross country'. The horse encounters roads and tracks (4.4 km), the steeplechase and the cross-country obstacle course.

One penalty point is awarded for every second over the set time for the first track course. The steeplechase is a 105-metre course with three brush fences that are jumped three times each. The riders incur penalty points for failing to finish in the set time. They also lose 40 points for a refusal or runout, and 120 points for a fall. A second refusal costs another 80 points, and a third refusal at the same obstacle, or a second fall, means elimination. The third segment is another roads-and-tracks section (7.92 km). In the cross-country (7.41km), horses and riders must clear up to 35 obstacles, again in a set time limit. The jumps include water, banks, drops and ditches, although most offer an easier but slower alternative route and the rider judges which one to take.

The horses that make it to the last day enter the show jumping. The medal contenders approach this tactically, trying to defend their positions. There are usually 10 to 12 obstacles in a 120 metres by 80 metres arena, which are easier than the jumps used for the separate showjumping. Knocking down a rail costs five penalty points, and a horse's refusal costs 10.

Did you know?

- A rider cannot use the same horse in both individual and team competition.
- Whips are not allowed in dressage. In the other events, they must be no longer than 75cm and cannot be weighted at the end. Blinkers are forbidden in all events.
- Some of the fences in the cross country are as much as 1.2 metres high.
- The gold medal-winning Australian team in Atlanta finished up with Wendy Schaeffer with a broken leg and Gillian Rolton with both a broken arm and collarbone.
- In the 1932 Los Angeles Games, only two countries managed to finish. The United States won the gold medal, the Netherlands silver, and the bronze went unclaimed.
- In 1936, the course at the Berlin Games was so difficult that only 27 of the 50 entrants in the individual competition finished.

Jargon buster

Cross-country
: Both the section of the cross-country day in the three-day event, and the new term for the speed-and-endurance test.

Dressage
: An Olympic equestrian event where each horse must perform a series of movements testing the rider's control of the horse and a panel of judges awards points.

Fence
: A vertical obstacle usually less than 1.2 metres (four feet) high and constructed with natural materials.

Jumping
: Short for 'showjumping', an Olympic equestrian event where each horse must clear a number of obstacles on a set course within a specified time.

Run-out
: A horse's attempt to escape the rider's control and avoid an obstacle it is supposed to jump.

Steeplechase
: A part of the cross-country test where horses run on a turf track featuring several low brush fences.

Fencing

Introduced: 1896
Scheduled: September 16-24
Venue: Sydney Exhibition Centre, Darling Harbour
Events: Men and Women: Individual/Team Foil and Epee

Introduction

Only electrons are spilled in fencing events these days as all the latest gadgetry is used to record hits by one fencer on another using electronic means. Strict safety precautions are taken, including special steels for blades, stainless steel masks and jackets stronger than kevlar. But fencing's spectator appeal is about to undergo big changes with the introduction of coloured uniforms, clear masks and, the International Fencing Federation has announced, a wireless hit-detection system to replace the wires introduced in Melbourne in 1956.

Three types of fencing weapons are used at the Games – the foil, epee and sabre and the match-ups, called bouts, are held on a 14-metre by 1.5-metre 'piste', the name for the playing area.

Fencers compete for 10 gold medals at Sydney. Men will compete as individuals and teams in the foil, sabre and epee. Women will compete as individuals and teams in foil and epee. Each competition has a single-elimination format. Teams consist of three fencers, and each duels each member of the opposing team.

Individual events will include about 40 contestants. All are seeded, based on World Cup rankings, and many receive first-round byes as the field is trimmed to 32. An elimination system then ensues.

Team events will involve eight to 12 teams comprising of three members. They, too, are seeded, based on the results of the individual competition, with many gaining first-round byes when more than eight teams are involved. The field is reduced to eight and an elimination tournament follows.

One of the highest-profile fencers at the Sydney 2000 Games probably will be France's reigning Olympic champion Laura Flessel-Colovic. Russia is emerging as the dominant nation in the men's competition. At the 1996 Olympic Games, Russia's men won medals in five of the six events, including four gold, two silver and a bronze.

Atlanta 1996

Event	Gold	Silver
MIF	Alessandro Puccini, Ita	Lionel Plumenail, Fra
MIS	Sergei Podnyakov, Rus	Stanislav Sharikov, Rus
MIE	Alexander Beketov, Rus	Ivan Trevejo Perez, Cub
MTF	Russia	Poland
MTS	Russia	Hungary
MTE	Italy	Russia
WIF	Lura Badea, Rom	Valentin Vezzali, Ita
WIE	Laura Flessel, Fra	Valerie Barlois, Fra
WTF	Italy	Romania
WTE	France	Italy

M=Men; W=Women; I=Individual; T=Team; F=Foil; E=Epee; S=Sabre.

Six men's and four women's golds were up for grabs in Atlanta at the Georgia World Congress Hall. Women's epee debuted in Atlanta and Laura Flessel of France arrived as favourite. Fencing officials wanted to make the sport more personable, so Olympic masks were changed to let the fencers' faces be seen.

In the sabre semi-finals Sharikov from Russia beat Touya from France 15-14 and fellow countryman Podnyakov made it an all-Russian final by beating Navarrete (Hungary) 15-7. Podnyakov took gold 15-12 while Touya beat Navarrete 15-7 in the bout for the bronze.

In the men's foil Italian Puccini beat Kim Young-Ho (South Korea) 15-4, Boidin (France) 15-13 and the other French contender Plumenail 15-12 on his way to gold. The bronze playoff went to Boidin, 15-11 over Wienand of Germany. In the individual men's epee Beketov (Russia) beat Trevejo Perez (Cuba). Bronze went to Hungary's Imre who beat fellow countryman Kovacs. An all-Russian final in the individual sabre resulted in gold for Podnyakov ahead of Sharikov 15-12. Bronze went to Touya (France), who beat Hungarian Navarrete 15-7. Russia featured in all three team finals and took gold in sabre and foil and silver in epee, Italy preventing a clean sweep.

The women's epee semi-finals resulted in guaranteed gold and silver for France when Barlois (France) beat Zalaffi (Italy) 15-6 and Flessel (France) beat Hungarian Szalay Horvathne (the eventual bronze medallist) 15-10. The final went the way of Flessel 15-12. In the foil semis, Vezzali (Italy) beat Modaine-Cessac, another strong French contender. and Romanian Badea beat eventual bronze winner Trillini from Italy 15-14. In the match-off for gold Badea beat Vezzali 15-10. Italy were the double finalists in the women's team competitions and they won one and lost the other. Foil went well with a win over Romania 45-33 but the epee final resulted in silver for Italy and gold for France (45-33).

Outline rules

Fencing is a contest between two combatants trying to touch each other in target areas with weapons to accumulate enough points to win the bout. The first fencer to score 15 hits wins in individual competition, and the first team to score 45 wins in team competition.

A bout begins with the referee calling "En garde!" and fencers cannot switch hands with the sword during the action. After a score, they return to this starting position. The combatants try to score hits while staying within the piste. Individual bouts consist of three three-minute segments with one-minute breaks between them. The winner is the first to score 15 hits, or the leader if neither reaches 15 before time expires (nine minutes).

Weapons are wired so that a system of lights registers any hit. The epee and sabre competition involve a red light and a green light, one for each fencer. When a hit occurs, the appropriate light shines to show the fencer who was struck. In the foil, a white light also shines when a hit occurs outside the target area.

If the score is tied after nine minutes, one minute of sudden-death extra time is added. To avoid cautious play, lots are drawn before the extra minute to determine a winner if nobody scores.

In team events, each team member fences against the three members of the opposing team. Unless time runs out in a bout, the first one ends when a team reaches five points, the second at 10 points, and so on up to 45 points, or nine bouts.

If a fencer puts both feet outside the side boundaries of the piste, he has to stand one metre back at the next restart. If a fencer puts both feet behind the rear limit of the piste, the opponent receives a penalty hit, or credit for another hit.

The foil is a thrusting weapon and the tip of the foil must hit the opponent in the torso, with a pressure exceeding 500 grams, for a fencer to score a point. In foil and sabre, only the attacking fencer (as judged by the referee) can score a point.

The epee, descendant of the duelling sword, is heavier than the foil. Only a hit with the tip of the sword, with a pressure exceeding 750 grams, can score a point. Hitting any part of the body, including the foot and the mask, counts as a hit. Both fencers score a point if a double hit occurs within .04 of a second.

The sabre, a modern version of the slashing cavalry sword, is both a thrusting and cutting weapon. Both the point and edge of the sabre score points. The target area is the waist up, including both arms and the mask.

The piste is a strip 1.5 metres wide and 14 metres long, with boundary and warning lines and a safety zone, where hits cannot be scored.

Did you know?

- After the 1924 Olympic Games team foil, an Italian and a Hungarian settled a scoring controversy with a real duel.
- At the 1982 World Championships the Soviet Union's Vladimir Smirnov, Olympic foil gold medallist, died after an opponent's sword pierced his mask.
- Before and after each bout, a competitor must salute the opponent, the referee and the audience by holding the sword's guard to the chin.
- Fencing is one of only four sports that has featured at every modern Olympic Games.

Jargon buster

Beat	A sharp tap on an opponent's blade to initiate or threaten an attack.
Feint	A false attack designed to force an opponent into a reaction that opens the way to a genuine attack.
Fleche	A running attack.
Forte	The stronger part of a sword blade, between the middle and the handle.
Hilt	The handle of a sword; also called the 'grip'.
Thrust	To extend the arm and sword toward the opponent.

Football

Introduced:	1900 men, 1996 women
Scheduled:	September 28 (final)
Venue:	Sydney Football Stadium (final)
	Adelaide, Brisbane, Canberra, Melbourne
Events:	Men and Women: Team

Introduction

The football tournament will start two days before the Games are officially opened to get through the large number of preliminary games. Matches are also scheduled for cities other than the host Sydney – Adelaide, Brisbane, Canberra and Melbourne are all staging games, with a semi-final at the MCG in Melbourne, and a quarter-final tie in the other three hosting cities.

In Sydney men's football will be celebrating 100 years at the Games. Women's football was introduced at the 1996 Olympic Games, where the final attracted a world record crowd of 76,000 people for a women's sporting event.

The men's tournament is contested by 16 teams, and the women's by eight. Professionals are allowed in the men's tournament but the rules restrict teams to players under 23 years old with the exception of three over age players. Australia qualifies automatically as host nation with the remaining 15 teams determined through regional competitions. The women's tournament, open to players at least 16 years old, will involve host Australia and the seven top-ranked finishers at the 1999 FIFA Women's World Cup, the United States, China, Brazil, Norway, Germany, Sweden and Nigeria.

The teams are divided into four pools for a round-robin preliminary tournament, with the top two teams from each group advancing to the quarter-finals (two pools to semi-finals for the women) and thence to the gold medal finals.

Eastern bloc teams dominated Olympic football after World War II, but since 1984 the competition has gradually opened up to professionals and the balance has shifted so that this time around World Youth champions Spain, 1996 gold medallists Nigeria, Brazil,

Argentina and Germany are favourites. The United States, as reigning Olympic and World champions, are likely gold medal contenders in the women's competition, ahead of China.

Atlanta 1996

Event	Gold	Silver	Bronze
Men	Nigeria	Argentina	Brazil
Women	Denmark	South Korea	Hungary

The round-robin section of the women's tournament saw early wins for China, USA and Germany while Norway drew 2-2 with Brazil. A USA win over Sweden took them to the semi-finals and China also progressed, winning 5-1 over Denmark. Brazil and Norway also booked semi-final places with wins over Japan and Germany respectively.

In the semi-finals China beat Brazil 3-2 while the US home team beat Norway 2-1, scoring a 'golden goal' in sudden-death extra time to mirror the progress of the men's gold-winning team Nigeria. The losing semi-finalists played for bronze and Norway came out winners 2-0 over Brazil.

A world-record attendance for a women's sporting even of 76,481 watched the United States win the first women's football Olympic gold medal with a 2-1 victory over China in the Sanford Stadium in Athens, Georgia. Shannon MacMillan and Tiffeny Milbrett scored the US goals and Michelle Akers and Mia Hamm provided the inspiration.

In the men's tournament there were early wins for Portugal and Argentina in Group A and they then drew with each other. There were more score draws in Argentina versus Tunisia and Portugal versus US. France and Spain won again. In Group B a parallel situation occurred when Spain and France opened with victories and then drew with each other.

In Group C Japan's team savoured their greatest moment when they beat a Brazilian side full of World Cup players. A defensive mix-up let in forward Teruyoshi Ito to tap in a simple goal in the 72nd minute. Brazil kept their medal hopes alive with a 3-1 victory over Hungary and finally made it to the last eight. Nigeria went top of their group after a second straight victory, 2-0 against Japan. Ghana eliminated Italy from contention with a 3-2 triumph in a tempestuous game

Norway beat Germany while Ghana and Nigeria booked quarter-final places with wins.

In the quarter-finals bursts of individual brilliance from Bebeto and strike partner Ronaldo gave Brazil a 4-2 win over Ghana to set up a semi-final meeting with Nigeria, who beat Mexico 2-0. Argentina quietly progressed on the other side of the draw.

Nigeria grabbed a 4-3 golden-goal victory over Brazil to take them to a final against Argentina. Ajax's Nwankwo Kanu (now with Arsenal), who had tied the scores in the final minute of normal time, scored the winner. Nigerian coach Jo Bonfrere had only withdrawn his resignation just before the Games, and could only afford a five-day build-up. In the bronze playoff Brazil beat Portugal 5-0.

Nigeria didn't relax after the semi but instead grabbed another last-gasp victory to take the gold 3-2 against Argentina. Emmanuel Amunike hit a controversial 89th-minute winner in front of a capacity 80,000 crowd. Nigeria conceded the opening goal in only the second minute and had to equalise twice before that last-minute goal.

Outline rules

Two teams of 11 players try to score goals by kicking or heading the ball into the opposition's goal. The team with the most goals, after two 45-minute halves of play, wins the game. The outfield players may not touch the ball with their hands or arms. The goalkeepers may use their hands within the rectangle around their own goal known as the penalty area. If a defender kicks the ball back to the goalkeeper, the goalkeeper may not use his hands,

The team captains toss a coin. The winner chooses which goal to attack in the first half of the match, while the loser kicks off. In the second half, the other team kicks off and teams change ends and attack the opposite goals. A goal is scored when the whole of the ball passes over the goal line, between the goalposts and under the crossbar.

A player is offside when he or she is in the opposition's half of the field and closer to the goal line than both the ball and two opposition players (usually the goalkeeper and one other player) when the ball is passed, and they are deemed to be interfering with play. A player is not considered to be offside if he receives the ball directly from a goal-kick, a throw-in, or a corner kick.

Players who interfere illegally with an opposing player are penalised and a free kick awarded. The ball is placed on the spot where the foul occurred, and opposing players must stand back at least 10 metres. If it is an indirect free kick, for routine offences, a team can score a goal only after it is touched by a team member. On a direct free kick, for more serious offences such as dangerous charging, striking, kicking or an intentional handball, the ball may be kicked directly at the goal.

If a defender commits a foul in his or her own penalty area, the attacking team is awarded a direct free kick in the form of a penalty kick. The kick is taken from the penalty spot 11 metres in front of the goal.

If a player commits a number of fouls or makes a particularly dangerous tackle (often from behind) then the referee shows the player a yellow card as a warning. For the most serious offences – including spitting, dangerous play, violence, an intentional handball or any other foul preventing a goal from being scored, the referee shows a red card and sends the player from the field (not to be replaced). A player is also sent off if he receives two yellow cards.

If a defender touches the ball last before it goes over the goal line outside the goal, the attacking team resumes play with a corner kick. If the attacking team last touched the ball before it went over the goal line outside the goalposts, the opposing team starts play with a goal kick. If the ball passes over the touchline, the team that did not touch it last resumes play with a throw-in from that spot on the touchline. Three substitutions per team per game are allowed.

In the round-robin (league) games, three points are awarded for a win, one point for a draw, no points for a loss. If the score is tied at full-time in a preliminary round match, the game remains a draw. In the knockout stages a sudden-death golden goal rule comes into effect, where the first goal scored during extra time wins the game. If nobody wins the game with a goal in two 15-minute extra periods, a penalty shoot-out follows. Each team gets five penalty kicks to decide the winner. If that leaves the teams still tied, a sudden-death shoot-out decides it. The first team to go behind loses.

A football field for international matches must be 100 to 110 metres long and 64 to 75 metres wide. The half way line crosses it, dividing it into two equal halves. It also dissects the centre circle, with its 9.1m radius from the centre of the field. A penalty area is marked at each end. Two lines at right angles to the goal line, starting 16.5m outside each goalpost, form the sides of the penalty area, also defined by the goal line and a line running parallel to it 16.5m inside the field of play. A goal area, where opponents may not charge the goalkeeper, lies within the penalty area and parallel to it, extending 5.5m outside each goalpost and running 5.5m into the field of play.

The goals stand 2.44m high (8 feet) and 7.32m wide (24 feet). The football must be 68 to 70 centimetres in circumference and not weigh more than 450g (16oz) and not less than 410g (14oz).

Did you know?

- The first women's Olympic final was held in Sanford Stadium in Athens, Georgia. It attracted a world-record attendance for a women's sporting event of 76,481.

Jargon buster

Advantage The referee allows play to continue even though an offence has been committed because it will benefit the team offended against.

Corner kick A kick from the corner of the field to team-mates lined up in front of the goal, awarded to the attacking team when the ball goes over the goal line outside the goal posts and the defending team touched it last.

Foul Any illegal interference with an opposing player, including kicking, pushing, shoving, tripping and dangerous or aggressive play.

Free kick A kick where the defence must stay 10 metres away.

Golden goal The first goal scored during extra time wins the game.

Hand ball An outfield player touches the ball with the hands during play.

Header To use the head to hit the ball.

Indirect free kick
 A free kick where a goal can be scored only after the ball has been touched by a team-mate first.

Offside A violation where a player is closer to the other team's goal line than any defenders except the goalkeeper when receiving a pass.

Penalty kick A free kick from directly in front of the goal with only the goalkeeper defending.

Save Preventing a goal.

Wall Defensive players stand shoulder to shoulder to shield the goalmouth

Gymnastics: Artistic

Introduced: 1896
Scheduled: September 26 - October 1
Venue: Pavilion 2, Sydney Olympic Park
Events: Men: Individual and Team
Women: Individual and Team

Introduction

In ancient times gymnastics was warming up for battle, in modern times it's a televisual spectacle with close-ups of the effort and emotion which the young competitors pour into their performances. The gymnastics 'family' now numbers three at the Games: artistic, rhythmic and, for the first time, trampoline. Artistic gymnastics is most familiar and it breaks down into a number of individual events.

Men compete in:
    floor   pommel horse   rings
    vault   parallel bars   horizontal bars

Women compete on the:
    vault   uneven bars   balance beam
    floor

The competition includes all-round events and team events, also scored over each apparatus.

Russia and China are the leading nations in artistic gymnastics, with Belarus, the Ukraine, Romania, the United States, France and Spain in the vanguard. Individuals to look for in the men's competition include China's Zhang Jinjing and Li Xiaoshuang, Russia's Alexei Bondarenko, Ivan Ivanenko of Belarus, and Spain's Jesus Carballo. In the women's watch for China's Ling Jie and Liu Xuan, Russia's Anna Kovalyova and Yekaterina Lobaznyuk, and the Ukraine's Atlanta all-around gold medallist, Liliya Podkopayeva.

A total of 98 men and 98 women will take part in these events and these have been drawn from the top 12 national teams for each sex, based on results at the World Championship. Two gymnasts from each of the countries ranked 13th through 18th at the championships and nine other gymnasts from high-placed nations also gain entry. One gymnast each from Africa, the Americas, Asia, Europe and Oceania is selected at the discretion of the Federation of International Gymnastics and other official bodies.

Atlanta 1996

Men's Event	*Gold/Silver*
Individual Combined	Li Xiaoshuang, Chn
	Alexei Nemov, Rus
Parallel Bars	Rustam Sharipov, Ukr
	Jair Lynch, USA
Floor	Ionnis Melissanidis, Gre
	Li Xiaoshuang, Chn
Horse Vault	Alexei Nemov
	Yeo Hong-Chul, Kor
Horizontal Bar	Andreas Wecker, Ger
	Krasimir Dounev, Bul
Rings	Yuri Chechi, Ita
	Szilveszter Csollany, Hun
Pommel Horse	Li Donghua, Sui
	Marius Urzica, Rom
Team Combined	Russia
	China

Women's Event	*Gold/Silver*
Individual Combined	Lilia Podkopayeva, Ukr
	Gina Gogean, Rom
Floor	Lilia Podkopayeva, Ukr
	Simona Amanar, Rom
Horse Vault	Simona Amanar, Rom
	Mo Huilan, Chn
Beam	Shannon Miller, USA
	Lilia Podkopayeva, Ukr
Asymmetrical Bars	Svetlana Chorkina, Rus
	Wengji Bi, Chn
Team Combined	USA
	Russia

In the women's competition Ukrainian Lilia Podkopayeva won the all-round title and took to the floor to win another gold in the individual, pushing Romania's Simona Amanar into silver. She also got silver in the beam. Amanar won her gold however in the vault. Russian Svetlana Chorkina took gold in the asymmetric bars. Shannon Miller wowed the home crowd when she won gold with a score of 9.862 on the balance beam. Kerri Strug, who won a gold with the US team, was carried to the podium by her coach, Bela Karolyi (once coach to Comaneci), after spraining her ankle on her last vault, causing her to withdraw. The US team scored 389.225 points to beat Russia, with 388.404, into second place, followed by Romania, China, Ukraine and Belarus.

There was a distinctly retro look to the winning line-up in the men's vault, harking back to the days of the Soviet Union. Now the individual countries were dominating. Gold went to Alexei Nemov from Russia, silver to H-C Yeo of South Korea, bronze to Vitali Scherbo from Belarus. The team event also reflected the strength of the former Soviet countries. Russia took gold with a total of 576.778 points, with China in silver position with 575.539 points and Ukraine in bronze position with 571.541.

The individual events did throw up talent from different nations. Greek Ioannis Melissanidis shaded the individual floor gold 9.850 points to Xiaoshuang Li's 9.837. The Chinese gymnast went on to put in the best overall performance on all apparatus to take the individual all-round gold.

In the pommel horse Swiss Li Donghua won gold while Yuri Chechi from Italy won gold in the rings.

Outline rules

Following a qualification round, the top six teams and top eight individuals in each area advance to the finals. Each team has six gymnasts, but only five perform on each apparatus. In the first round the scores for each apparatus are added for a total score for the all-round individual and team events. Scores from a second round of performances are added to the first set to determine the medals for the individual apparatus.

A gymnast makes one attempt at each apparatus, except in the women's vault when the results of two vaults are averaged to establish a score. Each gymnast determines the content of a routine, but must meet certain criteria regarding the type and difficulty of the skills. Two panels of judges rate the performances, one to give each routine a difficulty rating, another to mark each performance for its form and technical execution.

Gymnasts lose 0.10 points for small errors, 0.20 to 0.30 for medium errors and 0.40 for large errors. If a gymnast falls off – or onto – an apparatus, it should cost 0.50 points. A dismount from any apparatus must end in a standing position with the legs together.

A spotter (usually a team coach) may stand near the horizontal bars, rings, parallel bars and vault, but a gymnast is penalised 0.40 points if he or she needs help. On the horizontal bar and rings, a coach or fellow gymnast may help a gymnast into the starting position. The coach can't communicate with the gymnast during the performance.

The floor discipline is a chance for the gymnast to demonstrate a range of dance moves and circus-style tumbles in area just 12m square. Women have music, men don't.

The men's vaulting horse is 1.35m high, with a length of 1.6m and a width of 35cm. It runs longways to the runway. The gymnast sprints to the horse and performs one of a number of set vaults. The women's vault stands 1.25m high and across the runway. The horizontal bar (men) is made of polished steel and stands 2.55m high on uprights. The parallel bars (women) consist of two wooden rails resting on supports 1.75m above the floor. A routine on these apparatus is brief and intense. The pommel horse (men) is 1.05m high and set on two legs. The gymnast's routine takes place solely on the hands, on the top and using the two handles placed 40 to 45 centimetres apart. The rings (men) are two wooden rings suspended from the ceiling by cables and straps and hanging 2.55m above the floor. Strength moves are finished off by spectacular dismounts.

The uneven bars (women) consist of two bars, one situated 2.45m above the floor, the other 1.65m. Gymnasts push the range of moves on and between the bars to the limit and sometimes fall between the two. The balance beam (women) is a five-metre beam 10 centimetres wide and 1.25 metres above the floor. Gymnasts must use the entire length of the beam during their routine.

Did you know?

- Playwright Anton Chekov was one of the founders of the Russian Gymnastic Federation in 1883.
- When 14-year-old Romanian Nadia Comeneci was awarded a

- perfect 10 score at the 1976 Montreal Games, the first ever given, the scoreboard could only display to three digits so her 10.00s were displayed as 1.00s.
- In the 1976 Montreal Games Japanese gymnast Shun Fujimoto completed the pommel horse and the rings with a broken knee to help his team win their event by completing with five gymnasts as per the rules.

Jargon buster

Aerial	A manoeuvre where a gymnast completes a full rotation in the air.
Assemble	A jump where the legs are brought together in the air.
Beatboard	The springboard used in the vault.
Cabriole	A leap where one leg is raised to the front and the other leg is brought up underneath while beating against the standing leg in a ballectic fashion.
Composition	The structure of a gymnastics routine.
Compulsories	Routines that contain specific movements required of all gymnasts.
Cross	A rings position held as perfectly still as possible.
Dismount	A creative way of leaving an apparatus at the end of a routine and an important part of scoring.
Flic-flac	A spring backwards from feet to hands and back to feet; also known as a 'flip-flop' or 'back handspring'.
Release	To leave the bar to perform a move before grabbing it again.
Salto	A flip or somersault.
Tuck	The knees and hips are bent and drawn into the chest, with the body folded at the waist.

Gymnastics: Rhythmic

Introduced: 1984 individual, 1996 team
Scheduled: September 14-26
Venue: Sydney SuperDome, Sydney Olympic Park
Events: Women: Individual and Team

Introduction

Rhythmic gymnastics stems from group gymnastics, which still exists today in keep-fit clubs. In rhythmic gymnastics female gymnasts, accompanied by music, perform on a 13-metre-square floor area with rope, hoop, ball, clubs and ribbon. In the individual event they perform different routines with four of the five apparatus. Teams of five perform together, once using clubs and once with two using hoops and three using ribbons.

Sydney will welcome 84 rhythmic gymnasts, including 10 six-member teams and 24 individual competitors. Qualification was via a number of events including the World Rhythmic Gymnastics Championships which were held in Osaka, Japan, late in 1999, plus a number of wildcard entries to ensure a world-wide representation.

Historically the event has been dominated by the Soviet bloc of countries and Ukraine have been setting the trend in recent years with the 1997 world champion Elena Vitrichenko and Atlanta gold medallist Ekaterina Serebrianskaya at the fore. Russia, Bulgaria, Spain and Belarus are also challengers.

Atlanta 1996

Year	Gold	Silver	Bronze
Ind.	Yekaterina Serebrianskaya, Ukr	Yanina Batyrchina, Rus	Yelena Vitrichenko, Ukr
Team	Spain	Bulgaria	Russia

The 1996 Atlanta competition came down to a tight finish, when a single score gave Spain the gold medal in the team event, over the favoured Bulgarian group. The two teams were tied until the Spanish hoop routine, which featured a series of complex moves and thrilling exchanges, including one gymnast tossing her hoop high in the air and bouncing it off her chest into the hands of a team-mate. The successful routine gave Spain a 0.067 point edge. The women's all-round individual final saw the Ukraine's Yekaterina Serebryanskaya win with 39.683 points, from Yanina Batyrchina (Russia) and another Ukrainian Yelena Vitrichenko in silver and bronze.

Outline rules

Rhythmic gymnasts will demonstrate their skills with the rope, hoop, ball and ribbon and clubs, although clubs only feature in the team event. Each apparatus is worth points to the gymnast but the medals and placings are based entirely on total scores. The scoring takes into account the degree of difficulty in a routine, the artistic impression and execution of the routine.

The rhythmic discipline incorporates positions and leaps from classical ballet, including plies, jetes, attitudes and arabesques, and combines this dance element with the athletic side of gymnastics.

Gymnasts must use the entire floor area, should include a balance between left-hand and right-hand work and the apparatus should be in constant motion. Exercises should be between 75 and 90 seconds, with 0.05 points deducted for each second under or over the time allowed. An exercise must end simultaneously with the music.

One panel of judges looks at the difficulty level, one at the composition and a third at the artistic merit. The judges evaluate the choreography of the routine, the music, the choice of apparatus, body movements, originality and mastery.

When evaluating a performance, judges subtract 0.05 points for slight uncertainties or lack of precision, 0.10 points for small faults, 0.20 for medium faults and 0.30 for major faults.

Jargon buster

Axis throw A hoop throw where the hoop spins on its horizontal axis.
Boomerang throw
              A complex throw in which the gymnast pulls back on the ribbon, sending the cane flying towards her.
Mill   A small circling move with the clubs or rope.
Retro roll A roll of the hoop which returns to the gymnast.

Gymnastics: Trampoline

Introduced: 2000
Scheduled: September 22-23
Venue: Sydney SuperDome
Events: Men and Women: Individual

Introduction

Trampoline gymnastics debuts in the Sydney 2000 Games. Men and women will compete as individuals and each event will have 12 gymnasts, who will compete in a qualifying round and a final in one day. The competition involves both compulsory routines, displaying a specified set of skills, and optional routines chosen by the gymnast.

The main qualifying tournament for trampoline was the World Trampoline Championships in Durban, South Africa, in September 1999.

Russia, France and Belarus stand out in this discipline on the world stage and the medallists are expected to come from these countries. Great Britain and Germany will also be challengers.

Outline rules

The qualifying-round results are determined by adding the scores in both the compulsory and optional routines. The top eight competitors in each event advance to the finals,. The medals and places are determined by the final round only, consisting of a single optional routine, where the gymnasts select their 10 skills.

The recognised skills include various combinations of twists and somersaults in different positions. In the optional routines competitors try to maximise their scores with more difficult moves. The routines must include: one landing on either the front or back of the body, a single or double somersault, or something in between, with at least a 540-degree twist a forward or backward double somersault, with or without a twist, a forward or backward double somersault, including at least a full twist

Five judges score the execution, two judges rate the degree of difficulty, deducting points from a start score of 10. The gymnast with the most points wins. Certain faults draw automatic deductions, such as touching the trampoline bed with the hands (0.4 points) or the hands and knees (0.5 points). On the other hand certain moves earn difficulty points, for instance a full somersault is worth 0.4 points. Routines have to be performed in a certain order and even the optional routine must be submitted to the judges beforehand.

The trampoline is 5.05 metres long, 2.91m wide and 1.155m high. The bed is made from nylon or string material and is only about six millimetres thick.

Did you know?

- The ceiling of the competition venue must be at least eight metres high. Why? – to help prevent sore heads!
- In the early 1930s in the United States George Nissen built something similar to today's trampoline in his garage. He used it to help with his diving and tumbling and it ended up helping US pilots and navigators gain orientation skills in World War II, then helping US and Soviet astronauts adjust to different body positions in space.
- Great Britain held the first televised national championships in 1958 and London hosted the first World Championships in 1964.

Jargon buster

Adolph	A front somersault with three and a half twists.
Back	Backward somersault.
Barani	Forward somersault with a half-twist.
Bed	The spring part of a trampoline.
Fliffis	Any double somersault with a twist.
Quadriffis	Any quadruple somersault with a twist.
Randolph	A front somersault with two and a half twists; also known as a 'Randy'.
Rudolph	A front somersault with one and a half twists; also known as a 'Rudy'.
Triffis	Any triple somersault with a twist.

Handball

Introduced: 1936 outside, 1972 indoor
Scheduled: September 16-October 1
Venue: Pavilion 2, Sydney Olympic Park
Events: Men and Women: Team

Introduction

Handball is a popular sport on Continental Europe where league matches are well attended. It is a fast and physical seven-a-side game with passing and dribbling that can lead to lots of goals and crowd-pleasing action. Appropriately for this European game, the men's game debuted on turf football fields at the 1936 Games in Berlin and then appeared in its present indoor form in 1972 at Munich. In 1976 the women joined in and this division will grow to 10 teams in Sydney, with the men's field remaining at 12. Seven men's teams and five women's teams qualified from the 1999 World Championships and they joined Australia as hosts and the remaining teams who qualified through regional competitions. The qualifiers from that World Championship were Sweden, Russia, Yugoslavia, Spain, Germany, France and Egypt.

Teams play round-robin within one of two pools. The top four teams in each pool advance to the quarter-finals with knockout determining the two finalists who play for the gold and silver medals. The losing semi-finalists play for the bronze.

Current World Champions Sweden, runners-up Russia, and Yugoslavia are the men's favourites. Denmark, which followed its 1996 Olympic gold with a World Championship, remain the women's team to beat, with South Korea and Norway challenging.

Atlanta 1996

Event	Gold	Silver	Bronze
Men	Croatia	Sweden	Spain
Women	Denmark	South Korea	Hungary

In the women's tournament in the semi-finals, the championship underdogs Denmark defeated neighbours Norway 23-19 and went on to win gold after extra time against, South Korea 37-33. The Danish ladies could have won the gold medal at the final buzzer without the need for extra time when they were awarded a last minute penalty shot, but the free throw was saved to force the extra period. Hungary beat Norway 20-18 to take the bronze medal.

In the men's competition the semi-finals pitched Sweden against Spain and the Scandinavians came out top 25-20. Croatia beat France 24-20 to join them in the final. The game for gold and silver was a close-run thing with Croatia winning by the single goal 27 to Sweden's 26. Spain beat France to take bronze. Russia beat Egypt in the fifth and sixth place playoff.

Outline rules

Because handball has its origins in football the games are remarkably similar with the use of the hands replavinbg those of the feet. Thus free throws replaced free kicks, penalty throws replaced penalty kicks and so on. Players must pass, throw, catch and dribble a small ball with their hands while trying to score goals. The team with the most goals wins the game. A game consists of two 30-minute halves with a 10-minute half-time break. The pich is 40m x 20m and the goals are 3m wide and 2m high.

A player can make a pass to any team-mate who is at least three metres away, and the attacking team tries to work an opening to throw the ball past the opposing goalkeeper and into the goal. Only the goalkeeper may enter the D-shaped goal area that extends six metres out.

Players may use any part of their bodies except their lower legs and feet to stop, hit, catch or throw the ball. They can hold the ball for only three seconds before passing, dribbling or shooting. They may take only three steps after catching the ball. If they dribble, they can take another three steps.

A free throw can be a pass or direct shot. A penalty throw is awarded for a serious offence, such as illegal interference by a defender preventing a shot at goal or a defender playing the ball back into the goal area and the goalkeeper touching it. The offensive player takes the penalty throw from the penalty line seven metres in front of the goal. The goalkeeper may advance as far as the four-metre line.

If play stops for a reason where neither side is to blame, or the ball hits the ceiling, the referee throws the ball into the air, and a player from each team jumps for it.

Players cannot put the ball out of play deliberately. Players may be warned for fouls or misconduct with a yellow card, suspended for two minutes or disqualified from a match (red card). After two minutes, a substitute may replace the disqualified player. The highest form of punishment is exclusion, where a player is ejected and no replacement is allowed. Teams have five substitutes. Players may be substituted at any time, as often as desired. Each team is allowed a one-minute time-out per half.

Did you know?

- Spain's Onaki Urgangarin, a veteran of two Olympic Games – including a bronze medal in 1996 – is Duke of Palma de Mallorca after marrying into royalty.
- The ball is made of leather and ranges in circumference from 58 to 60 centimetres for men and 54 to 56 for women. It weighs 425 to 475 grams for men, 325 to 400 for women.
- Handball is probably based on a sport called Raffball.
- The first international handball match was played in 1925 with Germany beating Austria 6-3.

Jargon buster

Dribble	To move the ball by bouncing it on the floor.
Jump shot	A shot attempted while leaping.
Line player	An offensive player who plays largely around the six-metre line; also called a 'pivot'.
Running shot	A shot attempted while running.

Hockey

Introduced: 1908 men, 1980 women
Scheduled: September 16-30
Venue: State Hockey Centre
Events: Men and Women: Team

Introduction

Hockey has modernised greatly over the last few Games with high-tech pitches and specialist penalty-taking players amongst other attractions. For 2000 it has removed the offside rule to encourage more attacking play.

In the men's event, the two highest-placed nations in each of two leagues qualify for the semi-finals. The winners of the semi-finals meet in the final to play for the gold and silver medals, while the losers play off for the bronze. In the women's event, the top three teams from each pool advance to a medal pool round, which is another mini-league. The top two teams after the medal pool matches play each other for the gold and silver medals, and the third and fourth ranked teams play for the bronze.

Australia has dominated women's hockey for most of the past decade, winning Olympic gold medals in 1988 and 1996, the last two World Cups and five successive Champions Trophies. However, South Korea, Argentina, the Netherlands and Germany could offer strong challenges at the 2000 Olympic Games. The host nation – winner of the 1999 Champions Trophy – is also a leading contender in the men's division, while the Netherlands, the defending Olympic champions, is likely to do well again.

The defending Olympic champion and the host nation received automatic entries. The remaining teams qualified through regional elimination competitions and a qualifying tournament for each division, with the women competing in Great Britain and the men in Japan.

Atlanta 1996

Event	Gold	Silver	Bronze
Men	Netherlands	Spain	Australia
Women	Australia	South Korea	Netherlands

Great Britain's men started with three draws but kept the door to the semi-finals open by beating South Africa. The men's final Group B match saw them needing a victory to progress but Australia stopped them in their tracks 2-0. A rally against India 4-3 left them seventh in the standings. The medal action saw Spain beat Australia to get into the final with Holland who beat Germany 3-1. The Dutch took the gold with another 3-1 win and Australia beat Germany for bronze.

Great Britain's women lost to South Korea, drew with Holland and Spain, beat the US but lost to Australia. Captain Jill Atkins, the Great Britain captain, hammered in two late penalty corner goals to beat Germany 3-2 so that a victory over Argentina in their final group match (which included a hat-trick from Jane Sixsmith who scored the goal to send the team to Sydney) put Britain into the play-off for the bronze medal.

The South Korean striker, Chang Eun-Jung, the tournament's top goalscorer, helped put her team into the final against Australia. Britain played out a goalless bronze medal playoff. Chris Cook, Sue Fraser and Pauline Robertson had all beaten Jacqui Toxopeus from the penalty spot but the Dutch goalkeeper saved Kathy Johnson's effort to win the bronze for Holland.

In a repeat of the 1988 final, Australia swept to a 3-1 victory over South Korea and extended their unbeaten international run to 39 matches. With the score 1-1 at the break, Alyson Annan added her second goal when she converted a 44th-minute penalty, and then Katrina Powell scored with a brilliant reverse-stick shot.

Outline rules

Two teams of 11 players try to score goals by hitting the ball into the opponent's goal using hockey sticks. A game lasts 70 minutes and is composed of two 35-minute period halves. The team with the most goals wins.

In the round-robin section three points are awarded for a win and one for a draw. Wins, goal difference and goals scored are the first three tie-breakers used to determine standings.

Outfield players can only hit the ball with their sticks. The wooden, hook-shaped sticks are flat on the front face and rounded on the other. Players may only hit the ball with the flat side. The goalkeeper can use any part of the body to prevent a goal from being scored but must stay in the goal circle. Goalkeepers are well padded because the hockey ball is extremely hard!

Players may pass and dribble the ball with no general restrictions although their play must not be deemed dangerous. For example if they lift their stick above shoulder height then the referee (of which there are two – one in each half) may award a free hit against the offender. Free hits are given for any offences.

The goalkeeper's area is marked with a semi-circle or 'D'. A goal can only be scored if the ball is touched by a stick in this area before it enters the net. If a shot is taken from outside this line and goes into the net it does not count and the defending team is awarded a 22 yard hit.

If a defending player accidentally hits the ball over the back-line, the attacking team is awarded a long corner. The ball is actually placed on the sideline on a small mark close to the endline and the ball is hit into play. If, however, a defending player intentionally hits the ball over the back-line, the attacking team is awarded a penalty corner or short corner. In this case it becomes a case of five on five. Five defenders have to line up on the goal line (normally in or just outside the goal) while the attacking team places the ball on a mark to one side of the goal. One attacker hits the ball into play (injects) while the other players, standing outside the 'D' look to first stop the ball – this can be done with the hand – and then drill it into the net.

In all cases – as a safety matter – the ball must hit the backboard in the back of the goal to count. If a drilled ball hits the net above this board then the goal is disallowed. However, a flicked shot, as long at it is deemed non-dangerous by the referee – can be lifted into the net above the backboard.

When a defensive player commits an intentional offence within the goal circle that prevents an attacking play then a penalty stroke is awarded – a one-on-one with the goalkeeper. To count as a score, a shot must have been fired from inside the goal circle.

Offences can result in a green card warning, a yellow card five-minute suspension or red card ejection. A substituted player may return as a roll-on, roll-off substitution system is used.

The field of play, or pitch, is 91.4 metres long and 55 metres wide. A centre line running across the pitch divides it into two halves. On each end, an arc runs 14.6m from the goal, forming the D-shaped area called the goal circle. The goal is 3.66m wide between the goalposts and 2.14m high.

Did you know?

- India is the most decorated hockey nation with six golds. They won the golds during the period 1928 to 1956 during which period they won 30 consecutive games. Arch rivals Pakistan finally broke India's hold on the sport in 1960.
- The artificial surfaces which international and Olympic hockey is played on are actually filled with water!

Jargon buster

Back-line	The line marking the end of the pitch and including the goal-line between the goal posts.
Bully	Two players face each other, hit their sticks alternately on the ground and together three times, then jostle to control the ball. Very rarely used these days.
Centre pass	The opening pass of a half or following a goal.
Circle	Short for the 'striking circle', 'goal circle' or 'shooting circle, a D-shaped area in front of each goal and the only place a striker can score a goal from.
Dribble	To move while controlling the ball with the stick.
Flick	To push the ball with the stick and raise it slightly into the air. Also called 'scoop'.
Kicker	A protective device worn by a goalkeeper.
Push	To move the ball along the ground with the stick in a sweeping motion.

Judo

Introduced: Men: 1964, 1972; Women: 1992
Scheduled: September 16-22
Venue: Sydney Exhibition Centre, Darling Harbour
Events: Men and Women by weight divisions

Introduction

Judo made its debut in the 1964 Olympic Games at the request of Japan when the Games were held in Tokyo that year. However, it was dropped for Mexico in 1968 before returning on a permanent basis in 1972. The women had to wait until Barcelona in 1992 before they had their chance and there will be seven weight classes for both to compete in at Sydney. The divisions are as those listed in the Atlanta results below and the weight limits for each of these are: Men (60kg, 66kg, 73kg, 81kg, 90kg, 100kg, over 100kg); Women (48kg, 52kg, 57kg, 63kg, 70kg, 78kg, over 78kg).

Some 400 contestants – judoka – will compete for a variety of national teams at the Games with the top finishers in a variety of tournaments, including the World Championship, qualifying for the eight divisions. The final breakdown of numbers was not available at the time of writing but the greater balance of the judoka will be composed of men.

Both sexes will be drawn into two pools and each pool will be fought on a knockout basis with the two winners from each pool contesting the gold and silver medals. Two bronze medals will be awarded and these will be contested by a secondary tournament that involves all contestants that have lost to one of the two pools' semi-finalists. The winner in each of those groups faces the losing semi-finalist of the opposite group in the matches for bronze.

French heavyweight David Douillet, gold medallist in Atlanta, should be defending his title and is one contestant it is really worth watching out for, and not just because of his incredible size. He is likely to be France's only real challenger with the main thrust of the men's competition being provided by Japan and Korea, but with Germany likely to make an impact. Japan and Korea will also be the main contestants in the women's tournament with the Cubans also likely to fire a challenge.

Atlanta 1996

Men	Gold	Silver
Super Lightweight	Tadahiro Nomura, Jpn	Girolamo Giovanazzo, Ita
Half Lightweight	Udo Quellmalz, Ger	Yukimasa Nakamura, Jpn
Lightweight	Kenzo Nakamura, Jpn	Kwak Dae-Sung, Kor
Light Middleweight	Djamel Bouras, Fra	Toshihiko Koga, Jpn
Middleweight	Jeon Ki Young, Kor	Armen Bagdasarov, Uzb
Light Heavyweight	Pawel Nastula, Pol	Kim Min-Soo, Kor
Heavyweight	David Douillet, Fra	Ernesto Perez, Esp

Women	Gold	Silver
Super Lightweight	Kye Sun, Prk	Ryoko Tamura, Jpn
Half Lightweight	Marie-Claire Restoux, Fra	Kyun Sook-Hee, Kor
Lightweight	Driulis Gonzalez Morales, Cub	Jung Sun-Yong, Kor
Light Middleweight	Yuko Emoto, Jpn	Gella Van De Caveye, Bel
Middleweight	Cho Min-Sun, Kor	Aneta Szczepanska, Pol
Light Heavyweight	Ulla Werbrouck, Hun	Yoko Tanabe, Jpn
Heavyweight	Sun Fu-Ming, Chn	Estela Villanueva, Cub

One of the longest winning runs in Judo came to an end in Atlanta when North Korea's 16-year old Kye Sun beat Japan's Ryoko Tamura in the women's 48kg division to take the gold medal and with it end Tamura's 84-match winning streak. Amarilis Savon of Cuba and Yolanda Soler of Spain took the bronze medals. The last time that Tamura had lost a match was in the final of the 1992 Barcelona Olympics.

In the men's super lightweight final, Tadahiro Nomura was in the lead throughout the match and ensured victory with a late takedown. The men's bronze medals went to Richard Trautmann of Germany and Dorjpalam Narmandakh of Mongolia.

In the men's lightweight division Kenzo Nakamura, one of three brothers on the Japanese judo team, beat Kwak Dae-sung of South Korea in a split judge's vote for the gold medal. Nakamura scored an equalising point in the last ten seconds of the match and took a 2-1 decision. His brother Yoshio Nakamura wasn't as lucky, suffering the quickest defeat of the competition in the bronze medal match – being thrown to the mat in nine seconds by Frenchman Stephane Traineau.

France's Djamel Bouras and Japan's Yuko Emoto won judo gold medals in the light middleweight divisions. In the men's final, Bouras beat 1992 lightweight gold medallist Toshihiko Koga of Japan by a judges' decision. Meanwhile Emoto beat the 1993 world champion, Belgium's Gella Van de Caveye in the women's final. Soso Liparteliani of Georgia and Cho In-Chul of South Korea took the bronze in the men's division. The women's bronze medallists were South Korea's Jung Sung-Sook and Jenny Gal of the Netherlands. Belgium did experience gold success in the judo though with Ulla Werbrouck taking the women's light heavyweight title four years after she suffered a broken leg at the Barcelona Games.

South Koreans won both golds in the middleweight division. Cho Min-sun took the gold medal over Poland's Aneta Szczepanska. The men's winner was Jeon Ki-young, who defeated Armen Bagdasarov of Uzbekistan.

Estela Rodriguez Villanueva of Cuba was allowed to keep her silver medal in the heavyweight division despite testing positive for furosemide, a diuretic. China's Sun Fu-Ming won the gold.

Outline rules

The aim of a judo bout is to get your opponent into a position to allow you to score points. In general this involves putting the opponent into a position over which you have total control. Men's bouts last five minutes and women's bouts last four minutes and the first judoka to score a point in that time wins the contest. Half points can also be scored and if a full point is not scored, half a point can be the winning margin.

One of the most common ways of scoring is to throw an opponent. When a judoka does this then the referee is looking for him or her to implement it in a controlled manner. There are four different elements in the throw. How many of these elements are present determines the score awarded by the referee. For example a match-winning point – called an ippon – is scored if all elements are present while a half-point – called a waza-ari – is awarded if one of the four elements is missing. Holding an opponent still for 25 seconds secures an ippon, whilst a 20 second immobilising hold scores a waza-ari.

There are two other ways to score although these are not points-accumulating moves. A yuko demands that two elements of a throw are present or a judoka is held for 15-19 seconds and a koka is awarded if one element of a throw is effected or if the opponent is pinned for 10 to 14 seconds. A yuko and a koka are known as credits.

Any of these scores can also be awarded by the referee if he wishes to penalise one of the judoka – the most serious of these is called hansoku-make and results in an ippon being awarded against the perpetrator. For example, if one contestant deliberately bent back the fingers of another, he is likely to be disqualified.

Judo takes place on a special mat called a tatami which is 14m square and the judoka wear special judo uniforms called judogi. The judoka are distinguished by the colour of their judogi – one is blue and one is white.

Did you know?

- The defending gold medallist in Atlanta – David Shashaleshvili – did not get to defend his Olympic title. The Georgian went to the wrong venue for his first round match and found himself out of the tournament.
- Judo means 'the gentle way' in Japanese.
- Judo is the only Olympic sport where it is legal to choke an opponent or break an arm!
- Hillary Wolf, a Chicago actress who starred in the film Home Alone reached the quarter-finals of the judo competition in the 1996 Olympics!

Jargon buster

Chui   A penalty which results in a yuko.
Hansoku-make
             The most serious penalty, which results in disqualification by the issue of an ippon against the offender.
Keikoku   A penalty that sees a waza-ari, or half point, scored against the offender.

Modern Pentathlon

Introduced: 1912 men, 2000 women
Scheduled: September 30-October 1
Venue: Pavilion 2 (shooting, fencing),
Aquatic Centre (swimming),
Baseball Stadium (show jumping, running)
Events: Men and Women

Introduction

The Sydney Olympics sees modern pentathlon introduced for the women for the first time and some considerable time after the men's event was introduced in 1912. Previously a six-day event, it became a one-day event in Atlanta – a format that continues in Sydney. As the name suggests, the contestants have to take part in five sports – shooting, fencing swimming, show jumping and running (in that order). Thankfully all five can be staged within the confines of Homebush Bay.

A variety of qualification competitions took place prior to the Olympics to determine the men and women who would take part in the Games – with the World Championships at the heart of these – both the 1999 and 2000 events! The final field will have been whittled down to 16 pentathletes in both divisions.

Hungary has been the strongest nation in the modern pentathlon in recent years with Russia and France both pushing strongly. However, it was Kazakhstan who provided the 1996 Olympic champion. Poland, Italy and Great Britain will be amongst the strongest nations contesting the women's event.

Atlanta 1996

Gold
Alexander Parygin, Kaz

Silver
Eduard Zanovka, Rus

Bronze
Jano Martinek, Hun

Alexander Parygin of Kazakhstan won the men's gold medal in the most spectacular way possible by beating Eduard Zanovka of Russia to the line in the last ten metres of the final event – the cross-country – to snatch the gold medal from what looked like the certain grasp of the

Russian. Yards was all that separated the two after some 13 hours of non-stop competition.

Parygin, an outsider when the competition started, finished with 5,551 points, 21 points more than Zanovka, a bronze medallist at the 1992 Barcelona Games. To complete the symmetry Hungary's Janos Martinek, the gold medallist at the 1988 Seoul Games, took the bronze with 5,501.

However, at the start of the final discipline, the lead after four events belonged to Cesare Toraldo of Italy whose points converted into a 15-second lead over Parygin at the start of the 4,000m run. Zanovka hit back and over the final 500m the lead changed with Zanovka extending it to 100m at one point before Parygin found energy for his final glory burst.

Outline rules

Five events or 'disciplines' as they are known, form the modern competition. Each of the contestants – called pentathletes – earn points based on how well they perform in each of the disciplines. The competitor with the most points at the end of the day's five events takes the gold, with the silver and bronze medals being awarded to those finishing second and third in the points totals.

The events run roughly like this. First up is shooting where they have to fire 20 shots at a target some 10 metres away. They have a 40 second time limit for each shot and must be standing up. The target is a standard bull-ring target with 10 points being the inner ring score and one point the outer ring score. The shot score is then translated into pentathlon points. A score of 172 points on the target translates to 1,000 competition points with a 12 point adjustment made for each difference in the shot score either side of this.

Next up is fencing with an epee used for the duel where each pentathlete fights against each of the others. Each bout lasts for just one minute and the winner is the first to score a hit. If neither contestant registers a hit, both lose the bout. 1,000 competition points are scored if any pentathlete wins 70 percent of their bouts, with a mathematical formula being used to adjust the score, based on additional bouts won or lost.

The 200m freestyle is used for the swimming leg of the modern event with contestants seeded according to previously set times. However, the swimmers are racing against the clock, not one another.

A score of 1,000 points is achieved if the distance is swum in 150 seconds (men) or 160 seconds (women). A point adjustment for every one-tenth of a second faster or slower is made to the pentathletes' score.

After the first two disciplines are completed the scores are totalled and the pentathletes ranked in order of points. This is used to determine who will ride which horse in the next stage of the contest. Each pentathlete starts with a base 1,100 competition points and points are deducted as they make errors on the 450m course, which also has 12 jumps. The course has to be completed within a predetermined time limit and exceeding this incurs penalty points as does a refusal to jump a fence and so forth.

The final discipline is the cross-country race, which is run on a 750m course, of which four laps must be completed. The points scored by each of the pentathletes is totalled and they are ranked in order. The difference in points between the leader and those behind him or her is then converted into seconds. The pentathlete leading the ranking starts the race first and those behind him or her start after the time difference, as calculated, has elapsed. The idea behind this is that it now becomes a straight race to the finish line with the pentathlete crossing it first being the winner and taking gold, the person coming second winning the silver and the contestant coming third taking the bronze medal.

Did you know?

- Baron Pierre de Courbertin is said to be the founder of the Modern Pentathlon. The competition is based on the talents required by a courier in a battle.
- The original pentathlon was part of the ancient Games in 708BC
- The first athlete to fail a drug test at the Olympics was a modern pentathlete – Hans-Gunnar Liljenvall was over the blood-alcohol limit at the 1968 Games in Mexico City. He blamed it on beers he had drunk to calm his nerves!

Jargon buster

Bore The interior diameter of a gun barrel.
Canter The movement of a horse in which three legs are off the ground during each stride.
Corps-a-corps When two fencers are locked together so that neither of them can use their sword.

Rowing

Introduced: 1900 men, 1976 women
Scheduled: September 17-24
Venue: Sydney International Regatta Centre
Events: Men and Women various classes

Introduction

Steve Redgrave of Great Britain has done as much as any one individual to raise the profile of rowing in the UK and the rest of the world. Six-times World Champion, he has also won gold medals in the last four Olympics and will be returning in an attempt to add an amazing fifth in Sydney. Of course no one will forget how he told the world to shoot him if he ever went near a row-boat again after Atlanta! He will be looking to provide his own bullet after what must be his last Olympics – 20 years after he first competed in the Games!

Redgrave though could face his strongest challenge, moving as he is from the coxless pairs to the coxless four where the Australian team has dominated over the past four years and were the most successful nation in Atlanta on the basis of medals won.

Although rowing as a men's sport was introduced at the 1900 Games, the ladies only got their Olympic event added in 1976. Of the 16 events staged in Sydney, eight will be for the men and six for the women with the races grouped into sculling (oar in each hand) and sweeping oar (one oar in two hands) contests.

Teams qualified for the Sydney Olympics on the basis of performances in a variety of qualification events.

Atlanta 1996

Men	Gold / Bronze	Silver	Bronze
Single Sculls	Xeno Mueller, Sui Thomas Lange, Ger	Derek Porter, Can	
Double Sculls	Italy	Norway	France
Coxless Pairs	Great Britain	Australia	France
Quadruple Sculls	Germany	USA	Australia
Coxless Fours	Australia	France	Great Britain

Eights	Netherlands	Germany	Russia
Lightweight Double Sculls	Switzerland	Netherlands	Australia
Lightweight Coxless Fours	Denmark	Canada	USA
Women	*Gold*	*Silver/Bronze*	
Single Sculls	Yekaterina Khodotovich, Blr	Silken Laumann, Can Trine Hansen, Den	
Double Sculls	Canada	China	Netherlands
Coxless Pairs	Australia	USA	France
Quadruple Sculls	Germany	Ukraine	Canada
Eights	Romania	Canada	Belarus
Lightweight Double Sculls	Romania	USA	Australia

Steven Redgrave of Britain became only the fourth athlete to win a gold medal at four consecutive Olympics, teaming with Matthew Pinsent to win rowing's coxless pairs. The duo pulled out an early lead before holding off Australians David Weightman and Robert Scott for their second straight gold in the coxless pairs. Redgrave won his first two golds in the coxed pair (1984) and coxless pair (1988). It proved to be Britain's only gold rowing medal with the only other medal being bronze in the coxless fours.

There was some controversy surrounding the men's eights final, not least because some unfortunately difficult weather conditions put several of the competitors at a distinct disadvantage. The gold medal was won by the Netherlands, with Germany second-placed and Russia third.

In the ladies' division the world champion Australians, Megan Still and Kate Slatter, secured the coxless pair gold with Americans Missy Schwen, and Karen Kraft beaten out of their favourite's spot to take silver. Favoured Germany won the women's quadruple sculls in 6m27.48s, denying Canadians McBean and Heddle what would have been their fourth Olympic gold medal. They had to settle for bronze as the Ukraine took silver.

Romania won the women's eight race while Canada nipped ahead of Belarus, who finished third.

Outline rules

There are two types of rowing boat as far as the Olympics are concerned – boats are more correctly called shells. Sculls – where the rower has an oar in each hand, one on either side of the shell – and sweep oar – where the rower has one oar to row with. Beyond this, a boat can have one (single), two (double), four (quadruple) or eight (eights) rowers in it. Only the eight have a cox to steer the boat, the other craft are steered by one of the rowers who controls a rudder with the aid of a peddle.

The men and women compete in each of the same six divisions with the men also racing in coxless four and lightweight coxless four races.

Qualification for the semi-finals of the rowing races is done on a progression system. In this the top finishers in the heats move directly to the semi-final stage. The non-qualifying boats get another chance against the other heat 'losers' with the top finishers again moving forward. This is repeated until the required number of semi-finalists is decided.

The man-made course they row is on flat water and is 2,000m long. Flat water indicates it is free of wind and therefore waves. Six of the nine lanes available at Sydney will be used for each race.

A race is started after a two-minute pre-race procedure at the end of which a hooter sounds. If any crew false-starts the race is restarted and a second false start results in disqualification. At the finish line there are three judges who rule in close finishes – a hooter sounds to signal when the bow of each boat crosses the finish line. In the case of a dead heat both boats are awarded the same place.

Did you know?

- JC Babcock of the USA invented the seat on rollers which is now an integral part of any rowing boat.
- The depth of the water on the rowing lake is 3.5m.
- The buoys marking out the race lanes are colour-coded to indicate to rowers where they are on the course. The buoys are red for the final 100m.
- The rules do not demand that the boats keep to their lanes.
- The cox of a crew must be of the same sex as the crew itself.
- A race can be stopped if a boat suffers a mechanical problem within the first 100m of the race!

- Steve Redgrave is only the fourth person to win golds in successive Olympics. The others are Danish yachtsman Paul Elvstrom, Hungarian fencer Aladar Gerevich and American discus thrower Al Oerter.

Jargon buster

Aligner's hut	A small building near the start line where the starter is positioned.
Blade	The flattened end of an oar which is used to row through the water.
Boot	The device that holds the shell before the start of a race.
Bow	The forward section of a shell.
Cox	The person who steers the boat – short for 'coxswain'.
Feather	The process of rotating the blade of the oar so that it comes parallel to the surface of the water.
Keel	The main body of the shell which runs from box to stern.
Loom	The part of an oar between the blade and the handle.
Off keel	When the shell is unbalanced.
Port	Left.
Rating	The number of strokes a crew rows per minute – might be as many as 47 in the final stages of a race.
Regatta	A boat race.
Rudder	A board like device which is used to steer the boat.
Starboard	Right.
Stern	The back end of a boat.

Sailing

Introduced: 1900 (as Yachting)
Scheduled: September 16-30
Venue: Sailing Marina, Rushcutters Bay and Sydney Harbour
Events: Men, Women and Open – various classes

Introduction

Having previously been called yachting, the name 'sailing' is being used for the Sydney 2000 Games, in part to give it a more public image and also because the majority of vessels used are in fact small dinghies and sailboards.

The 2000 Games is one of those rare times when the sailing competition can be held in the host city. Sydney is tailor made for sailing and the whole Sydney Harbour area, with the backdrop of the Harbour Bridge, Opera House and spectacular coastline up to and beyond the Sydney Heads, will become a mass of fluttering white during the 15 days of yachting events. Wind and water are the two determining factors in any sailing event.

Located out of Rushcutters Bay there will be six different courses for sailing, four being within the harbour and two in the open sea beyond the Heads. There are 11 different events in all, fought out in nine classes of boats. Those classes are: 49er, 470, Europe, Finn, Laser, Mistral, Soling, Star and Tornado. Two races are held for men and women individually and the other classes are 'open' where men and women can compete side by side.

The master of the sport in modern times has been Denmark's Paul Elvstrom who won four Olympic golds from 1948 to 1960. Amazingly he competed in his eighth Olympics in Seoul in 1988 at age 60. Since then the United States has had the most success, with the northern European nations also making a strong showing. Australia was dominant in Atlanta and, with their local knowledge, it will be a major surprise if they do not dominate on home water.

Countries, not individual crews, qualify for the sailing events at the Olympic Games and places are allocated on performances in a variety of regattas held in the lead up to the games and no one nation may enter more than one boat in any event.

Atlanta 1996

Class		Gold	Silver
Finn	Men	Mateusz Kunierewicz, Pol	Sebastian Godefroid, Bel
470	Men	Ukraine	Great Britain
	Wom	Spain	Japan
Mistral	Men	Nikolas Kaklamanakis, Gre	Carlos Espinola, Arg
	Wom	Lai-Shan Lee, Hkg	Barbara Kendall, Nz
Europe		Kristine Roug, Den	Margit Matthijsse, Ned
Star	Open	Brazil	Sweden
Tornado	Open	Spain	Australia
Soling	Open	Germany	Russia
Laser	Open	Robert Scheidt, Bra	Ben Ainslie, Gbr

A gold medal at their third Olympics was the reward for Jochen Schumann and his German Soling crew as they swept past Russia in three races of the Open event. The German skipper took gold in Seoul in 1988 but missed out in Barcelona. The United States won the bronze, beating Great Britain 3-1 by overcoming a 1-0 deficit. The Brazilian Robert Scheidt missed the final Laser class race after being disqualified for twice false starting, along with a number of other boats, but still took the gold medal with 26 points. Ben Ainslie of Britain won the silver and Norway's Peer Moberg took the bronze. The Tornado class gold went to Spain's Fernando Leon and Jose Luis Ballester with 30 points, beating Australia's Mitch Booth and Andrew Landenberger. Brazil's Lars Grael and Kiko Pellicano took bronze. Finally, Brazil sailed away with the gold medal in the Star Class thanks to Torben Grael with a four-point advantage over silver medallists Sweden. Australia took bronze.

In the men-only events the 470 gold went to Ukraine's Yevhen Braslavets and Ihor Matviyenko, who didn't need to sail on the final day's events to be sure of their medal. Britain's John Merricks and Ian Walker won the silver, while Portugal's Vitor Rocha and Nuno Barreto claimed the bronze, which was also their country's first medal of the games. Nikolaos Kaklamanakis of Greece added an Olympic gold medal to his world championship in the men's Mistral.

As for the women, in the 470, Spain's Theresa Zabell and Begona Via Dufresne won the final race and the gold by beating silver medallists Yumiko Shige and Alicia Kinoshita of Japan by 11 points;

Ruslana Taran and Olena Pakholchik of Ukraine got the bronze. The Europe class gold went to Kristine Roug of Denmark and the silver to Margit Matthijsse of the Netherlands. Roug finished with 24 points, six less than Matthijsse's 30. America's Becker-Day claimed the bronze.

Lai-Shan Lee clinched the women's Mistral class to give Hong Kong its first medal of the Games, having built an insurmountable lead over defending Olympic champion Barbara Kendall of New Zealand. Alessandra Sensini of Italy took bronze.

Outline rules

Sailing in the Olympics falls into two categories – Fleet and Match racing. That said, virtually all racing is performed in the Fleet category and just one class is run under the Match racing banner. Essentially Fleet racing is where all boats compete with one another at the same time and the first boat to cross the finish line is the winner. Match racing is where two boats race it out one-on-one, but this only takes place at the latter stages of the Soling event.

Placements in races earn points. However, the lower you finish the more points you get!

In Fleet racing points are scored in the follow way. The winner earns one point, the runner-up earns two points, third place gets three and so on right down to the last boat. If a boat fails to finish the race then it is awarded one more point than the number of boats that entered the race. Thus if a race has 30 entrants and a boat failed to complete the course it would score 31 points. After five races each boat discards its worst result. Then after nine races each boat discards its worst two results. The gold medallist is then the boat that has the lowest aggregate score.

Match racing only applies to the Soling class and is held on a much shorter course. It is effectively a tactical battle where each boat tries to force the other into errors and incur penalties. Boats compete against each other on a round-robin basis. The qualifiers for the round-robin are decided by a series of Fleet races!

As already mentioned, there are nine classes of boat which compete in 11 different events.

Event	Sailing	
Mistral Sailboard	men	women
Europe Single-handed dinghy	women	
Finn Single-handed dinghy	men	
Laser Single-handed dinghy	open	
470 Double-handed dinghy	men	women
49er Double-handed, high-performance dinghy	open	
Tornado Double-handed catamaran	open	
Star Two-person keelboat	open	
Soling Three-person keelboat	open	

The most complicated rule in sailing is 'right-of-way' not least because it depends on where the boats are in relation to each other and what direction they are going in. The two most common right-of-way instances would be: when two boats on the same tack overlap (or are roughly side-by-side), the boat closest to the wind must stay clear; when two boats on opposite tacks meet, the port-tack boat must stay clear of the starboard-tack boat. If a boat breaks the right-of-way rule then they risk disqualification at the end of the race. However, if a boat realises it has breached the rule it can penalise itself by performing a 720 – that is sailing in two complete circles. The exception to this is the Tornado and 49er classes who only need to do a 360 – sail in one complete circle. In Match racing there are referees at hand and they will determine at first hand if a right-of-way infringement has been made.

There are two types of course – windward return and trapezoidal – and they are marked out by buoys (which normally must not be touched without a circle penalty being imposed) and it is the time taken for them to be sailed that determines their extent ranging from one hour for the Mistral and 49er class to two hours for Finn, Star and Soling classes. The other classes have a 90-minute limit.

Races have a set sequence for the start but essentially boats approach the start line together and must not cross it before the start horn is sounded – timing therefore is everything. If a boat crosses the line before the horn it must circle back and sail across the line again.

Did you know?

- Sailing was scheduled to be included in the first modern Olympic Games in 1896 but bad weather forced it to be abandoned and so the sport did not take part in the Games until four years later!
- Canada's Lawrence Lemieux received a special award after the 1988 Seoul Olympics when he rescued a fellow sailor who was swept away from his capsized boat.
- Some 3,000 categories of sailing are said to exist and each has its own set of rules!

Jargon buster

Bear away	Altering course away from the wind.
Beat	The sailing line into the wind.
Boom	The horizontal pole, to which the bottom of a sail is fixed.
Buoy	A floating marker in the water. Normally used to mark the course.
Forestay	The rigging used to secure the mast forward.
Going-about	When the boat turns into the wind and switches from the port tack to the starboard, or vice versa.
Jibe	The term used when the mainsail shifts from one side of the boat to the other, with the wind coming from behind.
Leeward	The side away from the wind.
Luffing	Changing course to sail towards the wind.
Mainsail	The largest sail on the boat.
Port	Left.
Starboard	Right.
Tack	Changing direction relative to the wind direction.
Windward	The side closest to the wind.

Shooting

Introduced: 1896 (missed 1904 and 1928)
Scheduled: September 16-23
Venue: Shooting Centre, Cecil Park
Events: Men and Women – various groups

Introduction

Shooting has been part of the modern Olympics since 1896 – but missed the 1904 and 1928 games – and has grown gradually down the years such that at the Sydney Games there will be 17 shooting events – composed of 10 for men and seven for women – and each is divided into four groups: shotgun, rifle, pistol and running-target events. Shooters may participate in more than one event if they achieve the minimum qualification requirement.

Women's skeet shooting has been re-introduced to the programme for the 2000 Olympic Games and China's Shan Zhan may well have a chance to add to the gold she won in Barcelona in 1992 but was unable to defend in Atlanta.

No single nation dominates the entire shooting event. Europe tends to excel in the men's rifle and pistol events with Australia and Italy on top in the men's shotgun. Ralf Schumann will be looking to shoot his way to a record third successive gold medal in the 25-metre rapid-fire pistol event. For the women's competition it is the Eastern European countries that have the most consistent competitors.

Up to 410 shooters will qualify through their countries for the Sydney Olympics. All but 28 of these will secure their places through major qualifying events in the lead-up to the games. The final places will be allocated by the International Shooting Sport Federation and will probably go to nations not represented at the games. No country can have more than two competitors per event entered via the normal qualification route. However, it is possible for a country to have a third entrant through a dozen places that are up for grabs using a points quota system.

Atlanta 1996

Men	Winner
Small Bore Rifle (Prone)	Christian Klees, Ger
Small Bore Rifle (3 Positions)	Jean-Pierre Amat, Fra
Rapid Fire Pistol	Ralf Schumann, Ger
Free Pistol	Boris Kokorev, Rus
Running	Ling Yang, Chn
Air Pistol	Roberto Di Donna, Ita
Skeet Shooting	Ennio Falco, Ita
Trap Shooting	Michael Diamond, Aus
Double Trap	Russell Mark, Aus
Air Rifle	Artem Khadzhibekov, Rus

Women	Winner
Sports Pistol	Li Duihong, Chn
Small Bore Rifle (3 Positions)	Alexandra Ivosev, Yug
Air Rifle	Renata Mauer, Pol
Air Pistol	Olga Klochneva, Rus
Double Trap	Kim Rhode, USA

Frenchman Jean-Pierre Amat, in his fourth Olympics, finally won the medal that had eluded him in previous Games. Indeed just 0.1 of a point cost him bronze in Barcelona, but at Atlanta he took gold in the three position small bore rifle competition, setting an Olympic-record score of 1,273.9. This added to the bronze he had just won in the air rifle event. Sergey Beliaev of Kazakhstan won the silver (1,272.3) and Wolfram Waibel Jr. of Austria the bronze (1,269.6).

A world record was just missed in skeet, with Italy's Ennio Falco coming within one target of equalling it, but he was more than happy in winning the gold with a score of 149. Miroslav Rzepkowski of Poland won the silver with a score of 148 and Benelli beat Ole Rasmussen of Denmark in a shoot-off for the bronze. Falco hit all 125 targets in the five qualifying rounds and missed only one of the clay disks in the final round of 25 shots.

Germany ended its Olympic gold medal drought thanks to two shooters. Christian Klees set a world record in winning the men's 50-metre free rifle prone event, while defending Olympic champion Ralf Schumann won the 25-metre rapid fire pistol, setting an Olympic-record score of 698 points in the process. Slovakia won its first ever

Olympic medal when Jozef Gonci won the bronze in the rifle prone event.

Australia, which hadn't won a shooting gold medal since 1900, picked up its two in four days. Russell Mark won the double trap event after Michael Diamond had won the first by winning the trap. Russia's Artem Khadzhibekov set an Olympic record on the way to taking gold in the air rifle event with 695.7 points.

In the women's events a 17-year old Californian was making most of the headlines. Kim Rhode won the gold medal in women's double trap scoring 141 points, two more than Germany's Susanne Keirmayer of Germany who took silver after a shoot-off with Deserie Huddleston who took bronze. Li Duihong scored an Olympic Record 687.9 points in winning the 25-metre sport pistol. Yugoslavia's Alexandra Ivosev captured gold in the 50-metre three-position rifle and also took bronze in the air rifle event.

Outline rules

Olympic shooting is divided into four events. In the shotgun events shooters fire at clay targets while in the running target event shooters fire from a distance of 10 metres at a moving target as it moves across a two-metre opening. The rifle and pistol competitions are held on shooting ranges with competitors aiming at targets from distances of 10 metres, 25 metres and 50 metres. Each of these is discussed in a bit more detail below.

The shotgun event is divided into trap, double trap and skeet competitions. In the first two divisions if the clay target isn't released on the shooter's signal he can refuse to fire at it. In the skeet competition the clay pigeon must be released within three seconds of the shooter's signal. For a shotgun shooter to register a hit at least one visible piece must be shot from the clay saucer. In trap events one target is released, in double-trap and skeet two targets are released and the shooter aims to hit both with separate shots.

In the rifle and pistol events entrants earn points based on where they hit the 10-ring target. With rifles, shooters fire from standing, kneeling and prone positions while pistol shooters use only a standing position. In both cases the competitor with the most points scored at the end of the competition wins. For the final there are more rings on the target and final-round scores are added to the qualification-round scores.

Normally, a bulls-eye scores 10 points and the outer ring scores one point. If a shot hits between rings then normally the higher score is awarded. Ties are broken by comparing the previous ten shots or more, or by having a shoot-off.

In the running target event, competitors shoot from a standing position at a moving paper target from a distance of 10 metres. This is done in 'slow' and 'fast' run forms which determines how quick the target moves across the opening which is 2.5 and 5 seconds respectively.

Did you know?

- Karoly Takacs won a world championship with Hungary's pistol shooting team in 1938 but lost his right – shooting – arm when a grenade exploded in it. Ten years later he won two gold medals in the rapid-fire pistol event, having taught himself to shoot left-handed.
- Prior to the 1984 games in Los Angeles all shooting events were open to both men and women.
- At the 1900 Games shooters aimed at live targets – pigeons.

Jargon buster

Air pistol	A pistol that uses compressed air or carbon dioxide to fire lead pellets.
Air rifle	A rifle that uses compressed air or carbon dioxide to fire lead pellets.
Airgun	A rifle or pistol that uses compressed air or carbon dioxide to fire lead pellets.
Bore	The inside diameter of a gun barrel.
Bunker	The concrete area from which clay targets in trap shooting are fired.
Crossfire	A shot fired at the target of another shooter.
Gauge	The unit used to measure the bore of a shotgun.
Lost	When a shooter has not hit his shotgun target.
Magazine	The chamber into which cartridges are placed.
Rifle	A firearm into which spiral grooves are cut in the inner surface of the barrel to give the bullet a rotating motion to make its path more accurate.
String	A number of successive shots, normally five or 10.

Softball

Introduced: 1996
Scheduled: September 17-26
Venue: Softball Centre, Blacktown
Events: Women

Introduction

Softball made its debut at the 1996 Atlanta Olympic Games as a women-only sport and remains in place as such for Sydney 2000. Despite its recent introduction into the Games it has been played as a sport in its own right for over one hundred years and evolved in the United States as an indoor form of baseball – although it is now played mostly outdoors – and has become a popular summer sport in schools around the world. The major differences from baseball are that it is played on a smaller field, the ball is bigger and is also bowled (pitched) under-arm.

The USA have dominated the sport although Australia managed to inflict a defeat on the US in 1996 and will have home advantage. Given that the Japanese are baseball crazy, it is not surprising that their women's teams are also increasingly strong, as are China.

As in Atlanta eight teams will contest the fast-pitch competition – Australia, Canada, China, Cuba, Italy, Japan, New Zealand and the USA – all qualifying through various regional tournaments except the Australians who qualified as hosts. Each nation plays one another once on a league basis with the top four forming the semi-finals. The team finishing top of one league plays the team finishing second while the team finishing third plays the team finishing fourth. The loser between teams one and two then plays the winner between teams three and four to determine the right to play the previous winner between teams one and two, for the gold medal.

Atlanta 1996

Gold	Silver	Bronze
USA	China	Australia

It would have been one of the biggest surprises of Atlanta if the USA had not taken the Olympic gold medal – they did so by defeating China 3-1. Their road to the final had seen them chalk up an 8-1 record.

Shortstop Dot Richardson, a 34-year-old orthopaedic surgeon, was the star of the final and went 2-for-3 and hit a home run in the fourth just inside the fair pole in right field, her third homer of the tournament. The Chinese held up play for almost 10 minutes as they protested the ball had gone foul. TV showed it was good though. When play resumed, Julie Smith reached base on a throwing error and Cornell hit a drive to deep centre that allowed the US to go 3-0 up after Sheila Cornell had hit a deep drive that scored another run in the third-inning. Starting pitcher Michele Granger struck out eight and allowed three hits before giving up a double to Liu Xuqing in the sixth.

The Chinese beat Australia 4-2 to reach the final and Australia won the bronze medal.

Outline rules

A softball game consists of seven innings with the two teams contesting the game taking turns at batting and fielding. The aim is to score runs and the team with the most runs at the end of seven innings is the winner. If the scores are equal at the end of seven innings additional innings are played until one side has taken the lead after both sides have taken the same number of extra innings. However, if the game is still tied after the ninth inning, each team starts each subsequent innings with a runner on second base.

An innings lasts three outs. That is, when the fielding team has retired or 'got-out' three batting players, the teams swap roles. Players on the batting team take turns at batting in order and continue to do so until three of them are out. If a batter hits the ball then she must run (unless it is a foul ball as described below).

The batter stands on 'home-plate' and to score a run he must run and touch the three bases spread out in a diamond shape – with home plate forming the fourth base of the diamond. The batter must touch each base with hand or foot. The most spectacular run is called the 'home-run'. Here the batter hits the ball beyond the boundary and automatically advances around all bases to score. However, a batter can also score by advancing around the bases by being aided by other batters. For instance, a batter might only hit the ball well enough to reach first base. Once there, she can stop. The next batter comes into play and when she has hit the ball, the first batter can attempt to run home or to any of the bases between the base she is on and home.

A batter can be given out in a variety of ways. If she hits the ball and it is caught before hitting the ground it is out. If the batter hits the ball or is running between bases a fielder can gather the ball and touch the player with the ball for an out – this is called 'tagging'. A player can also be given out if the ball is thrown to the base where she is running to. However, if there is no player running to the base behind her she can attempt to run back to her originating bases (but not home plate) to be safe. In this instance the fielders will aim to run in and touch the ball on the runner. Watch out for players trying to steal bases. Crafty players try to run from one base to another quite often before the pitcher bowls the ball. Providing the ball isn't hit foul, this is quite legal but the player faces getting out. If the ball is foul the player is allowed back to their previous base.

A player can also be promoted to first base from home plate by drawing a 'walk'. The ball pitcher has to throw the ball at the batter so that it arrives across the width of the home plate base and at a height between shoulders and knees. If it does this and the hitter fails to hit the ball then it is called a 'strike'. If the batter faces three strikes she is out. If the ball is pitched outside this 'strike-zone' it is deemed a 'ball'. If the pitcher bowls four balls to an individual batter the batter automatically walks to first base. If a member of the batting side is already on first base they are promoted to second base. Equally a player on second base would be walked onto third and if someone was also on third base they would be promoted home to score a run.

If a player hits the ball in the air – called an air-ball – and it is caught then any players already on bases can only run after the ball is caught. If they run before the ball is caught they must get back to their previous bases – but could be run-out in the process!

Extending from home plate either side of the batter are single lines. This is the foul-line. If a batter hits the ball and it falls behind the foul line then it is called a foul ball and counts as a strike against the batter. However if the ball is caught behind the foul line the batter is out. A player cannot commit a third strike on a foul ball and so in these cases the ball is simply re-pitched.

The Softball diamond's bases are 60 feet apart and although the main field is grass the running areas are composed of a special 'dirt'. The pitcher stands on a rubber plate 40 feet from home plate from where the ball is bowled under arm. The outfield boundary fence must be at least 200 feet from home-plate.

Did you know?

- The USA once had a nine-year, 106-game winning streak. China brought it to an end in 1995.
- Australia staged the first-ever world championship for women in 1965 with the host nation beating the USA 1-0.
- Softball was originally called kitten ball.
- The average fastball of the top pitchers in softball travels at speeds from 105 to 115kph
- There is little that is soft about Olympic softball. One pitch at Atlanta was clocked at 118 kilometres per hour. Considering the pitcher stands 12.2 metres (40 feet) from the batter, and the hardest-throwing baseball pitchers throw 160 kilometres per hour from 18.4 metres (60.5 feet), softball batters have essentially the same time to react as their baseball counterparts.

Jargon buster

Ball	A pitch outside the strike zone that the batter does not try to hit.
Base	One of the three safe stations for the batter or baserunner.
Baseline	The direct line between each base, along which the baserunner generally must run.
Baserunner	A batter who has reached base safely.
Bases loaded	Bases are said to be loaded when there is a baserunner on each base.
Batter	The player trying to hit the pitch.
Bunt	An attempt by the batter to tap the ball instead of swinging at it.
Catcher	The fielder positioned behind home plate who catches the pitches.

Curveball	A pitch thrown with a rotation that makes the ball curve – the technique is to try and make the ball curve late.
Double play	A play in which two outs are made with one pitch.
Flyball	A ball hit in the air to the outfield.
Foul ball	A ball hit outside the foul lines.
Grand slam	A home run with a baserunner on each base, scoring four runs.
Home plate	The five-sided slab of whitened rubber, 17 inches wide, the batter stands beside to hit the pitch.
Home run	A hit by a batter, which usually goes over the outfield fence, that enables him to run around all the bases safely.
Pitcher	The player who throws the ball to the batter.
Sacrifice	A bunt that allows a baserunner to move to the next base while the batter gets out.
Single	A hit that allows a batter to reach first base.
Steal	A baserunner's successful advance from one base to the next on his own, usually during a pitch that is not hit.
Strike zone	The area over home plate between the batter's armpits and the top of his knees, where a pitch is called a strike even if he does not swing the bat.
Strikeout	An out where the batter gets three strikes.
Walk	An automatic advance to first base for the batter after the pitcher throws four balls.

Swimming

Introduced: 1896
Scheduled: September 16-23
Venue: Sydney International Aquatic Centre
Events: Men and Women – 16 events in each

Introduction

Swimming is contested in both men's and women's categories with 16 events for each, involving four different strokes and a variety of distances. The sport has been in the modern Games since 1896 and in those early Games they were open events when most swimmers used a style called The Trudge, which the front crawl developed from.

The four strokes used are freestyle (crawl), backstroke, breaststroke and butterfly. Backstroke made it into the Games in 1900 and breaststroke followed eight years later. However, it wasn't until 1956 in Melbourne that the butterfly became an official Olympic discipline.

Freestyle events are swam at 50, 100, 200, 400, 800 and 1500 metre distances, with the 800m event being for women only and the 1500m event the sole domain of the men. The other three strokes are raced at 100 and 200 metres, while all four strokes are combined in the 200m and 400m individual medley events. These are rounded off by a variety of relay races – 4 x 100m freestyle, 4 x 200m freestyle and 4 x 100m medley.

The United States has dominated Olympic swimming down the years – who can forget Mark Spitz's record haul of seven gold medals at Munich in 1972? However, in Atlanta 19 different countries won swimming medals.

The Americans will be strong in Sydney but the Australians will be full of anticipation. Watch out for the Russian swimmer Alexander Popov who will could win a third straight 50m/100m double gold. Also Australia's Susan O'Neill and American Jenny Thompson will attempt to win third consecutive golds.

Qualification for the Games is on a two-tier basis determined by pre-set times designated A and B. If a country wishes to enter two swimmers in an event then they must both set A times. If only B times are achieved then the country can only enter one swimmer in the event.

There is no fixed limit to the number of swimmers that will be at Sydney but somewhere close to 800 are expected and these will be whittled down.

Each race has a maximum of eight swimmers. Preliminary heats in the 50m, 100m and 200m lead to semi-finals and finals based on the fastest times. In relays and individual events of 400 metres or more, the eight fastest finishers in the preliminaries advance directly to the finals.

Atlanta 1996

Event	Men's Golds	Woman's Gold
50m Freestyle	Alexander Popov, Rus	Amy van Dyken, USA
100m Freestyle	Alexander Popov, Rus	Le Jingyi, Chn
200m Freestyle	Danyon Loader, NZ	Claudia Poll, Crc
400m Freestyle	Danyon Loader, NZ	Michelle Smith, Irl
800m Freestyle	–	Brooke Bennett, USA
1500m Freestyle	Kieren Perkins, Aus	–
100m Backstroke	Jeff Rouse, USA	Beth Botsford, USA
200m Backstroke	Brad Bridgewater, USA	Krisztina Egerszegy, Hun
100m Breaststroke	Frederick Deburghgraeve, Bel	Penelope Heyns, RSA
200m Breastroke	Norbert Rozsa, Hun	Penelope Heyns, RSA
100m Butterfly	Denis Pankratov, Rus	Amy van Dyken, USA
200m Butterfly	Denis Pankratov, Rus	Susan O'Neill, Aus
200m Medley	Attila Czene, Hun	Michelle Smith, Irl
400m Medley	Tom Dolan, USA	Michelle Smith, Irl
4 x 100m Freestyle	USA	USA
4 x 200m Freestyle	USA	USA
4 x 100m Medley	USA	USA

They did it in LA in 1984 and they did it again back in their own pools. The USA swept all the swimming relays – men and women. It culminated in a world record in the men's 400-metre medley, winning in 3 minutes, 34.84 seconds. The women did their part by winning the 400 freestyle in Olympic record time.

In the women's events Krisztina Egerszegi of Hungary became the first swimmer in Olympic history to win five gold medals in individual events when she captured the 200-metre backstroke. The victory also tied Egerszegy for the record of winning the same race in three consecutive Olympics. Australia's Dawn Fraser did it in the 100m freestyle in 1956, 1960 and 1964 but had no other golds.

Amy Van Dyken was another record setter. The US swimmer became the first American woman to win four golds in one Olympics, taking the 50m freestyle, 100m butterfly and two more in two of the relays. Sixteen-year old Brooke Bennett got the 800m freestyle gold in 8 minutes, 27.89 seconds.

Ireland's Michelle Smith won three gold medals and a bronze at the Games. She took the 400m freestyle almost a second ahead of Germany's Dagmar Hasa and finished almost three seconds in front to take the 400m medley event. She took the 200m medley event with possibly her best swim of the Games, coming from fourth to first. The bronze came in the 200m butterfly, which she had been expected to win, but she later admitted to being too tired to sustain a challenge.

The title of world's fastest man went to Russian Alexander Popov who won both golds from the 50m and 100m freestyle events, beating American Gary Hall Jnr in both. In the long distance 1500m freestyle Australian Kieren Perkins defended his Olympic title and finished ahead of countryman Daniel Kowalski. The bronze went to Graeme Smith of Britain.

Outline rules

Each race has a maximum of eight swimmers and where required preliminary heats in the 50m, 100m and 200m events whittle the field down to semi-finals and finals based on the fastest times set in them. In relays and individual events of 400 metres or more, the eight fastest finishers in the preliminaries qualify for the finals.

Individual medley races are held over distances of 200m and 400m. In these the swimmers use the four different strokes for each leg of the race (50 metres or 100 metres each respectively) using first backstroke and then followed by breaststroke, butterfly and freestyle. In the medley relay, a different swimmer swims each leg of the course using butterfly, backstroke, breaststroke and freestyle in turn.

For the semi-finals and finals, lane four is allocated to the fastest qualifier with lane five being awarded to the second fastest qualifier with positions moving out from these for the next fastest times set.

As the Olympic swimming pool is 50 metres long, races are a series of lengths or laps of the pool and vital seconds can be gained or lost at the turn as the swimmer finishes one length and starts another. This is normally effected by a tumble-turn which, for the freestylers and backstrokers, involves touching the end of the pool with any part of their bodies as they turn and pushing off with their feet. In the individual medley races the swimmer must stay on his or her back until they have touched the end of the pool before switching to the breaststroke.

Starting is all-important but it is also the most tense start of the race, not least because in Olympic Games a false start, ie, going before the start is signalled, results in automatic disqualification! There is little room for swimmers to appeal because pressure plates in the starting blocks are used to log starts electronically. To keep in line with the more high tech approach there is a touch pad at the end of each lane so that judges can ensure that a relay swimmer does not take over until the incoming swimmer has actually finished their leg. A relay team will be excluded if any swimmer takes off earlier than three hundredths of a second before the incoming swimmer arrives. Virtually no room for error!

To finish the race breaststroke and butterfly swimmers must touch the pool end with both hands. However, freestylers and backstrokers only need to touch the pool end with one hand to have been deemed to have finished the race.

The four strokes will be familiar to most readers but here are a few points you may not be aware of. In freestyle some part of the body must be above the surface of the water at all times apart from the start where the swimmer must not stay under the water for more than 15 metres. In backstroke the feet and toes must be kept below the water's surface in the starting position. In breaststroke the swimmer's head must break the surface of the water during each complete stroke. Finally, in butterfly, both arms must be swung forward together, and both feet must move together.

Did you know?

- The 1900 and 1904 Games both had underwater swimming events. In 1904 it was called the 'plunge for distance'.
- The maximum distance a swimmer is allowed to stay under water at the start of a race is 15 metres.
- American men have won the 4 x 100m medley relay in every Olympics except for 1980, when the US boycotted the Moscow Games.

- The Sydney Olympic Pool is 50 metres long and three metres deep. It also has 10 lanes although the two outside lanes on each side will not be used. The water temperature will be controlled between 25 and 27 degrees Celsius.
- A rope, called the false-start rope, is dropped into the water to indicate to a swimmer that a false start has occurred – just in case they do not hear the hooter!

Jargon buster

Break	A false start at the beginning of a race or a relay racer starting before the previous swimmer has completed their leg.
Dolphin kick	The most common kick used in the butterfly stroke.
False-start rope	A rope dropped into the water about 15 metres from the starting end of the pool to stop any swimmer who does not hear a false-start signal.
Medley	An event where all four strokes are combined.
Negative split	Indicates that the swimmer swam the second half of the race faster than the first half of the race.
Split	The time taken by the swimmer to complete a single length of the pool.

Synchronised Swimming

Introduced: 1984
Scheduled: September 24-29
Venue: Sydney International Aquatic Centre
Events: Women Team and Duet

Introduction

It is probably the least understood of the Olympic sports but equally it is also one of the most demanding – not least in the quite incredible breath control required by those taking part in this women only event. The ability to time graceful movements in total synchronisation is aided because water is such a great conductor of sound – underwater speakers let the swimmers know where they are in their routine.

Synchronised swimming didn't make its full medal debut in the games until 1984 and it comes in two basic flavours for the Olympics – duet and team. Since its introduction Canada and the USA have won every gold and silver medal, not just in the Olympics but at all major events. Total domination. However, with many of their big stars retiring after Atlanta the balance of power has swung the way of Russia, with Japan and France challenging also. These teams will be amongst the favourites for medals in Sydney, along with Italy but the US and Canada are also expected to try to bounce back.

The judging for synchronised swimming resembles the judging for figure skating. Two panels of five judges assess a performance, one panel scoring technical merit and the other assessing artistic impression. In both cases, each judge awards marks out of a possible total of 10.

Atlanta 1996

Gold	Silver	Bronze
USA	Canada	Japan

The USA maintained their dominance of synchronised swimming by taking the gold medal in Atlanta. They finished with a score of 99.720 points which included nine perfect 10s for their freestyle routine.

Canada took the silver with a score of 98.367 and Japan the bronze with 97.753.

Outline rules

Synchronised swimming is judged by two panels of five judges who award marks out of ten. One panel awards marks on technical merit and the other panel marks for artistic impression. The format is the same as for figure skating.

Eight teams, each comprised of eight swimmers plus one reserve, will contest the team event while 24 pairs of swimmers will contest the duets. The team competition is a straight battle between the eight teams and each has to perform a technical routine and then a free routine. After a preliminary round of technical routines and a free event the top 12 pairs go through to a final round where they perform their free routine again.

The technical programme is composed of a set number of routines that have to be performed in a pre-defined order. Teams and duets can select their own music though. The free routine is aimed to make the maximum impression on the judges and technical and artistic elements must be combined to best effect and must last for five minutes in the team event and four minutes in the duet events. Again the choice of musical accompaniment is down to the countries participating. Judges are looking to score points under a variety of headings including level of difficulty, execution, technical merit and of course, synchronisation! Equally penalty points can be deducted if any infringement of the rules takes place or a particular routine was not included in the technical event.

Swimmers can start their routines on the side of the pool – called the 'deck' – but this deck work cannot last longer than 10 seconds. When the routines are completed the highest and lowest scored from each panel of judges is thrown out. The resultant three scores are averaged and a variety of weighting multiplications is implemented to produce a final overall score. In fact the scoring has become so complicated it is computer driven!

Did you know?

- The USA, Canada and Japan have won every medal awarded in synchronised swimming in the Olympics. Canada has two golds and five silvers. US swimmers have won four golds and two silvers in individual and duet competition.
- All seven of Japan's medals have been of a bronze hue.
- In Atlanta there was only a team event.
- Synchronised swimmers must not touch the floor of the pool.
- If a tie occurs then results are recalculated to three decimal places rather than the normal two.

Jargon buster

Boost	The swimmer aims to get as much of her body above the surface by rising up through and out of the water.
Cadence action	Identical movement performed by each swimmer, one after the other as quickly as possible.
Continuous spin	The swimmer rotates completely at least twice while descending.
Float	Two to eight swimmers connect together on the surface.
Nose clip	Plastic clip that is placed on the nose to allow swimmers to move freely underwater.

Table Tennis

Introduced: 1988
Scheduled: September 16-25
Venue: State Sports Centre, Sydney Olympic Park
Events: Men and Women: Singles and Doubles

Introduction

Think table tennis and you automatically think China – whether you follow the sport or not. The Chinese have dominated 'ping-pong' at the last three Olympics and there is no reason to expect any different in Sydney. A mesmeric sport, there can not be many people who have not played the game at some point in their lives and thus we all have an affinity for the game which started life well over a hundred years ago.

Surprisingly the game only entered the Olympics as recently as the 1988 Games in Seoul and since then China have won all six women's gold medals and four of the six men's gold medals that have been up for grabs. The 1996 Olympic men's champion Liu Guoliang will almost certainly be looking to retain his title but may be pushed by the world number one in the lead-up to the Olympics, Vladimir Samsonov of Belarus. Wang Nan and Li Ju, are expected to be in the medal hunt at Sydney but will probably face stiff competition from Chen Jing of Taiwan.

The Sydney 2000 tournament will involve 64 men and women competing in the singles and 22 pairs for the doubles. For the singles events the top 20 players in the International Table Tennis Federation (ITTF) ranking qualify automatically but may not include more than two players from any one nation for the men's or women's games. The various governing bodies based on each continent select the balance of the numbers with at least three other players qualifying through a qualification tournament. At this stage no country can have more than three players, in total, representing it at the Games. The same federations then select 22 pairs for both doubles events with a maximum of two pairs per country.

The top 16 seeded singles players and top eight seeded pairs for each sex automatically qualify for what is called the 'main draw'. The balance of the singles players – 48 men and 48 women – are drawn into pools of three with the winner of each of the pools advancing to the main draw. The doubles is played on a similar basis. The main draw will then consist of 32 singles players and 16 doubles teams for both sexes. These are then drawn and play on a straight knock-out basis.

Atlanta 1996

		Gold	Silver
Men	Singles	Liu Guoliang, Chn	Wang Tao, Chn
	Doubles	China	China
Women	Singles	Deng Yaping, Chn	Chen Jung, Tpe
	Doubles	China	China

China completed a sweep of the Olympic table tennis gold medals in Atlanta. Star of the show was Deng Yaping who completed her second consecutive table tennis double by taking the singles and doubles titles just as she did in 1992. She beat Taiwan's Chen Jing in five games – 21-14, 21-17, 20-22, 17-21, 21-5 – to take the singles and teamed up with Qiao Hong, to beat fellow nationals Liu Wei and Qiao Yunping in four games – 18-21, 25-23, 22-20, 21-14.

In the bronze medal match Qiao, who lost to Chen in the semi-finals, took third over another Chinese, Liu Wei, 21-17, 15-21, 21-19, 21-11. The doubles bronze went to South Korea's Park Hae-Jung and Ryu Ji-Hae.

In the men's tournament Liu Guoliang took gold, winning the men's singles over team-mate, Wang Tao 21-12, 22-24, 21-19, 15-21, 21-5. In the bronze medal match, Germany's Joerg Rosskopf defeated Petr Korbel of the Czech Republic 21-17, 19-21, 21-18, 21-19. Rosskopf was the only non-Asian medallist in table tennis.

Outline rules

Table tennis is played between two players – singles – or between teams of two players – doubles. Using a table tennis table, they stand at each end of the table and look to hit the ball over a small net and onto the opponent's side of the table, using a small bat.

The aim is to score points by forcing the opponents into a position such that they cannot return the ball legally. The three most common ways of this happening are: the opponent cannot get to and return the ball (hitting an out-right winner); the opponent returns the ball but hits it into the net on their side; or the opponent returns the ball but is unable to land it on the other side of the table. Note that the ball is only allowed to bounce once on any side of the table – if it bounces twice then the team that made the shot wins the points. The team that hit the last legal shot scores the point. Note that if the ball hits the edge of the table after being returned it is deemed good.

The first player or team to reach 21 points wins the game, provided there is a lead of at least two points. Thus a game cannot be won 21-20. If the scores are tied at 20-20 – also called deuce – the two sides continue playing until one goes up by two clear points. In the Olympics the preliminary round matches are best of three games while the main draw games are played as the best of five games.

As with most games of this type serve can be all important and some of the moves players perform at this stage of the match can be quite spectacular! To start the serve the player must rest the ball on the palm of his hand so the opposition can see it and must toss it at least 16cm into the air before hitting the serve, at which point the bat and ball must be behind the end line and above the table level. The ball must hit the table on both sides of the table. If the ball hits the net on the way across it and bounces on the opponent's side of the table, it is ruled a net serve and it is retaken.

In singles the serve can hit anywhere on the other side of the table. In doubles the serve must always go from right-hand corner to right-hand corner and the receiver returns it. Play must then alternate between players, thus when the ball is returned the server's partner must be the next to hit the ball. If this sequence is broken the point is awarded to the other side.

Service is changed after every five points, while in doubles the previous receiver becomes the new server. Where games are tied at 20-20 then serve alternates between sides. The team serving has its score called first by the umpire.

To ensure games move along at a reasonable rate the Expedite Rule is available to umpires. Effectively a game should be completed within 15 minutes – if it is not then the umpire will tell the players he is implementing the expedite system and for the rest of the game the server must win the point by the 13th stroke of the rally. If the server does not then the umpire stops the rally and awards the point to the receiver. Of course in these cases the receiver is trying to return the ball – because he will win the point if he or she does so 13 times, whereas the server is going all-out to win. The only time the Expedite Rule is not introduced is if both sides have scored 19 points each or more.

The table tennis table is 2.74 metres long and 1.525 metres wide and is 76cm above the floor. The net is 15.25cm high and positioned across the centre of the table.

Did you know?

- Some glues are banned from use on table tennis bats as they can make the ball travel up to 20 mph faster!
- Table tennis is known by a variety of names around the world – the most popular are ping-pong, gossima, whiff-whaff and flim-flam.
- The International Table Tennis Federation was formed in 1926 with Great Britain, Germany and Hungary the early drivers of the sport.
- Unlike tennis, in table tennis, players may not volley, or hit the ball before it bounces.

Jargon buster

Backspin	When the ball is spinning in the reverse direction to which it is travelling – implemented by striking the ball with a downward movement of the bat.
Block	A defensive return shot where the returner simply blocks the ball with the bat.
Deuce	A term to indicate that the game is level and at a point where one of the two sides needs to win two points in succession to win the game.
Kill	A powerfully hit shot with such speed it is almost impossible for it to be returned.
Sidespin	A sideways spin put on the ball by striking it with a sideways movement of the bat.
Smash	A shot that is hit hard, normally at a sharp angle to the table, in an effort to win the point.
Topspin	When the ball is spinning in the direction to which it is travelling – implemented by striking the ball with an upward movement of the bat.

Taekwondo

Introduced:	2000
Scheduled:	September 27-30
Venue:	State Sports Centre, Sydney Olympic Park
Events:	Men and women at various weight divisions

Introduction

Taekwondo makes its debut at the Sydney games. As an organised sport it is just 42 years old but it has a history that dates back, coincidentally, 2000 years. This will be its first full appearance although it has appeared twice as an exhibition sport – first in 1988 and then in 1992.

The Olympics will include four divisions each for men and women. The men will fight at weights of 58kg, 68kg, 80kg and over 80kg while the women will compete at weights of 49kg, 57kg, 67kg and over 67kg.

The men's competition will contain 52 competitors and the women's 48 athletes with places at the Olympics being decided by special qualifying tournaments, with hosts Australia getting a place in each division automatically.

The tournament is run on a straight knock-out basis right through to the final to decide the gold and silver medals. However, the qualifiers for the bronze medal are decided by a rather convoluted method. The two losing semi-finalists qualify for a second round of match-ups along with all those that lost to the two finalists, who match-up to leave two more qualifiers who fight it out with the losing semi-finalists to decide who will match-up for the bronze medal. Well, I said it was convoluted.

The Koreans – from North and South – dominate the sport they invented. However Iran have been amongst the challengers to the supremacy of the Asians, including the other strong contenders China and Taiwan.

Outline rules

A taekwondo contest involves two contestants who are distinguished by the colour of their uniform of dobok. Wearing blue is the 'Chung' and wearing red is the 'Hong'. The aim is for the fighters to score points by landing kicks on the opponent's head and body or by delivering punches to the body. A match can be won in a number of ways: by knocking out an opponent; by scoring more points than the opponent; by default if the opponent incurs three penalty points or by the disqualification of an opponent. A contest takes place over three rounds of three minutes, with a one-minute interval between rounds.

If a match finishes in a tie on points then the referee decides which contestant showed the greater initiative and awards them the match. However, if it is the gold medal match then a fourth, sudden-death round is started with the contestant to score the next point declared the winner. If no points are scored then at the end of the extra round the referee's decision is taken.

Scoring progresses a point at a time with one point being awarded each time a competitor makes a legal strike on his opponent. The body protector each athlete must wear marks scoring areas. Some examples of scoring strikes are: a strike on the head, the abdomen and each side of the body.

A team of three judges sits and rules whether a point scoring strike has taken place, a majority decision is enough for the strike to score. For a strike to count it must also have been delivered in a legal manner, for example with the front of the knuckles of the index and middle-fingers of a clenched fist, or with parts of a foot below the ankle. These are things the judges are looking for as well.

Penalty points are also a big factor in a taekwondo contest. Three of them in one contest mean automatic disqualification – this is rare – but contests can be so tight that a single penalty point can often be the difference between winning and losing. There are two types of penalty – the kyong-go and the gam-jeom. Kyong-go is the most common and is in effect a warning that carries with it a half-point penalty. However, it only counts if the same contestant receives a second kyong-go and then has the full penalty point awarded against him. The referees will give a kyong-go for offences such as holding or pushing.
Much more serious is the gam-jeom, which is an immediate one-point penalty and this is awarded for more serious offences such as attacking an opponent's face with the hands or throwing an opponent.

If an opponent is knocked down then the referee starts a 10-second count which can lead to a knock-out if the downed party does not get up or looks unable to continue.

Did you know?

- Taekwondo staged its first championship in 1973.
- Taekwondo means 'way of hands and feet'.
- The sport is practised by more than 50 million people worldwide.
- Taekwondo originated in Korea.
- No taekwondo fighter who has been knocked out by a blow to the head is allowed to compete for 30 days.

Jargon buster

Chung	The contestant wearing blue.
Deuk-jeom	A single point.
Dobok	The uniform worn by both contestants.
Gam-jeom	An automatic penalty point.
Hong	The contestant wearing red.
Kal-yeo	The command to break, or move away from an opponent.
Keu-man	The command to stop the contest.
Kyong-go	A warning carrying a half penalty point.
Yeo-dul	Eight in Korean – used to indicate a mandatory eight-count that is issued to any contestant who is downed.
Yeol	10 in Korean, issued at the end of a knock-out count.

Tennis

Introduced: 1896-1924, 1988
Scheduled: September 19-28
Venue: Tennis Centre
Events: Men: Singles and Doubles
Women: Singles and Doubles

Introduction

Many people are not aware that tennis as a sport was part of the original modern Olympic Games. It was introduced in 1896 and remained an integral part of the fabric of the competition until 1924 until debates over professionalism, amongst other on-going disputes, saw it omitted for the following 64 years. How ironic that the best-paid professionals of all-time were invited back when the sport was re-introduced in Barcelona in 1988.

The lure of Olympic Gold should ensure that just about every major name on the tennis circuit is competing in Sydney, with singles and doubles competitions for both sexes. There will be 64 players taking part in each of the events – 32 pairs for the double. The competitions will be fought out on a rubberised hard court surface at the Tennis Centre at Homebush Bay and will be fought on a straight knock-out basis. The top 16 players in each singles event are seeded – eight on each side of the draw, as are the eight top-ranked doubles teams.

Qualification for the Games was dependent on world ranking. The top 48 ranked players following Wimbledon qualified automatically, although no more than four players from any one nation in either the men's of women's events are allowed with three singles players and one doubles team being the limit. Lower ranked players will be admitted to make up the balance of the 48 players. The remaining places are allocated by the ITF (International Tennis Federation) and were due to be allocated to players from countries not represented after the initial qualification process.

As far as potential winners for each event goes, for the men's tournament Australians Pat Rafter and Mark Philippoussis will be among the favourites on home rubber but the Brits will be looking at Henman (a medal winner in Atlanta in the doubles) and Rusedski to produce their best. But with the likes of existing gold medallist Andre Agassi, Spain's Carlos Moya, and Russia's Yevgeny Kafelnikov looking to make an impact, the field will be strong.

American Lindsay Davenport will look to defend her ladies' title with vigour but Switzerland's Martina Hingis will also be aiming for gold. The spotlight as ever however, is sure to be on Russia's Anna Kournikova, and not just for her tennis exploits.

Atlanta 1996

	Gold	Silver
MS	Andre Agassi, USA	Sergi Bruguera, Esp
MD	Mark Woodforde/Todd Woodbridge, USA	
		Tim Henman/Neil Broad, Gbr
WS	Lindsay Davenport, USA	Arantxa Sanchez-Vicario, Esp
WD	Gigi Fernandez/Mary Jo Fernandez, USA	
		Jana Novotna/Helena Sukova, Cze

M=Men; W=Women; S-Singles; D=Doubles.

Top seed Andre Agassi, who easily disposed of his Spanish opponent Sergi Bruguera in three straight sets 6-2, 6-3, 6-1, won the men's gold medal. Bruguera, unseeded, didn't help his cause by committing no less than 60 unforced errors and only managed to break the American's serve once in the match. The bronze medal turned out to be India's first in any sport since 1980 when Leander Paes beat Brazilian Fernando Meligeni 3-6, 6-2, 6-4.

Agassi's gold win was matched by fellow American Lindsay Davenport who also beat Spanish opposition in the form of Arantxa Sanchez-Vicario in two sets 7-6, 6-2. At 6 foot 3 inches she towered over her opponent although a 8-6 tie-breaker was needed for her to take the first set before she went on to romp to gold in the second set.

Jana Novotna had two set points against her in the opening set but she went on to win the Olympic bronze by beating Mary Joe Fernandez 7-6, 6-4. It was Novotna's third Olympic medal, but the first in the singles. She had accounted for top seed Monica Seles in the quarter-finals.

Mark Woodforde and Todd Woodbridge of Australia won the gold in the men's doubles, defeating Brits Tim Henman and Neil Broad 6-4, 6-4, 6-2. It was the Woodies' first gold and came on the back of four straight Wimbledon championships. Marc-Kevin Goellner and David

Prinosil of Germany won the bronze in men's doubles, beating Jacco Eltingh and Paul Haarhuis of the Netherlands 6-2, 7-5.

Americans Mary Jo Fernandez and Gigi Fernandez, who held off the challenge of Czechs Jana Novotna and Helena Sukova 7-6, 6-4, 6-4, won the ladies doubles. The Spanish pairing of Sanchez-Vicario and Conchita Martinez won the bronze by beating Dutch duo Manon Bollegraf and Brenda Schultz-McCarthy.

Outline rules

Matches are played as singles (between two individual players) or as doubles (between two teams of two players). Using a racquet, the tennis ball must be hit over a central net but kept within the bounds of the tennis court that is marked by white lines. The ball is allowed to bounce only once on each side of the court (although a player can hit it before it bounces – called a volley) after which the player has to attempt to hit it back over the net into their opponent's side of the court. The process of doing this a number of times is called a rally. The object of the game is to score points by putting the opponent in a position such that he or she cannot return the ball legally back across the net.

All matches are played as the best of three sets with the final in each of the two men's divisions being the best of five sets. A set is won by winning a required number of games, which in turn are won by scoring points.

The points naming system can be the most confusing aspect of tennis. The sequence of points is: Love, 15, 30, 40, Game. In effect 0, 1, 2, 3, Game. A game starts with the score 'Love-all'. If a player wins a point it becomes '15-Love' or 'Love-15'. The order of the score is important – the player who is serving is always scored first. So '15-Love' indicates that the server won the point. A game can only be won if the player wins by two clear points. Thus if the score is 40-40 the next point will not win the game. At 40-40 the score is called 'Deuce'. The next point won becomes advantage point, ie, 'Advantage Henman'. In this case if Henman won the next point he would win the game. If Henman lost the next point the score would revert to Deuce.

Sets are won by the first player to win six games and have a two game advantage. Thus if Henman was winning games 5-4 and then won the next game he would win the set 6-4. A set cannot be won 6-5. In this case an extra game would be played. If the game score then went to 6-6, a tie-break would be played, unless it was the final deciding set in which case the match would continue until one player or team wins two successive games.

A tie-break is a game that is scored incrementally from one to seven. The first player to reach seven and be two points ahead wins the tie-break game. If there is no two point advantage the tie-break continues until one player achieves a two-point advantage.

Service is a big weapon in tennis – especially in the men's game – and the service stays with each player for one game at a time, swapping between them for alternate games. The server stands behind the base or end line of the court and has to deliver the ball over the net so that it bounces into a marked service court diagonally opposite them on the opponent's side. The opponent's task is to return the serve and from there the rally is fought. The first serve in every game comes from the right side of the court, after which the server alternates from left to right sides. Most players serve over arm but it is quite legal to serve under arm and there are some famous incidents of this happening to flat foot opponents! In a service, as well as during a rally, the line is part of the area of play and if the ball touches any part of the line it is in-play.

In a tie-breaker, the player who was due to serve the next game serves the first point. The opposing player serves the next two points, then all players continue, rotating the serve two points at a time. Players change ends after every six points played – in normal play the players change ends after the very first game of a match and then every two games.

If a server fails to get the ball in the service court it is called a fault. The server can do this once, because he gets a second serve. If this then results in a fault the server loses the point. If a service ball hits the top of the net but falls into the service court this is termed a 'let' and the server is allowed to take the service again, ie, they are not charged with a fault. A third type of service fault is called the foot fault. This occurs if the server's feet touch the ground on or ahead of the baseline during a serve.

A tennis court is 78 feet long and 27 feet wide for singles. For doubles the court is widened to 36 feet. The service court line extends across the court 21 feet back from the net. The service net is 3 feet high in the middle.

Did you know?

- The first tennis court was mapped out in 1858 in Birmingham, England.
- The father of Atlanta gold medallist Andre Agassi, Mike, boxed for Iran in the Olympics of 1948 and 1952. Boxing under the name of Emanoul Aghassi, he entered the bantamweight competition but was eliminated in the first round at each Games.
- John Boland went as a spectator to the 1896 Games in Athens and ended up winning a tennis gold medal for Ireland!
- In Atlanta 1996, Australians Todd Woodbridge and Mark Woodforde won their doubles semi-final last set 18-16 before continuing on to take the gold medal.
- A player loses the point if the ball touches his body or if he touches the net or net posts with any part of his body. A player also loses the point if he or she touches the ball before it crosses the net.

Jargon buster

Ace	A point scoring service that cannot be returned by the opponent.
Approach shot	A shot that is hit towards the far end of the court to allow the player to approach and dominate the court from near the net.
Back court	This is the area between the service line and the baseline.
Break serve	When the receiving player wins the game served by his opponent.
Deuce	The term to indicate the score is tied at 40-40.
Double fault	The term to indicate a player has served a second successive fault.
Forecourt	This is the area between the net and the service line.
Ground strokes	The shot or stroke played after the ball has bounced on the stroke maker's side of the court.
Let	The term when a serve touches the top of the net but still progresses into the service court. The serve is retaken and does not count as a fault.
Smash	A returned shot that is taken from over the head, ie, smashed hard back into the opponent's half of the court.

Triathlon

Introduced: 2000
Scheduled: September 16-17
Venue: Farm Cove and Harbour front
Events: Men and Women

Introduction

The triathlon makes its debut as an Olympic sport at Sydney. Its popularity has helped make it one of the youngest disciplines to be included, less than 30 years after the first versions were staged in the United States. Triathlon is three race events in one – a test of stamina and fitness. For Sydney it will consist of a 1.5km swim around Farm Cove on the Harbour front, and a 40km cycle race followed by a 10km run; the route for these two goes around the Royal Botanic Gardens and along to Woolloomooloo Bay before heading into town and back down to Circular Quay and the Opera House. The course is about 5km long so eight laps will be required for the cycling leg and two for the run.

There will be a women's and a men's event, with the ladies having the privilege of going first. The women are expected to take a bit over two hours to complete the course with the men being around 15 minutes quicker.

A maximum of 50 athletes will compete in the men's and women's events and qualification is through world rankings, although this is limited to a maximum of three entrants per event – as hosts, Australia receive three qualifiers in each event automatically. That said the Aussies currently dominate the sport in both sexes and will expect the likes of Greg Bennett, Chris McCormack and Chris Hill to be battling out for the men's gold and Michellie Jones, Loretta Harrop, Emma Carney and Jackie Gallagher to be doing the same for the ladies. However Hungary and New Zealand have shown impressive form in the men's division with France also being a contender for the women.

With the top triathletes being so close in terms of performance, races can be won and lost in the period between finishing one leg and starting another. This is called the transition period and how efficiently the competitors react at this point can be all-important.

Outline rules

Essentially the first to reach the finishing line at the end of the 10km run is the winner.

The 1.5km swim gets things underway, with the triathletes diving from a large pontoon and then following a triangular course marked out by buoys and ropes. Although most choose to use freestyle (crawl) as their mode of locomotion there is no rule stating what stroke must be used, but this is generally the quickest and it takes the men around 20 minutes to complete the course.

Once out of the water the competitors immediately get on their bikes for the 40km ride which takes around one hour to complete. Competitors must complete the whole course by bike unless they suffer a flat tyre, in which case they can run with the bike to a tyre change station. There will be six of these positioned around the course where for the first time a tyre change crew will do the job for them – previously competitors had to effect their own tyre change.

With the cycle leg completed it is straight on to the 10km run, which takes around 30 minutes. Triathletes must complete the race on foot, ie, an exhausted triathlete is not allowed to crawl across the finish line!

Competitors have to adhere to the rules strictly and they face penalties if they are deemed to have committed any sort of infringement. Normally the punishment is to hold the transgressor up for a period of time, normally 30 seconds, at the end of the leg. To do this the official will normally show a yellow card to the competitor. If a competitor is shown a red card it means disqualification. Two yellow cards during a race results in an automatic red card. Typically a yellow card will be shown if one competitor deliberately impedes another.

Did you know?

- Up until five years ago it was illegal for triathletes to ride their bike in the slipstream of the cyclist in front – called drafting.
- Swimming caps are compulsory for the swim.
- Wet suits are not allowed if the water temperature is above 20 degrees C and compulsory if the water temperature is below 14 degrees. Race officials decide on whether wet suits are worn if the water temperature is between these two.

- Bikes are checked 24 hours before the race to ensure they comply with the rules. If there are any infringements, athletes are allowed to make the necessary modifications.
- Runners must wear shoes during the running leg.

Jargon buster

Attack — A term used to indicate a burst of acceleration.

Draft — When a cyclist positions himself behind another to get in the slipstream, thus taking advantage of less wind resistance.

Drift — Moving off the cycling line, normally when a corner is taken too fast.

Freestyle — The most common style of stroke used in the triathlon – more commonly called the crawl.

Ironman — This is the name of the long-course triathlon – 2-mile swim, 110-mile bike ride and 26-mile run.

Leg — A triathlon is made up of three races and each race is called a leg.

Peloton — The main group of riders in the cycle race.

Pontoon — The floating wooden platform from which the swimming race is started.

Transition area — The change-over area, where the bikes are parked. The area triathletes use to change clothing and move from one phase to another.

Volleyball

Introduced: 1964
Scheduled: September 16-October 1
Venue: Sydney Entertainment Centre, Darling Harbour. Buring Pavilion, Sydney Olympic Park
Events: Men and Women teams

Introduction

The success of beach volleyball in the Atlanta Olympics gave the indoor game the scare that it probably deserved. A century after it was invented the indoor game has been brought into the new millennium with several new rule changes. The most important of these is the introduction of the libero. Not an Italian defender but indeed a specialist player – who will wear a distinctive uniform – and who will be available only in the back court but who cannot play in the front court or serve. The idea is that this specialist player will be able to implement longer rallies and therefore more spectacular play. Another major rule change is that the non-serving team can score points when the opposition are serving and that the first four sets are now played to 25 points (previously 15).

For the Games both the women's and men's tournaments will consist of 12 teams which will be drawn into two pools of six teams. The teams will play each other once on a round-robin basis with the top four teams in each pool progressing into a straight knock-out competition from the quarter-finals to the final. Teams that are eliminated will play-off with other eliminated teams to determine the top eight placings.

The men's competition is normally the most keenly contested with Brazil, China and Russia always strong although Italy have been the most consistent team over the past ten years winning everything except the Olympic gold, taking silver behind the Dutch team in Atlanta. The women's game has been dominated by the Cuban team and they are sure to be the favourites in 2000.

Qualification for the Sydney Olympics was determined by a series of qualification and play-off tournaments that started with the Volleyball World Cup that was held in November 1999.

Atlanta 1996

	Gold	*Silver*	*Bronze*
Men	Netherlands	Italy	Yugoslavia
Women	Cuba	China	Brazil

The Dutch team beat the Italians in the men's final in a five set thriller to take the gold medal in Atlanta. Over the previous year there had been little to separate the two teams, the Dutch ousting the Italians in five sets to take the World League final just a few months earlier. And this final couldn't have been any closer, the Dutch winning the fifth and deciding set 17-15 to take the game 15-12, 9-15, 16-14, 9-15, 17-15. It turned into a battle of wills between Holland's Bas van de Goor and Italy's Andrea Giani at the centre of almost every play.

Yugoslavia took the bronze, having returned from Olympic banishment to win its first men's volleyball medal, beating Russia in four sets 15-8, 7-15, 15-8, 15-9, a remarkable achievement given that they finished sixth in their only other Olympics, in 1980. The Yugoslavs played the game without their skipper Dejan Brdovic, who returned home after his 14-month-old son died of a brain tumour.

In the ladies competition Cuba became only the second country to win consecutive Olympic women's volleyball gold medals when they beat China in four sets 14-16, 15-12, 17-16, 15-6. Hitter Mireya Luis was the star of the show, ably aided by blockers Magalys Carvajal and Ana Ibis Fernandez.

Brazil won its first Olympic women's volleyball medal beating Russia 15-13, 4-15, 16-14, 8-15, 15-13 to take the bronze, leaving the Russians (formerly Soviet Union) without a medal for the first time in the eight Olympics in which they had competed. During that time they had won four gold and two silver medals.

Outline rules

There are six players per team who position themselves on the court either side of the net, with three players lined up across the forecourt (just behind the net) and three lined up in the back court. The object of the game is to score points by touching the ball down in the opponent's side of the court. To enable a team to do this they can touch the ball three times on their side of the court without it touching the floor on their side of the court. They cannot, however, hold the ball nor can the same player touch it twice in a row. A team wins the point if they get the ball to touch the floor on the opponent's side of the court, but within the bounds of the court; if the other team fails to get the ball back over the net or if the other team hits the ball out of court without it first touching in the court. A team also can lose the point if a player touches the net with his or her body. It is not counted as a hit if a player blocks the ball and only the front three players may block the ball.

When a team gains service all the players rotate one position in a clockwise motion. The player who rotates into the back right hand corner takes service. Service may be over or under arm and must be from behind the end line, but the player may land within the court after the serve. The serve can be to anywhere inside the opponent's half and it continues until the server's team loses a point. When the service is lost it transfers to the opposition who start by rotating their players through one position.

Up to six substitutes can be used per set played and each sub can only enter the game once each set. A sub can only replace a player who started the set and can themselves only be replaced by the same player. In addition to this the new libero player is free to sub anywhere in the back row. The libero – who must wear a distinctive uniform to distinguish him from the others– can only play in the back court and cannot serve.

Each match consists of five sets. The first four sets are played to 25 points and the fifth set is played to 15 points. However, a team must win by two clear points to take the set. Each team is allowed two time-outs per set.

The volleyball court is 18 metres long by nine metres wide and is separated in half by a net which is 2.43m high for men and 2.24m high for women. The lines are included in the court.

Did you know?

- The original name for volleyball was Mintonette.
- The former Soviet Union was the only other country to win consecutive women's Olympic titles, doing so in 1968 and 1972.

Jargon buster

Ace   This is a clean serve that lands in the opponent's court without being touched.

Block	When a front player jumps at the net to stop an opposing player spiking the ball.
Chuck	When the ball is pushed or thrown rather than hit.
Dig	When both arms are placed together to push a hard-hit ball back into the air – digging-out.
Fault	An error which results in the loss of the rally, ie, serving the ball out of court.
Heater	A hard-hit shot or spike.
Kong	A one-handed block.
Spike	The process of performing an over-arm smash of the ball into the opponent's half of the court.

Water Polo

Introduced: 1900 men, 2000 women
Scheduled: September 16 - October 1
Venue: Ryde Leisure Centre,
Sydney International Aquatic Centre
Events: Men and Women: Team

Introduction

The women will play water polo as an Olympic event for the first time in Sydney. Given that it has existed as a men's sport in the Olympics since 1900 it does seem strange that it has taken so long for the ladies to get involved in what is one of the most physically demanding team sports at the Games.

In the men's competition 12 teams will qualify for the Games, while six will be the total number for the first women's tournament. The men's tournament will start as a round-robin with two pools (sic) of six teams with the top four teams (ie, two eliminated from each group) advancing to the quarter-finals where the tournament evolves into a straight knock-out competition. In the women's competition the top four teams from the round-robin pool advance to the semi-final stage.

Spain won the gold medal in Atlanta and the Spanish men, along with Russia, Italy and Hungary, are sure to be amongst the challengers – in fact only once has the gold medal travelled outside Europe. The first women's gold medal could go to the host nation but Russia and Italy will be early favourites.

Eight of the 12 places for men's teams were awarded on the basis of rankings and World Cup performances, plus Australia as host. The remaining four places will have been decided by an Olympic qualifying competition that was held in May.

Atlanta 1996

	Gold	*Silver*	*Bronze*
Men	Spain	Croatia	Italy

Spain won the gold medal in water polo by defeating Croatia 7-5. The bronze medal went to Italy, who beat Hungary 20-18. The bronze medal match had all sorts of problems associated with it and ended in acrimonious circumstances with players fighting and fans being evicted from the Atlanta Aquatic Centre. With one second left to play on the clock and Italy leading 16-15, several of their players, wearing full-length blue towelling robes, jumped in the pool to start celebrating.

However, as they entered the water the clock stopped at 0.02s and led to a penalty being awarded to the Hungarians which they duly scored to leave the game tied. This led to a disruption of the match, followed by two three-minute periods of extra time before Italy won.

Outline rules

Two teams of seven-a-side battle it out in the pool with the object being to score more goals than the opposition. A goal is scored by throwing the ball (just like a football) into the opponent's net. The ball can be passed between players or a player can decide to go on a dribble and a goal can be scored in just about any way – although the use of a clenched fist is not allowed and only goalkeepers are allowed to touch the ball with two hands. Players are not allowed to kick the ball and will be banished to the sin-bin (see below) if they do so.

The pool of play is marked by ropes and measures 30m by 20m for men and 25m by 17m for women. Games are normally played in 50m Olympic pools and the water depth must be a minimum of 2m – in Sydney it will be 3m. The goals, which float on the water, are 3m wide and 90cm high. Players are not allowed to touch the sides or the bottom of the pool and therefore have to spend the whole game either swimming or treading water! Substitutes can be used at any time.

A game is made up of four periods each of seven minutes, with a two minute break inbetween periods. The clock stops when a foul or rule violation is called and so a typical game will last a bit over the hour. If the scores are tied, two three-minute periods of extra time are played. If there is still no separation a third extra period is played until a winning 'sudden-death' goal is scored.

The game is started with the ball floating in the middle of the pool and after the signal to start the game the two teams rush to take possession of it. Once in charge of the ball the attacking team has 35 seconds to get a shot on goal. If they fail to, then possession of the ball goes to the defending team. For a goal to be scored the whole of the ball must cross the line and a goal can be scored from any part of the pool. If a ball goes out of play then the team that did not touch it last gets possession. In these cases it normally results in a pass-on from the side rope. This is the way that the game is restarted after a foul has been committed. Examples of fouls include holding the ball with two hands, holding the ball underwater while being tackled and obstructing an opponent who does not have the ball. If the foul is deemed to be unsportsmanlike then the offending player is sent to a sin-bin where he is exiled for 20 seconds (a long time in water polo) or until a goal is scored or possession changes back to his team. Splashing water in an opponent's face is an exclusion foul. A penalty throw can be awarded if a foul occurs within the 4m area of the goal which stopped the player from shooting at goal.

Jargon buster

Ball under	When the ball is held underwater and the referee calls a foul.
Dead time	The time after a foul has been called and before the game is restarted – the clock is stopped.
Double dead-time foul	Simultaneous fouls by both an offensive and defensive player during dead time.
Driver	Usually the fastest swimmer in the team, who looks to get the ball into a shooting position.
Drop	When players drop back to defend their goal.
Hole set	In football terms this is the team's centre-forward.
Sink	When a player is pushed under water when he is tackled.
Stalling	The foul called when a team doesn't get a shot off in 35 seconds.

Weightlifting

Introduced: 1896 men; 2000 women
Scheduled: September 16-26
Venue: Sydney Exhibition & Convention Centre
Events: Men and Women – various weight divisions

Introduction

If one thing is guaranteed for the Sydney Olympics – it is in the weightlifting competition where no less than 15 new records will be established. Why so certain? Simple, the weight divisions for this Games have been changed from those in all previous Olympics – 15 new classes means 15 new records!

Weightlifting rules are simple and watching muscle-bound men and women lift almost three times their own body weight above their head can be quite hypnotic. Weightlifting as a men's discipline was on the agenda for the first Olympics in 1896, but Sydney will see the women's weightlifting for the very first time. In that particular category expect China to dominate and possibly sweep the board, with only the Hungarian ladies likely challengers to total supremacy.

In the men's competition the Greeks will be the ones to watch and it is possible that Akakios Kakhiasvilis and Pyrros Dimas could pick up their third successive gold medals – a feat previously performed by Turkey's Naim Suleymanoglu.

There will be 176 male and 74 female entrants who qualified via their national team's world championship ranking and decisions of the organising body.

Atlanta 1996

Weight	Gold	Silver
Flyweight	Halil Mutlu, Tur	Zhang Xiangsen, Chn
Bantamweight	Tang Ningsheng, Chn	Leonidas Sabanis, Gre
Featherweight	Naim Suleymanoglu, Tur	
		Valerios Leonidis, Gre
Lightweight	Zhang Xugang, Chn	Kim Myong-Nam, Pkr
Middleweight	Pablo Lara, Cub	Yoto Yotov, Bul
Light Heavyweight	Pyrros Dimas, Gre	Marc Huster, Ger
Middle Heavyweight	Alexei Petrov, Rus	Leonidas Kokas, Gre
First Heavyweight	Akakidei Khakiashvilis, Gre	
		Anatoli Khrapaty, Kaz
Second Heavyweight	Timur Taimassov, Ukr	Sergey Syrtsov, Rus
Super Heavyweight	Andrej Chemerkin, Rus	Ronny Weller, Ger

In Atlanta the weightlifting competition featured just the men in ten divisions and during the Games 15 world records were set. The title of world's strongest man was won by Andrey Chemerkin. The Russian broke the world record in the clean-and-jerk on his final lift to win the Super Heavyweight gold medal with a total of 457.5 kilograms. Silver went to Ronny Weller of Germany (455kg) with Australia's Stefan Botev taking the bronze (450kg).

Alexander Kurlovich of Belarus and Manfred Nerlinger of Germany failed in their attempts to make Olympic weightlifting history. Kurlovich was trying to become the second lifter to win gold medals in three Olympic Games. He finished fifth at 425kg. Nerlinger was trying to win a medal in his fourth straight Olympics, but was sixth with a total of 422.5kg. Only one other lifter, American Norbert Schmensky, has accomplished that feat, between 1948 and 1960.

Timur Taimassov won gold in the Second Heavyweight class, lifting 430.3kg thanks in part to a world-record effort in the clean-and-jerk. Russia's Sergey Syrtsov took the silver medal and Nicu Vlad of Romania secured the bronze. Greek lifter Akakidei Kakhiashvilis broke the world record for the First Heavyweight division and won his second Olympic gold medal in the process by lifting a total of 420.3kg.

In the Middle Heavyweight division Russia's Aleksey Petrov took gold just two months after gaining a reprieve from a lifetime ban. Leonidas Kokas of Greece won the silver medal and Germany's Oliver Caruso the bronze. Light Heavyweight Pyrros Dimas, of Greece, won his second straight Olympic weightlifting gold medal and set a world record by lifting 392.8kg. Marc Huster, of Germany, won the silver medal and Poland's Andrzej Cofalik the bronze.

Tang Ningsheng gave China their first weightlifting gold medal in 12 years when he won the Bantamweight division. That inspired Zhang Xugang to set three world records in the Lightweight division to give China a second gold of the Games with a total lift of 357.5kg. North Korea's Kim Myong-nam, had to settle for silver, with Hungary's Attila Feri taking bronze.

The lifter dubbed 'Pocket Hercules' because of his size and power – Turkey's Naim Suleymanoglu – made Olympic history by winning his third gold medal. Suleymanoglu set two world records in the Featherweight division. He needed the world records, because silver medallist Valerios Leonidis of Greece also broke the previous world marks. Another Turk, Halil Mutlu, raised his own world snatch record on his way to winning the Olympic Flyweight division.

Outline rules

For Sydney new weight divisions are introduced as well as a weightlifting tournament for the women. The ten divisions there used to be for the men have been reduced to eight for lifters in the following weight categories: 56kg, 62kg, 69kg, 77kg, 85kg, 94kg, 105kg and over 105kg. The women's lifting will be organised into seven weight divisions: 48kg, 53kg, 58kg, 63kg, 69kg, 75kg, and over 75kg.

There are two types of lift – snatch and the clean-and-jerk. In the snatch the lifter has to take the bar from the floor to above their head in one movement and fully extend their arms in the process. In the clean-and-jerk the end result is the same but the lifting process takes place in two stages. First the bar is taken to the shoulders (the clean) – with the lifter dropping into a squat position at the same time. The lifter then stands up maintaining the bar on their shoulders, before they then attempt to lift the bar above their head (the jerk). Again the arms must be fully extended. In both cases the result must be that the feet are parallel to the body and the lifter steady. There are three referees and a majority decision determines if the lifter has been successful. They signal by means of white (successful) and red (failure) lights.

Each competitor gets three attempts at the snatch, and three attempts at the clean-and-jerk. The lifter increases the weight on the bar as they wish and the heaviest successful lift in each category is scored. Scoring is done by combining the best weight in each category. If the competitor lifted 120kg in the snatch and 90kg in the clean and jerk, the total weight scored would be 210kg. If competitors finish on the same weight then the lifter who has the lower body weight is deemed the winner.

The weights on the bar are increased in increments of 2.5kg per successful lift at the discretion of the lifter. The bar itself is made of steel and weighs 20kg (men) and 15kg (women) and is just over two metres long.

Did you know?

- Turkey's Naim Suleymanoglu weighed under 64kg and stood less than five feet tall and could lift nearly three times his body weight. He won three consecutive Olympic gold medals and was seven-time World Champion.
- If two lifters lift the same weight and have identical body weights then the winner is the first to lift the weight!

Jargon buster

Bomb out	When a lifter fails to make a final score by not making a scoring lift in either the snatch or the clean-and-jerk.
Chalk	The powder lifters put on their hands prior to a lift as a means of improving their grip on the bar.
Disc	The name given to each weight on the bar.
Fixation	The term used to define the moment when the bar becomes held over the lifter's head.
Platform	The wooden stage on which the lifters compete.
Press	The term given when the bar is taken to the shoulders and after a two-second pause for the referee's approval, then lifted above the head.
Six-for-six	Three successful snatches and three successful clean-and-jerks in straight attempts.

Wrestling

Introduced: 1896
Scheduled: Greco-Roman – September 24-27
                Freestyle – September 28-October 1
Venue: Sydney Exhibition & Convention Centre
Events: Men – various weight divisions

Introduction

Wrestling is perhaps the oldest sport of all. It predates even the original Olympics and there is evidence that organised events took place over 5000 years ago! Now it is a fixture of the modern Olympic Games and there is even talk of a women's competition being added to the 2004 Games when they arrive back in Greece.

There are two types of wrestling – Freestyle and Greco-Roman and they are essentially the same – the difference is only in what the legs are allowed to do. Basically Greco-Roman wrestlers are not allowed to use or attack the legs whereas Freestyle wrestlers make use of single-leg and double-leg tackles. Visually this means that the Greco-Roman encounters are more akin to Judo with the competitors using body lifts and throws to get their opponents onto the floor.

The European nations have dominated Greco-Roman wrestling in recent times and there has been no more dominant competitor than the Russian Alexander Karelin. With three straight Olympic gold successes behind him he could well add a fourth at Sydney and he is famed for what has become known as the Karelin Lift, a move where he throws opponents over his shoulder! The Freestyle is always a much more open affair and no one nation has been totally dominant.

For Sydney the competition takes on a new format – the previous ten weight divisions in both styles are being replaced by eight new divisions in each style. The divisions are defined by maximum body weight and will be: 54kg, 58kg, 63kg, 69kg, 76kg, 85kg, 97kg and 130kg.

Each class will contain 20 wrestlers, who will have qualified through a variety of pre-Olympic tournaments. They will then be drawn into six groups, composed of two four-man groups and four three-man groups. There is no seeding – the draw for the pools is open. Each wrestler fights within the group on a round-robin basis with the winners from the four three-man pools progressing to the quarter-finals. The two winners from the quarter-finals join the two winners from the four-man groups in the semi-finals. The victorious semi-finalists fight for gold and bronze while the defeated wrestlers wrestle for bronze.

Atlanta 1996

Greco Roman

Weight	Gold	Silver
Light-Flyweight	Sim Kwon-Ho, Kor	Aleksandr Pavlov, Blr
Flyweight	Arman Nazaryan, Arm	Brandon Paulson, US
Bantamweight	Yovei Melnichenko, Kaz	Denis Hall, US
Featherweight	Wlodzimierz Zawadzki, Pol	Juan Delis, Cub
Lightweight	Ryzsard Wolny, Pol	Ghani Yalouz, Fra
Welterweight	Feliberto Aguilera, Cub	Marko Asell, Fin
Middleweight	Hamza Yerlikaya, Tur	Thomas Zander, Ger
Light Heavyw't	Vyachetslav Oleynyk, Ukr	Jacek Fafinski, Pol
Heavyweight	Andreas Wronski, Pol	Sergei Lishtvan, Blr
Super Heavyw't	Alexander Karelin, Rus	Matt Ghaffari, US

Freestyle

Weight	Gold	Silver
Light-Flyweight	Kim Il, Prk	Armen Mkrchyan, Arm
Flyweight	Valentin Jordanov, Bul	Namig Abdullaeyev, Aze
Bantamweight	Kendall Cross, USA	Giga Sissaouri, Can
Featherweight	Thomas Brands, USA	Jang Jae-Sung, Kor
Lightweight	Vadim Bogiyev, Rus	Townsend Saunders, USA
Welterweight	Buvaisa Saityev, Rus	Park Jang-Soon, Kor
Middleweight	Khadshimurad Magomedov, Rus	Yang Hyun-Mo, Kor
Light Heavyw't	Rasul Khadem Azghadi, Irn	Maharbeg Chadartsev, Rus
Heavyweight	Kurt Angle, USA	Abbas Jadidi, Irn
Super Heavyw't	Mahmut Demir, Tur	Alexei Medvedev, Bul

Wrestling was one of the big successes of the Atlanta Games, drawing bigger than anticipated crowds who were not disappointed in the performances and stories it turned up. Bruce Baumgartner, looking for his fourth Olympic medal in the freestyle super heavyweight division, had to settle for the bronze version this time as Turkey's Mahmut Demir beat Bulgaria's Alexei Medvedev in the final.

While it was disappointment for Baumgartner, it was glory for the former Soviet Republic of Armenia who had its first taste of Olympic glory of any kind when Armen Nazaryan won the flyweight gold medal. Poland had a taste of double gold when Ryszard Wolny won the lightweight division and Andrzej Wronski won the heavyweight division and they immediately dedicated their wins to the memory of Eugeniusz Pietrasik, head of the Polish Olympic team, who collapsed during the opening ceremony and died of a heart attack.

In the freestyle divisions the USA chalked up three gold successes. Kendall Cross, who had to beat a world champion just to qualify for the Games, beat Giya Sissaouri of Canada 5-3 to take the bantamweight title, and then Tom Brands won the featherweight title by beating Jang Jae-sung of South Korea 7-0. The hardest earned of them though was won by Kurt Angle in the heavyweight division. After eight minutes of overtime he was still tied with Abbas Jadidi, but got the referee's decision over the Iranian. Townsend Saunders could have made it a clean sweep of the four finals that the Americans were contesting when he lost to Vadim Bogiev of Russia in the lightweight division.

There was also controversy in the flyweight final which was won by Bulgarian Valentin Dimitrov Jordanov at the ripe old age of 36. In sudden-death overtime, the Bulgarian pulled his Azerbaijan opponent Namik Abdullayev out of bounds. The referee whistled, Abdullayev relaxed and a point was then awarded to Jordanov. The Azerbaijan fighter protested vehemently as he felt his opponent was not in control when the point was awarded. The result stood though.

In super heavyweight Alexander Karelin, possibly the greatest wrestler of all-time and known as Siberian Bear, needed overtime to beat off the unwavering challenge of Iranian-born Matt Ghaffari

Russia's Makharbek Khadartsev failed in his bid to win a third consecutive gold medal in the light heavyweight division, losing 3-0 to world champion Rasul Khadem of Iran for what was the country's first gold at the Games.

Outline rules

A wrestling match or bout can be won in one of four ways, a fall, technical superiority, on points or by majority vote. If a fall takes place then victory is immediate. A fall is when a wrestler can pin his opponent's shoulders to the floor long enough for the referee to determine that he is in control. A technical superiority win takes place when one wrestler takes a 10-point lead over the other. A points win occurs when the bout comes to an end – the winner is the wrestler with the most points. Finally, a majority vote takes place when the bout is deemed tied in which case the referee, the judge and mat chairman take a majority vote to decide the winner.

Wrestling bouts consist of two three-minute rounds, with a 30-second break between the two rounds. If the score is tied, or if neither wrestler has scored three points, an extra round of three minutes is fought. Wrestlers score points in a number of ways and it is the referee who determines when points are won, although both judge and mat chairman must also concur. Equally points can be deducted – penalty points – if a wrestler is deemed to have committed an offence. Points are scored when certain holds are implemented or if an opponent is thrown. Three of the more common of these and the points they carry are listed below:

1 point	Lifting opponent off his feet and planting him on mat in a controlled manner.
2 points	Turning an opponent's shoulders so that they face the mat and are at an acute angle to it.
5 points	Throwing an opponent in the air.

For the Olympics in Sydney wrestling bouts take place on an octagonal mat which is formed from a 12-metre square. In the very centre is a circle which is where each bout starts. Outside this is a seven-metre diameter yellow circle called the wrestling area, which not surprisingly is where the competitors fight it out. A metre beyond this is a red zone which indicates to the wrestlers that they are near the bounds of the competition area.

Did you know?

- In most events in the Games the host nation normally receives a place in the competition. However, this does not happen in Sydney for the wrestling competition.
- Wrestlers must shave on the day of the competition. Beards are only allowed if they are deemed by the referee to be 'mature' and unless hair is short it must be tied back!
- Each wrestler has to have a handkerchief with him – normally tucked into their jockstraps – to wipe away saliva etc!
- Wrestlers may not speak to their opponents during bouts.

Jargon buster

Arm throw   When the opponent is thrown over the shoulder by the arm.
Body lock   A hold effected by the arms around the opponent's body, before he throws the opponent onto the mat.
Bridge   Used by a wrestler when he is trying to avoid a fall or being pinned to the mat, in which he arches his back to lift his shoulders off the mat.
Bridge out The process of rolling onto the stomach from a Bridge position.
Danger position
            When a wrestler's back is less than a right angle to the mat.
Grapevine   Also called the cross-body ride, it is when a wrestler uses his legs to turn his opponent.
Souple   The hold used to make a spectacular throw.
Takedown   Used to indicate that an opponent has been taken from a standing position to the ground.

Sydney 2000 Dates

Event	Dates
Archery	17-22 September
Athletics	22 September – 1 October
Badminton	16-23 September
Baseball	17-27 September
Basketball	16 September – 1 October
Beach Volleyball	16-26 September
Boxing	16 September – 1 October
Canoe/Kayak Slalom	16-20 September
Canoe/Kayak Sprint	26 September – 1 October
Cycling: Mountain Bike	23-24 September
Cycling: Road	26-30 September
Cycling: Track	16-21 September
Diving	22-30 September
Equestrian: Dressage	25-27 September
Equestrian: Jumping	21 September – 1 October
Equestrian: Three-day Event	16-22 September
Fencing	16-24 September
Football	13–28 September
Gymnastics: Artistic	26 September – 1 October
Gymnastics : Rhythmic	14-26 September
Gymnastics: Trampoline	22-23 September
Handball	16 September – 1 October
Hockey	16-30 September
Judo	16-22 September
Modern Pentathlon	30 September – 1 October
Rowing	17-24 September
Sailing	16–30 September
Shooting	16-23 September
Softball	17-26 September
Swimming	16-23 September
Synchronised Swimming	24-29 September
Table Tennis	16-25 September
Taekwondo	27-30 September
Tennis	19-28 September
Triathlon	16-17 September
Volleyball	16 September – 1 October
Water Polo	16 September – 1 October
Weightlifting	16-26 September
Wrestling	24 September – 1 October